ANNE F

Irish Writers in their Time

Series Editor: Stan Smith

This innovative series meets the urgent need for comprehensive new accounts of Irish writing across the centuries which combine readability with critical authority and information with insight. Each volume addresses the whole range of a writer's work in the various genres, setting its vision of the world in biographical context and situating it within the cultural, intellectual, and political currents of the age, in Ireland and the wider world. This series will prove indispensable for students and specialists alike.

1. Patrick Kavanagh
(Editor: STAN SMITH)

2. Elizabeth Bowen
(Editor: EIBHEAR WALSHE)

3. John Banville
(JOHN KENNY)

4. Jonathan Swift
(BREAN HAMMOND)

5. James Joyce
(Editor: SEAN LATHAM)

6. W.B. Yeats
(Editor: EDWARD LARRISSY)

7. Oscar Wilde
(Editor: JARLATH KILLEEN)

8. Anne Enright
(Editors: CLAIRE BRACKEN and SUSAN CAHILL)

For Nessa

Anne Enright

with all best wishes [signature: Anne Enright]

Edited by
CLAIRE BRACKEN
and
SUSAN CAHILL

[signature: Claire Bracken]

[signature: Susan Cahill]

IRISH ACADEMIC PRESS
DUBLIN • PORTLAND, OR

First published in 2011 by Irish *Academic Press*

2 Brookside,
Dundrum Road,
Dublin 14, Ireland

920 NE 58th Avenue, Suite 300
Portland, Oregon,
97213-3786, USA

This edition © 2011 Irish Academic Press
Chapters © Indvidual Contributors

www.iap.ie

British Library Cataloguing-in-Publication Data
An entry can be found on request

978 0 7165 3080 0 (cloth)
978 0 7165 3081 7 (paper)

Library of Congress Cataloging-in-Publication Data
An entry can be found on request

Printed by Good News Digital Books, Ongar, Essex

Contents

List of Contributors

Claire Bracken is Assistant Professor of Irish Literature and Culture in the English Department at Union College, New York, where she teaches courses on Irish literature and film. She has published articles in *Irish Postmodernisms and Popular Culture*, *Irish Literature: Feminist Perspectives*, and *Facing the Other: Interdisciplinary Studies on Race, Gender and Social Justice*. She is co-editor of a forthcoming collection *Theorizing the Visual: New Directions in Irish Cultural Studies* and is currently working on a monograph entitled *Irish Feminist Futures*.

Susan Cahill is a Post-Doctoral Research Fellow in the UCD John Hume Institute for Global Irish Studies, University College Dublin, working on Irish Children's Literature by Women Writers, 1870–1920. She has published articles on contemporary Irish fiction, gender and the body, Irish children's literature, and on fairytale cinema. She is currently co-editing a book on the Irish author, Colum McCann. Her book, *Irish Literature in the Celtic Tiger Years 1990 to 2008: Gender, Bodies, Memory*, will be published by Continuum in 2011.

Patricia Coughlan, a Professor of English at University College, Cork, has published widely on Irish writing, including several essays on early modern colonial discourse, Irish Gothic, and twentieth-century work (Beckett, Bowen, Kate O'Brien). Edited or co-edited collections include *Spenser and Ireland* (1990), *Modernism and Ireland: the Poetry of the 1930s* (1995) and *Irish Literature: Feminist Perspectives* (2008). Recent work on contemporary literature includes articles on Banville, Peig Sayers and life-writing, Edna O'Brien, Ní Chuilleanáin, Ronan Bennett, and others. During the 2000s she led a State-funded research project on women in Irish society. She is completing a study of subjectivity, gender and social change in Irish literature since 1960.

Elke D'hoker is a lecturer at the University of Leuven, Belgium. She has published a critical study on John Banville (2004) and edited essay collections on narrative unreliability (2008) and Irish women writers (forthcoming). Her research domain is that of Irish and British fiction and her articles have appeared in journals such as *Contemporary Literature, Critique, Modern Fiction Studies, Irish University Review, Etudes Irlandaises, Journal of the Short Story in English* and *Irish Studies Review.* She has been a visiting research fellow at the Institute of English Studies of the University of London (2006–07) and a visiting scholar at Boston University and Boston College (Spring 2008).

Kristin Ewins is Lecturer in Modern and Contemporary English Literature at the University of Salford. She has published on twentieth-century women's writing, political activism and popular fiction.

Heidi Hansson is Professor of English Literature at Umeå University, Sweden. Her main research interest is women's literature, and she has previously published in the fields of postmodern romance, nineteenth-century women's cross-gendered writing, and Irish women's literature. Among her works is a full-length examination of the nineteenth-century writer Emily Lawless, *Emily Lawless 1845–1913: Writing the Interspace* (2007) and the edited collection *Irish Nineteenth-Century Women's Prose: New Contexts and Readings* (2008). She has published several works on the Nordic North in nineteenth-century travel writing, and is currently working on a study of Irish fiction and nostalgia.

Gerardine Meaney is Vice-Principal for Research and Innovation in the College of Arts and Celtic Studies, Director of the Centre for the Study of Gender, Culture and Identities and of the IRCHSS funded Graduate Research and Education Programme in Gender, Culture and Identities. She is the author of *Gender, Ireland and Cultural Change* (2010), *Nora* (2004), *(Un)like Subjects: Women, Theory, Fiction* (1993), a co-editor of the *Field Day Anthology of Irish Writing: Women's Writing and Traditions,* volumes 4 and 5 (2002) and of numerous articles on gender and Irish culture, with particular emphasis on Film, Literature and Drama.

Anne Mulhall is a College Lecturer in the School of English, Drama and Film at University College Dublin where she teaches and researches in feminist, queer and psychoanalytic theory, Irish literary and cultural studies, women's cultural production, and migration studies. She has forthcoming essays on queer and feminist theory, contemporary Irish writing, migration and cultural change and Irish visual culture. She has co-edited (with Noreen Giffney and Michael O'Rourke) a special feature on the work of Bracha L. Ettinger for the journal *Studies in the Maternal* (2009) and, with Moynagh Sullivan and Wanda Balzano, *Irish Postmodernisms and Popular Culture* (2007).

Matthew Ryan teaches cultural and literary theory in the Centre for Comparative Literature and Cultural Studies at Monash University. He has published articles on contemporary Irish literature and culture. He has a particular interest in the work of Colm Tóibín, Deirdre Madden, John Banville, Philip Ó Ceallaigh, and, of course, Anne Enright. His current research includes work on a book which considers the relations between the novel form, the self, the nation and globalization, as they appear in recent writing from Ireland. He lives in Melbourne, Australia.

Hedwig Schwall teaches and researches in contemporary Irish literature, psychoanalytic theory and European art. She is the director of the Leuven Centre for Irish Studies and president of EFACIS, the European Federation of Associations and Centres of Irish Studies.

Acknowledgements

We would like to thank all our contributors for their hard work and dedication. Much appreciation to Lisa Hyde from Irish Academic Press for being such an encouraging and supportive editor, and Heather Marchant for her detailed proofing. In addition, we are very grateful for the advice and support of colleagues and friends, in particular Gerardine Meaney, Anne Mulhall, John O'Neill, and Emma Radley. Thanks to all our colleagues in the School of English, Drama and Film, UCD and the Department of English, Union College.

We are also especially grateful to our wonderful families and friends for their interest, care, support, and good humour throughout the process of editing and writing this book, particularly our partners Glen and John. Finally, an enormous thanks to Anne Enright. The book would not have been possible without her generous support and enthusiasm, not to mention her inspirational writing, which we admire so very much.

The editors and publishers wish to thank the *Irish University Review* for permission to reprint a revised version of Patricia Coughlan's essay "'Without a blink of her lovely eye": *The Pleasure of Eliza Lynch* and Visionary Skepticism' and Litteraria Pragensia Press for a revised and lengthened version of Susan Cahill's article '"Dreaming of upholstered breasts", or, how to find your way back home: dislocation in *What Are You Like?*', which first appeared under the title, 'Doubles and Dislocations: The Body and Place in Anne Enright's *What Are You Like?*'.

CHAPTER ONE

Introduction

CLAIRE BRACKEN and SUSAN CAHILL

Anne Enright is one of the most innovative and exciting writers in Ireland today, whose work encompasses a wide range of genres, themes and interests. With her dark humour and wry tone she displays an ability to be remarkably funny while engaging with serious subjects and themes. The recognition for her novel, The Gathering, by the Man Booker judges in 2007, her substantial body of work, and her incisive fictional engagement with contemporary Ireland prove this to be a timely moment to critically explore her œuvre. In this collection, leading scholars in the field examine her work in relation to style, her situation in a postmodern and experimental tradition in Irish and non-Irish writing, her engagement with culture and social change, tradition and modernity, memory, gender and sexuality. The book also includes an extensive interview with Anne Enright and a bibliography of primary and secondary sources.

Born in Dublin in 1962, Anne Enright grew up in the suburbs of that city, attending St Louis High School in Rathmines.[1] Both her parents, Cora and Donal Enright, were civil servants. She moved to Victoria, Canada in 1979 to complete her high school education at Pearson College, an institution of academic excellence which has a highly competitive, scholarship-only admissions policy. Enright returned to Ireland in 1981 to study for a BA degree in English and Philosophy at Trinity College, Dublin. Throughout her university career, she was heavily involved in the arts. In addition to writing plays and scripts, Enright was also interested in drama, commenting, 'I spent all my time in the student theatre'.[2] It was at Trinity that Enright developed her interest in

1

ANNE ENRIGHT

psychoanalysis, a major influence on her work:

> I see how important my reading in psychoanalysis is to my work.
> I read all of Freud when I was in college and sort of loved Freud's
> work and laughed at it as well. But it's a great way to think about
> things and he's also a wonderful writer and stylist.[3]

She graduated in 1985 and then took up a Masters scholarship at the
University of East Anglia to study creative writing with Angela Carter
and Malcolm Bradbury. Enright's first fiction publication came in 1989:
four short stories ('Smile', 'Felix', 'Thirst' and 'Seascape') in *First Fictions
Introduction No. 10*.[4] *The Portable Virgin*, a collection of surrealist and stylistically experimental short stories, published in 1991, was well received
and won the Rooney Prize for Irish Literature.

Returning to Ireland from the UK, Enright worked for the national
broadcaster, RTÉ, for six years.[5] For four of those years, she was a producer and director of the popular television series *Nighthawks*, which no
doubt was influential in the creative development of Enright's first novel
The Wig My Father Wore, based as it is on a central character, Grace, who
works as a television producer in Dublin on 'LoveQuiz', a 'Blind Date'-
style show. Published in 1995, she had by this time substituted her RTÉ
career for one of full-time writing. The novel, described by Colm Tóibín
as 'post-feminist' and 'post-nationalist',[6] was shortlisted for the *Irish
Times/Aer Lingus Irish Literature Prize*. Postmodern in style, the novel
opens with an angel, Stephen, arriving at the door of Grace, the narrator
of the novel. Stephen promptly moves in with Grace, who is immediately attracted to him, and his presence has profound effects on her
physicality; as he becomes more corporeal, Grace's body reverts to a
child-like state. Indeed, Enright describes it as a '*bildungsroman*, in
reverse'.[7] The magical surrealism of the novel has led to comparisons
with writers such as Angela Carter and Gabriel García Márquez.
Formally, the novel borrows from televisual techniques; as Enright says
of it, 'Some of the book feels as though it is happening in rewind, and the
reader might find it disjointed, though you can't write about television
without fast cutting.'[8]

In the late 1990s, Enright participated in a group project which saw
seven writers working together to produce the novel *Finbar's Hotel*.
Spearheaded by Dermot Bolger (the other writers were Enright, Roddy

Doyle, Hugo Hamilton, Jennifer Johnston, Joseph O'Connor and Colm Tóibín) each writer composed one chapter, presented anonymously, on the subject of the demolition of the fictional Finbar's Hotel. It was released in 1997. The year 2000 saw the publication of Enright's very successful novel *What Are You Like?*, the story of twins, Maria and Rose, separated at birth following their mother's death, and their unconscious search for each other. The winner of the Encore Prize of the Society of Authors and the Kerry Ingredients Listowel Writer's Week Prize, this book was also shortlisted for the Whitbread Award. Following the state-sanctified protection of the unborn child, Anna, the twins' mother, is not informed of her terminal brain tumour, and is kept alive in order that the twins survive. Maria is raised in Dublin with her father, Berts, and his new wife, Evelyn. Rose is put up for adoption and raised in England, Berts being unable, after the death of his wife, to contemplate raising two children. Similarly episodic in style to *The Wig My Father Wore*, eschewing a chronological narrative structure, and focalized through a variety of characters, the novel intersperses the stories of Berts and Evelyn, Maria's childhood and her 20s in New York, Rose's childhood and adulthood in England, and, hauntingly, Anna's first-person narrative from beyond the grave. The novel rehearses themes of trauma, grief and loss, and the twins' experiences of dislocation and unhappiness uncannily mirror each other throughout the narrative.

Enright moved from fiction to personal memoir, writing of pregnancy and motherhood in *Making Babies: Stumbling into Motherhood*, which was released in 2004. This witty and poignant account of the trials and difficulties, as well as the joys, of mothering provides a remarkable combination of frank anecdote and reflective philosophy. The experience of pregnancy is given detailed fictional representation in Enright's novel, *The Pleasure of Eliza Lynch*. Published in 2002, it concerns a real-life Irishwoman who was the lover of the late-nineteenth-century Paraguayan dictator Francisco López. The novel destabilizes linear chronology by holding two timelines simultaneously — Eliza's first-person narrative, while pregnant, on board a ship travelling to Paraguay, and the narrative of Dr Stewart, which runs from their arrival in Paraguay until the devastating end of the War of the Triple Alliance (1864/5–1870). Enright plays with this morally suspect figure from history, neither condemning nor redeeming her, and the novel charts her progression from individual to national object, obscured by the mythologizing impulses of her iconic status. Eliza's excessive consumerism – she is, for a time, the richest woman in the world – is a subtle comment on the Celtic Tiger Ireland during which time the book was written.

With *The Gathering* (2007), Enright returns to her own time and place – contemporary Dublin. This haunting novel, concerned with memory and the past, is told by mother of two, Veronica, as she attempts to deal with her grief stemming from her brother Liam's suicide. Weaving an intricate structure that allows the narrative to move effortlessly between the time-spaces of Veronica's past and present, the novel presents Veronica constructing imagined memories of the relationships between her grandmother (Ada), grandfather (Charlie), and their landlord (Nugent). And it is through the fabrication of memory that Veronica is enabled to articulate a 'truth' of the past, a 'truth' which speaks to the reason for Liam's suicide: his sexual abuse by Nugent: 'It is time to put an end to the shifting stories and the waking dreams. It is time to call an end to romance and just say what happened in Ada's house, the year I was eight and Liam was barely nine.'[9] *The Gathering* won the 2007 Man Booker Prize, in addition to being shortlisted for the 2008 Booksellers Association Independent Booksellers' Book Prize and the 2008 Hughes & Hughes Irish Novel of the Year.

Enright's most recent publications are two collections of short stories, *Taking Pictures* and *Yesterday's Weather*, both of which were released in 2008. *Taking Pictures* is a new collection of short stories, one of which, 'Honey', won the inaugural Davy Byrne Award in 2004. *Yesterday's Weather*, which was issued by the US publisher Grove Press, is a compilation of new and old material, bringing together stories from *First Fictions* and her first collection, *The Portable Virgin*, with stories from *Taking Pictures*. Of the nineteen stories in *Taking Pictures*, all but one have a female protagonist. Speaking in interview, Enright has said that while these women have very 'constrained lives', 'their minds run free',[10] and *Taking Pictures* is notable for its fluidity of detailed psychic introspection. Enright is currently working on a new novel, which is due to be published in 2011.

THEMES/STYLE/INFLUENCES

Enright's literary career to date precedes and spans the Celtic Tiger Ireland of the 1990s and early 2000s. Her work comments directly on the Irish cultural climate of these years and investigates contemporary Ireland and societal change, considering the shifts in the cultural imaginary and the relationship between past and present, remembering and forgetting. The majority of the writing is set in contemporary urban Ireland, the time-space associated with the protagonists of *The Wig My Father Wore*, *What Are You Like?*, *The Gathering*, and many short stories. While the historical fiction *The Pleasure of Eliza Lynch* tells a story of late-nineteenth-century Paraguay, Enright draws correlations between it and the contemporary period:

> Eliza is a greedy girl. I did think that Eliza was about the boom, when I was writing it, but nobody else noticed that. Stewart at one stage says that he thinks that her real talent was for shipping. You know, that she could do this amazing consumer thing in the middle of all the mould and this very organic, semi-tropical place I made up. She could do that – I mean it's not Manaus [city in Brazil] but it was tropical enough – so she was better at it than all the girls these days with their Louis Vuitton.[11]

Matthew Ryan's essay in this collection considers Enright's work in the specific context of contemporary cultural change, arguing that the self in her fiction is caught in tension between two competing forces in Celtic Tiger Ireland: a global drive that disembodies and alienates, and a local desire that seeks to embody and situate. Through an analysis of the relations between materiality and abstraction in Enright's work (an analysis which includes the practice of writing itself), Ryan suggests that striking the right balance between the two might just be the answer to the question of selfhood in contemporary Irish culture.

The engagement of Enright's work with the conditions of Ireland's present is matched with a similar interest in the past, evidenced most clearly in *The Gathering*, which moves from the Celtic Tiger period to encompass moments that stretch back through the twentieth century, charting the timeline of the post-colonial state. An interest in recovering what has been silenced and repressed structures Enright's writing, an ethical impulse that is given representation in Grace's pulling down of the bedroom wallpaper in *The Wig My Father Wore*. As Enright herself states: 'Well, it's all buried under the wallpaper. We are living in it; it's in bits, it's half-mad, the wallpaper and all the historical bits and scraps which are all real things.'[12] Kristin Ewins's essay explores this feature of 'living in' the past through an analysis of the physical nature of history in *The Gathering* and the short story 'Switzerland', arguing that history is written on the body. She connects images of the physicality of the past with metaphors of the diaspora to consider the complexity of Irish national identity in Enright's work, which is structured by a desire to be both there and not there, simultaneously 'home' and 'away'.

In the opening lines of *The Gathering*, Veronica says that she needs to 'bear witness to an uncertain event'.[13] This desire to 'bear witness' to the past, something which runs throughout Enright's work, is not an attempt to uncover the truth (it is an 'uncertain event' after all), but rather to open space for other stories and voices, repressed in the past, to be heard. Hence, in *What Are You Like?*, the dead mother Anna is given a chapter in which to speak from the grave/ground, just as in *The Pleasure of Eliza Lynch*, Eliza, a figure obsessively and routinely spoken *about* in his-stories, is brought to life by Enright and given an 'I' speaking position in the narrative's boat sections. It is clear then that in Enright's work the past can be associated with concealment. In this respect Patricia Coughlan has noted, referring to *The Wig My Father Wore*, that the 'wig' stands in for processes of covering so endemic to the Irish past. Symbolic objects of concealment are identifiable across Enright's work: for example, the 'carpet' that covers the dead mother Anna in *What Are You Like?*;[14] the 'dresses' which make Eliza into a consumable object of desire in *The Pleasure of Eliza Lynch*; and the 'garage' in *The Gathering* which is the possible 'house' of Liam's abuse. There is no major gap between signifier and signified. An object whose purpose it is to cover is used as a symbol of concealment, thus enabling Enright to articulate all the more insistently that which has been made absent in/by the past.

Memorial practices are also discussed in Gerardine Meaney's essay, which considers mourning in *The Gathering* and the short story 'Little Sister'. She establishes the Antigone-Ismene myth as the frame through which to read sibling grieving in both texts, arguing that Enright's fictions allow us to extend the interpretative paradigms associated with this myth, by creating space for both life and the future in the midst of traumatic memory and the past. In Meaney's reading, the 'uncanny' becomes the embodiment of a living past in the present that enables an openness to the future, thus connecting with Enright's comments that:

> You kind of think of history as what happens after people are dead, it is the story that is told when there is no one left who remembers, no one there to contradict it. And yet history is something that has to be broken open again and again and retold, even though officially it's something that has stopped. But as we continue, history shifts and changes all the time.[15]

All of her novels enact a disruption of linear and chronological time, with past times interrupting and breaking 'open' the narratives. Claire Bracken analyzes such temporal fluidities, exploring the figuration of the car in *What Are You Like?* and *The Gathering* as embodying non-sequential movement through past, present and future. This is part of the essay's more general study of the machine in Enright's work, and Bracken considers the relationship between female characters and machines as constructing a feminine self in modernity, one example of which is the pregnant woman in the short story 'Shaft'.

Motherhood is a central theme throughout Enright's fictions and she is explicit in her desire to deal with 'the iconized mother figure in Irish literature ... They are very often dead, or left out of the narrative.'[16] It is not just the fictional mother that concerns Enright, however, but also the cultural silence surrounding the embodied experience of pregnancy and motherhood: 'What I am interested in is not the drama of being a child, but this new drama of being a mother ... about which so little has been written. Can mothers not hold a pen?'[17] Her 'apology' at the beginning of *Making Babies* is a tongue-in-cheek reference to this silence and the tendency to privilege mother as object, iconic mother, mother-Nation, rather than mother as subject: 'Speech is a selfish act, and mothers should probably remain silent.'[18] Enright's work deals with the gap in the symbolization of motherhood as a subject position. She details the embodied experience of pregnancy and motherhood in *Making Babies*, and, in her fiction, mothers speak from beyond the grave, from the occluded position they have been designated. It is this cultural repression of the mother as subject that both Anne Mulhall and Susan Cahill focus on in their essays. Mulhall, through analyses of *The Wig* and *What Are You Like?*, points to a persistence of ghosts and untimely hauntings in Enright's work, linking these spectral presences specifically with Enright's interest in animating the buried maternal presence in the Irish literary tradition through alternate means of representation and signification. Similarly, Cahill investigates the effects that occlusion of the mother from our cultural imaginary has on mother-daughter relations and female subjectivity through her discussion of the twins' feelings of alienation and loss in *What Are You Like?*. She highlights the dislocations at work in the novel as indicative of the trauma felt by this obscuration of the maternal body.

The body itself is a central concern of Enright's work. As she writes in *Making Babies*, 'I have always paid close attention to what the body is and what it actually does'.[19] For Hedwig Schwall, it is this intimate focus on the body, instrumental in Enright's 'female aesthetic',[20] that offers a paradigm for thinking about feminine intersubjectivity and human interaction. Schwall also specifically focuses on Enright's treatment of religion in *The Gathering*, highlighting Enright's critique of a Catholic ethos that represses and silences an embodied female subject, which is countered through Enright's 'revolutionary stylistics'.

Enright's style is explored by Elke D'hoker in her essay, which focuses on Enright's short fiction. Given the seventeen-year gap between the publication of the two short story collections, it is illuminating to consider the development of Enright's style through a comparison of the two. D'hoker situates Enright's short fiction within the Irish short story tradition, relates the work to developments in international feminism towards concerns with difference and otherness, and charts a move from her earlier experimental style, what Patricia Coughlan calls, 'A certain deliberate excess of linguistic effect over fictional cause',[21] to a more realist mode at work in *Taking Pictures*. It is a move that Enright describes in her interview here as one aimed towards her readers, in her words, 'a more generous impulse'. Despite this 'impulse towards the real', she notes that 'language itself, obviously, is not real. It doesn't want to be real',[22] and texts such as *The Gathering* explicitly explore the unreliability of history, memory and representation.

Stylistically, Enright's work has been characterized by innovation, experimentation and a close attention to language itself: 'I find that ... language strains toward metaphor. And I follow on.'[23] She explains her surrealism as linguistically informed: 'I might make the metaphor radical, like I have an angel knock on the door instead of saying he looked like an angel.'[24] A major influence on her work are the word games and surreal fantasy of Lewis Carroll's *Alice's Adventures in Wonderland*, which she cites as her favourite book from her childhood,[25] and can be clearly seen to inform Grace's father's linguistic idiosyncrasies in *The Wig*. Other notable influences include Angela Carter, particularly in her early work, and Joyce, from whom Enright says she pilfers freely.[26] *The Gathering*, for example, is particularly informed by *Dubliners*. In various interviews, Enright has mentioned the wide range of her inspirations from myths and fairy tales to American and Canadian realism, such as the work of Cormac McCarthy and Alice Munro. Schwall captures this range when she writes that Enright

> has antennae to catch the almostness Rilke specialized in, and combines this with the suggestive epistemology of John Banville, the witty distance of A.L. Kennedy, the physicality of Jeannette Winterson, and the incisiveness of Sylvia Plath. One could almost say that her prose is more anatomy than analysis.[27]

Enright's work is decidedly postmodern in its emphasis on fragmentation, metafiction, parody, parataxis, linguistic play and privileging of performative and 'atomised' identities.[28] Coughlan, in her 2004 article on Irish feminism and postmodernity, groups Enright with other contemporary Irish women writers such as Anne Haverty, Éilís Ní Dhuibhne and Mary Morrissy, who share a postmodern aesthetics and politics and call into question the assumptions of a masculinist Irish literary tradition. To this list we could also add the work of writers such as Claire Kilroy, Lia Mills, Emma Donoghue and Claire Keegan.

However, analyses of Enright's work need not just be read in terms of the Irish context, as Heidi Hansson argues in her essay. Hansson worries that over-emphasis on the local might limit readings of the novels and calls for a broadening of frames of reference that might include such categories as women's literature, postmodern literature, historical literature, postnationalist literature and world literature, the last of which she discusses at length in relation to *The Wig*. Attention to both the local and the global runs though all the essays in this volume, and is particularly evident in Patricia Coughlan's essay on *The Pleasure of Eliza Lynch* in which she contextualizes the novel in relation to Paraguayan history. She also reads *Pleasure* as a postmodern comment on modernist narratives of colonial dislocation, such as Joseph Conrad's *Nostromo*, offering investigations of embodied feminine agency and explicitly foregrounding the material world of bodies, death, food, sex and consumption – these are concerns that run throughout Enright's work. As Coughlan argues, *Pleasure* 'presents experience as discontinuous, while inescapably concrete because based in the bodily', and this materiality of Enright's postmodernism is note-worthy. Her experiments in style matter:

> The difference in my postmodern impulse is that I actually mean it. There's a sincerity to my discourse that isn't in most postmodern writing (although I'm not particularly interested in the labels). If you look at [*Making Babies*] … where there is a description of a child crying and it's like 'hnang hnang hnang'. And it goes on for the whole page. That would be a very postmodern thing to do – to play with the typeface, but it was literally a very honest attempt to explain what it is like to listen to a crying baby.[29]

Making Babies is Enright's one non-fiction book publication, although since the beginning of her writing career she has produced opinion pieces in, for example, the *Irish Times*, *The London Review of Books* and the *Guardian*. The essays in this collection engage productively with this journalism, which combines Enright's wit with an incisive look at current affairs and contemporary culture. Perhaps the most infamous is her piece, 'Disliking the McCanns', which came under intense and hysterical media scrutiny following her 2007 Booker win. The article gave complex consideration to the public reaction of the McCann case,[30] whereby Enright embodies the voice of 'dislike' that structured responses to the couple, suggesting the reason for negative reaction to be symptomatic of psychological projection ('Distancing yourself from the McCanns is a recent but potent form of magic. It keeps our children safe'),[31] a point the media failed to capture and Enright and her piece became a target of tabloid attack.[32]

Enright's identification of the psychological response on the part of the public illustrates her abiding engagement with psychoanalytic discourse. Many of our contributors respond to this through their use of theorists such as Sigmund Freud, Jacques Lacan, Julia Kristeva, Luce Irigaray, Gilles Deleuze, Judith Butler, Bracha Ettinger and Rosi Braidotti. The first essay of the collection is concerned with Enright's short fiction from her first publication, *The Portable Virgin*, to her most recent *Taking Pictures*. Following this the essays deal chronologically with her novels from *The Wig My Father Wore* to *The Gathering*, and the book concludes with three essays that provide overviews of her work. We share with all our contributors an admiration for Enright's remarkable work, with its playful prose and insightful commentary. Refracted through Enright's eyes, the sinews and fibers of human life take shape in new and startling ways. Above all, Enright's fiction constantly surprises with its incisive and darkly witty take on our contemporary world.

NOTES

1. For further biographical information, see: M. Felter, 'Anne Enright', in *Dictionary of Irish Literature, Revised and Enlarged Edition* Vol. 1, ed. R. Hogan (Westport, CT: Greenwood, 1996.), pp.410–1; C. Moloney, 'Anne Enright', in *Twenty-First-Century British and Irish Novelists*, ed. Michael R. Molino (Detroit, MI: Gale, 2003); S.E. Stenson, 'Anne Enright', in *Irish Women Writers: An A-Z Guide*, ed. A.G. Gonzalez (Westport, CT: Greenwood, 2006), pp.120–4; and 'Anne Enright', in A.O. Weekes, *Unveiling Treasures: The Attic Guide to the Published Works of Irish Women Literary Writers* (Dublin: Attic Press, 1993), pp.120–1.

2. A. Enright, 'Muscular Metaphors in Anne Enright: An Interview by Hedwig Schwall', *The European English Messenger*, 17, 1 (2008), p.21.

3. A. Enright, 'Interview by Claire Bracken and Susan Cahill', in this volume, p.30.

4. See A. Enright, 'Smile', 'Felix', 'Thirst', and 'Seascape', in *First Fictions Introduction 10* (London: Faber and Faber, 1989), pp.121–50.

5. A. Enright, 'Anne Enright interview by Caitriona Moloney', in *Irish Women Speak Out: Voices from the Field*, ed. C. Moloney and H. Thompson (Syracuse, NY: Syracuse University Press, 2003), p.52.

6. C. Tóibín, 'Introduction', in *The Penguin Book of Irish Fiction*, ed. C. Tóibín (Harmondsworth: Viking, 1999), p.xxxiii.

7. Enright, 'Anne Enright interview by Caitriona Moloney', p.59.

8. Ibid., p.64.

9. A. Enright, *The Gathering* (London: Jonathan Cape, 2007), p.142.

10. A. Enright, Interview by Matthew Sweet, *Night Waves*, BBC Radio 3, 11 March 2008.

11. Enright, 'Interview by Claire Bracken and Susan Cahill', p.28.
12. Enright, 'Interview by Caitriona Moloney', p.64.
13. Enright, *The Gathering*, p.1.
14. See Susan Cahill's essay in this collection for a discussion of the carpet in *What Are You Like?*
15. Enright, 'Interview by Claire Bracken and Susan Cahill', p.31.
16. Enright, 'Interview by Caitriona Moloney', p.61.
17. A. Enright, *Making Babies: Stumbling into Motherhood* (London: Jonathan Cape, 2004), p.42.
18. Ibid., p.1.
19. Ibid., p.2.
20. Enright, 'Muscular Metaphors', p.22.
21. See P. Coughlan, this volume, p.107.
22. Enright, 'Muscular Metaphors', p.22.
23. Ibid.
24. Ibid.
25. Ibid., p.18.
26. See Enright, 'Interview by Claire Bracken and Susan Cahill', pp.23–4.
27. H. Schwall, 'Anne Enright, *The Gathering*', *Irish University Review*, 37, 2 (2007), p.597.
28. See P. Coughlan, 'Irish Literature and Feminism in Postmodernity', *Hungarian Journal of English and American Studies*, 10, 1–2 (2004), pp.175–202.
29. Enright, 'Interview by Claire Bracken and Susan Cahill', p.18.
30. The McCann case refers to the disappearance of British 3-year-old Madeleine McCann from her holiday apartment in Portugal in 2007. The incident received widespread media coverage as well as speculation concerning her parents' implication in the disappearance.
31. A. Enright, 'Diary: Disliking the McCanns', *London Review of Books*, 29, 19 (2007), p.39.
32. For an example of a more balanced media reaction to the piece, see S. Lee, 'Anne Enright was Spot On about McCann Mania', *Daily Telegraph*, 22 October 2007.

CHAPTER TWO

An Interview with Anne Enright, August 2009

CLAIRE BRACKEN and SUSAN CAHILL

You've had so many interviews, especially since your Booker win — is there one question you're constantly asked?

I was thinking about talking to you earlier and I realized that I have been emptied out by the whole process. I've actually no thoughts any more at all and I think that's a reasonably hopeful place to be actually. I've sort of worn out my opinions now. I need a new set. I don't necessarily believe anything I used to say anymore — not that I believed it much at the time! You're often being interviewed by people who don't read, so that's just mad because there's no connection. They endlessly ask what it's like to win the Booker. 'Increasingly tedious, because I have to talk to people like you, who don't read books!' And I also find questions about reputation extremely difficult. Reputation is not something that is in my control, it's not in the writer's control, although there is, I think, some kind of feedback loop involved with issues of reputation. Books happen one reader at a time. The writer's relationship is with the individual reader, not with the crowd. It's very difficult to tease apart and for a lot of the public stuff, like winning awards, the writer is fairly passive. You can only control what you do, which is write a book, and you have to relinquish that attempt to control how it's perceived.

When you talk about reputation, are you specifically referring to the perception of your work?

Well it's interesting to think about the kind of questions you're asked over a lifetime's writing. People have always got some sort of agenda, harmless or otherwise, some sort of theory. When I started out, I was always asked about 'Irish writing'. So for the whole of the eighties I was discussing Ireland and Irishness and how problematic that was as an idea, or how interesting, or how encouraging, or how energized you were, annoyed you were – all the contradictions involved. I never really got a gendered approach in the whole interview thing because they couldn't do two categories at once, and 'Irish' was a more interesting, or easier, or more fashionable discourse, it seemed, than 'woman'. So you weren't a woman writer, you were an Irish writer. But you know, I am a woman, sometimes, for weeks at a time, and I am only Irish of a Tuesday. And the thing about the Booker is that it takes you out of those two boxes and it puts you into another box, which is Booker winner. They forget about your gender and your Irishness, pretty much, and just call you successful instead. Or they put you into a story about the British novel, or the novel after empire. So it shifts a little bit.

We'd like to ask a really general question about your writing process? How do you begin – with an image, an idea, an agenda, or a particular form, or tone or mood?

The whole sort of area of genetic criticism terrifies me, because I don't know how I begin particularly. I just sort of pootle along, you know. Inspiration – this idea of things descending, or things coming from some-where else is worrisome for me, because if ideas are bestowed then they can also be withheld. Whatever the mechanism is it's not externalized like that for me.

How important is rhythm to your writing?

Well, certainly the voice and the cadence of the voice is very important. That is where it happens. That is where the energy is. I get a bit bored with my rhythms actually, I try not to make them sound fatuous. But on this book that I'm writing at the minute, I'm a bit worried about her voice. You know you have the character, some essence, and you have the character's problem and after that you sort of stick bits on. The character walks into your head, and then there is – what kind of shoes are they wearing? And you have to build the voice, you have to do exercises, almost, get a bit more flexibility into the voice. Say, give her an M.A., no, don't give her an M.A. See how that works. So I'm building the character, it's quite like improvisation, it's quite like the actors' room. There are certain things you know, and know very clearly – you are often answering a question that was posed by the last book. I realized at the end of The Gathering that although the book is saturated in a kind of off-tone sexuality, although it is full of desire, we don't know what Veronica wants. So this time, I thought, well, we know what this one wants. This is like a whole new problem. So that's what I'm doing! You say, I haven't done that yet, or I haven't done it properly. Then, of course at the end of it you say: oh no, it's all the same old, same old. Here we go again. And I thought it was new and I thought I was pushing out the envelope.

The new novel? When is it due out?

Well, I never had deadlines before. I did a deadline once and it was a disaster and I never did a deadline again. I sort of took my ball and ran away and wouldn't play any of those games. But I'm doing a deadline on this one. I'm also using a different method, because I'm starting at the beginning and really holding the line and it's chronological and that's all very interesting as a discipline, so I'm enjoying all those kind of constrictions as it were. It's anchored in a particular place. It's chronological, but it is involved in ideas of chronology as well and there is a kind of worry about cause and effect.

It could be argued that your work has moved from an experimental to a more realist style. Would you agree?

Yeah, absolutely. Yes! And that's what I wanted to do. I mean the grand theory being that of course cubism was Picasso's great contribution, but nobody looks at those pictures any more. What we like is the Blue Period, a sentimental, lyrical stage, and then what we really like is the last Neo-Classical work, which is informed by the cubist thing and it's fabulous! Fantastic! So, that's my line on it basically. That said, it's not something I can do all that much about. It's as much about weakness as about strength, in a way. I mean, I write from a very deep place, or I try to. And I didn't necessarily want those earlier books to be so fragmented. So I want to be more in control of the process without being too much in control – I think that books that are overly controlled are dead. Maybe it's the wrong way to go. I probably should be saying: 'No I am a wild creature and everybody must make a greater attempt to understand me.' But that's not my impulse. My impulse is very strongly toward the reader and so that's where I'm going.

Relating that to your two short story collections – one of our contributors, Elke D'hoker argues that The Portable Virgin is more experimental and Taking Pictures is more realist. Do you also see a development in terms of a theme or of tone?

I don't know if it's better to be less experimental, or worse. I suspect it's probably worse, in a way [Laughs]. Anyway, who do you love? Do you love Bohumil Hrabal, this wonderful Czech, absurdist writer, or do you love Alice Munro? Of course, you can love both of them. The early stories, they achieve their own metaphor and they stop. So the people in those stories are artefacts of language. They only exist in those sentences. They don't exist outside those sentences. And maybe I get tired of that, maybe it's time to have people who have a life independent of your sticking them down on the page. If you look at the woman in the bingo story ['Luck be a Lady', The Portable Virgin], where she's obsessed by numbers and then all the numbers make sense it's this kind of post-Pynchon paranoia. I find it extremely interesting to use something like Pynchon in a female context, in somebody, a woman, who's playing bingo. That was very exciting to me at the time. But she is squished, you know what I mean? That's what she is. She's this person with an addiction to numbers. Even her skirt is too tight and I've stuck diamante on her ears! But a lot of the stories [in The Portable Virgin] are about freedom as well or about women breaking out of systems. So, yes these are very interesting themes. Whereas the woman in 'Yesterday's Weather' – she is in a hotel room with a crying baby – the strength of the recognition that story gets from people who have had children is very gratifying. It's very gratifying when people say 'oh yes, that story' and you know that you're telling a story that's currently available, but that hasn't been said properly before. I mean, things become more available to general speech and discussion, so the idea of creaming off these things is fun. It's good, it's nice, it's a more generous impulse as well, which I like.

I think what really struck us about Taking Pictures is that you do feel closer to the characters.

Right. The characters aren't always very likable though. I mean, the woman in 'Until the Girl Died', she'd drive me up the wall if I had to be around her for any length of time. I couldn't have her in a novel. I couldn't do a novel with her.

To return to your point about women breaking out of systems, Colm Tóibín called you a post-feminist writer. What does that term mean to you? Or would you consider yourself a post-feminist writer?

Well, Colm was just being fun. He was just being mischievous, which was great. And also because I think that was quite early on. But writers, in marketing terms, need a label and people found it difficult to label me.

It's been really taken up – a lot of essays quote it.

Right, you know you do wonder whether Ireland ever had a proper feminism, to have a post-feminism so quickly. Irish feminism had to fight so hard to claim control of the female body, that it didn't have time to fight for the female career. It was never as involved with money as British or American feminism. Personally, I am a feminist, I have always been a feminist, but I am not a deliberately feminist writer. I've never been an ideologue, because fiction suffers from ideology. Ideology is a very tertiary way of discussing the world. And the writer wants to look at things in a primary way, to make them new again. So you want to go under that existing discourse, linguistically, as well as every other way. The 'post' thing, might hook in with postmodernism. I had just written The Wig My Father Wore, which was like 'What! What is that?' It was a different kind of animal. Not that anyone cared all that much. Not many people were exclaiming! [Laughs] But it needed some kind of label and 'post-feminist' might do. The difference in my postmodern impulse is that I actually mean it. There's a sincerity to my discourse that isn't in most postmodern writing (although I'm not particularly interested in the labels). If you look at the baby book [*Making Babies: Stumbling into Motherhood*] where there is a description of a child crying and it's like 'hnang hnang hnang'. And it goes on for the whole page. That would be a very postmodern thing to do – to play with the typeface, but it was literally a very honest attempt to explain what it is like to listen to a crying baby. So I realized then that whatever postmodern impulse I have, it is an attempt to be more honest and not less. It's not an attempt to be clever, it's an attempt to be honest. So I was the only sincere postmodernist I know! On the other hand, I don't know what is 'post' about my feminism particularly. I'm not sure what the term means.

Well perhaps, in popular terms, the association of women with consumer spending. And in theoretical terms, a refusal of the collective feminine 'we', a non-identity politics of sorts.

In the way that Colm might have used it, apart from just to annoy everyone and give them something to think about, it would be – after that feminist discussion of the seventies and early eighties. Perhaps.

Because Grace at the beginning of *The Wig* has the career...

Yeah, you see, I did do the handbags certainly, but I looked at handbags as strange and peculiar objects in a way. My relationship to objects is not a consumerist one. It's not a relationship to money. It's a relationship to the object itself. It's almost infantile. So I'm pre-money, put it that way. Post-feminist, pre-money! Whereas the consumerism you see in other kinds of female fiction is a lot about purchasing power. So Grace has it all, but you don't see her going to the shops much, you know.

And *The Wig* came out just before the Celtic Tiger period …

I was always out of sync because I wrote *The Wig My Father Wore* after I'd given up a job, a very good job, as I subsequently realized. In the late eighties there was no boom, no one had a job, but I had, like Grace in *The Wig*, a good job and a car and a lot of freedom. I had a lot of things that people might think are a good thing to have. Then when the boom started, I was a starving artist in my garret. And I spent most of the boom raising babies out in Bray, which is far from cappuccino bars. So I've always been slightly out of sync.

Claire Kilroy said in an interview a few months ago: 'Recessions are good for creativity'. She said 'Writers don't have money. In a boom, that makes you a pariah. I think it affected Ireland's literary and artistic output. People who might have written got full-time jobs instead and it displaced their creativity.'[1]

Well, Claire would know; she would have more experience of it than I would, being a slightly different generation. I suppose there was a time that if you were clever in Ireland you wrote a book, whereas if you were clever in New York you went to film school, or later, into banking. But you have to ask — what did the boom do? What difference does money make to people? Certainly the lack of money is very stressful and difficult. Ireland used to have this idea that we were lovely warm friendly people because we were poor, so when we got rich all that would be lost. But you know, I never believed that 'lovely poor people' argument in the first place. And I don't think something essential was lost.

This current book I am writing is based during the boom and I did look at what boom and recession did to American letters. I thought Richard Yates's *Revolutionary Road* was one of the best of those American books about the suburbs. It was grounded in the fact that those guys came back from a war, so it made sense. So the blandness of the suburbs was something to be desired. It was something that was necessary.

I wasn't wildly enthusiastic about the boom. I didn't actually believe it, especially towards the end, there was something too frantic and aggressive about the story people were telling, the money story. But it was very, very sad to see it go. I don't know if recessions are good and bad for ... I don't think they're good for anything really. But certainly in my generation, anyone who stayed in Ireland was in the arts. That was basically also known as being on the dole, right. Because there was no other job. If you wanted any kind of job, you got on a plane. If you stayed in Ireland, as my generation of fellow students did in Trinity, then you were in the theatre, you were in the arts and that's what you were doing.

You are talking at the Mountains to the Sea Festival [September 2009] on whether the idea of a national literature has any meaning in the current age of globalization. Could you talk a little about this?

I get asked so much about Irishness that it makes me more than a little cross. I get cross with people who have large ideas about what a nation is. Or narrow ideas, when you think about it. So I have no time for ideas of authenticity that are based on nationhood. Someone once said to Gloria Steinam: 'You don't look like forty'. And she said, 'This is what forty looks like'. So, when people say 'You're Irish in this way' or 'You're not Irish in that way', I say 'This is what Irish looks like. This is what an Irish woman writes like.' And I write very passionately for an Irish audience. I think that the Irish audience is ignored in all of these conversations about how Irish you can be if you publish abroad or are successful abroad. No one talks about the Irish readership, which is huge and extremely important to Irish writers. Too much credence is given to the mediators between the Irish writer and the Irish audience, I mean the commentators and critics. That isn't Ireland. The readers are very interested, very involved, very engaged. When I wrote that baby book, I thought, well nobody who thinks they're somebody will read this book. I will have direct access to the Irish audience without any intermediary having a large opinion about it, because nobody in Ireland who thinks they're important will read about babies. So, there I have absolute, frank, conversational access to my readers with that book, which is great. So, that's all I have to say about that.

These are very interesting comments about readership and audience.

Well, how dare people tell us what it is to be Irish! How dare they! It's just something they insert between the book and the reader, a distorting lens. It's just an excuse to complain. There's a game of withholding that goes on in Irish life that gets more complex and absurd the more acclaimed the writer becomes abroad. And, when you think about it, it must be a very fruitful game, a very interesting game, because we are obliged to do better and better elsewhere. And so we do.

And there are so many expectations about what constitutes Irishness and the Irish novel.

Can I tell you what I do? – and no one has ever noticed this except for one little student, who came up to me in Malta, of all places – I use in my paragraphs, I mean sometimes so much that it annoys me, the kind of patterns of assonance and half rhyme that were used by the Irish poets and by Austin Clark that I loved so much at school. I should say that more, shouldn't I? When I talk about Irishness. But I am not allowed to own all that. Whoever owns the Irish bardic poets, it's not me.

But also, yes, writers always find themselves trying to break out of stereotypes of one type or another and deconstruct, pulling down, deconstructing things. I mean, that's one of the writer's jobs – to pull things down, start new.

What would you see your work as pulling down?

Well, I don't know. I mean, certainly ideas of Irish womanhood. Someday I'll call a book, 'It's not the Rose of Tralee'. So certainly that, yes.

And is that one of the reasons that so much of your work is concerned with motherhood?

No, that was an accident. That was an existential accident really. Yeah, that was a discovery. I never thought that that was going to be a factor particularly. But once I kind of cottoned on to it, and thought 'wow, this is a great subject'. All beliefs, nearly all kinds of national and religious belief, involve, finally, women staying at home. I mean, even fascist Germany was very involved in the idea of motherhood and hausfrauish-ness. So that is part of the deconstructive project. When I started out – and

I have to reiterate that all my opinions are at the moment in abeyance – I don't believe anything I say anymore because I don't know where I am really, or I'm in a kind of a new place, or a blank place, or an interestingly sort of fresh place – but certainly when I started off, when I was 18, 19, 20, I thought that it was part of my job to say things that Irish women had not said previously. It was certainly part of my job to do that. I don't know if that's what I'm doing now, but it was one of my original impulses.

And was foregrounding the body in your writing part of that impulse?

Well, you could say that all religious wars are fought over women's bodies and of course it was very interesting to come of age in the Eighties when the wars were about abortion, divorce, contraception. And it was very clear what it was all about. Certainly in retrospect, it was extremely clear what it was all about. But I think that extends beyond an Irish or a Catholic context, that ownership of the body. The imperative I feel to turn my women into subjects is part of a broader set of problems about gender and the objectification of women. We're always breaking out of those stereotypes or images, or we're always insisting on our subjectivity. And we're relentlessly turned into objects. And you could say that about other power structures, that we objectify the poor. It's not just the gender power structure. But all of these things are interlinked. It's about power, I suppose. About fighting back. So, when you say 'why is the body so important in the work?', I say, I don't know! Well, of course, we have nowhere else to be, right. So, the body is where we are, the body is the problem. You know, Yeats chained to a dying animal, all that kind of thing. The body dies, so it isn't just a modern problem. It is a very long-term issue [Laughs]. We didn't discover it, like, last year, you know, with plastic surgery! For me, it's not a problem of the mirror because my characters aren't very involved with the mirror. It's the problem of the body as it is experienced rather than as seen. But certainly, if you think about gender, you say well, what is the difference between men and women? It is first of all anatomical, so ok, that we know. The body is something that we can know, that is in some way true. The rest of it we don't know. And then you say, well, are women anatomically better designed for washing dishes? No! What does the anatomy actually do? That's interesting too.

Even at the level of language, the body seems bound up in the type of words you use. There's a type of writing that tries to abstract the body, but writing is actually a very embodied thing.

Yes, there's a lot of meat, a lot of gristle. I did a word search on 'meat' in The Gathering and took out about six 'meats'. And in The Gathering the opposition was between meat and blossom and plants. I tell students that you have to have one of the five senses in all of your sentences and then your reader is helpless. If you put a ball in, the reader has the sense of a ball. If you put a red ball in – the reader can't help but see the ball or can't help but have an experience of red. So if you use the senses then you're getting beyond your reader's conscious response, which I like to try to do. I regret the fact that I'm so cheerful about writing things that people find a bit strong sometimes, because I feel that that magnetizes the attention. If you put a taboo word into a sentence people just go 'Ohh!' They're hard wired. We're so sexually alert. If you put a taboo word into a sentence, the brain just goes nygiong, nygiong, nygiong. And you're half way down the page before you are reading properly again. So it overburdens the thing a little and so I have to be aware of that and perhaps be a bit more cautious. This next narrator is very coy. She won't say a damn thing. She says 'I can't name it. I can't name it', she says, 'It's love'. [Laughs] 'I'm in love.' And that's funny too. She says 'I'm not going to say it! I'm not going to say it!'

You have said that 'Joyce did not throw a shadow, he cast a great light. He made it possible to write about anything at all.'[2] Could you comment on Joyce's influence on your work?

I'm very louche about intertextual references. I mean, I steal and I stick things in and I don't think it's either mischievous or reverential or anything, it's just there, it's just part of the stuff, it's part of the available language and you can't ignore it. I suppose a lot of contemporary writers would put in references to television or cinema, but I don't do much contemporary, because it labels the work too strongly or narrows it down, socially. Joyce is a resource, he is a great resource. In *The Gathering*, when I wrote about 1925, well, you can't escape *Dubliners*. And I did read other contemporary work from that time but none of it reads properly after you've read *Dubliners*. It's like looking at old lino, at the retro patterns. You read Frank Duff, say, or you read people who aren't writers, to try and hear their social cadences, the things unsaid, the things that are known when you speak, that don't have to be articulated. But none of them produce the emotions that Joyce does, the atmosphere or the poignancy. He has it all, he's just really good. So that's your source, that turns into your source. I can't think of anybody in contemporary terms that would be available in a hundred years' time in that way. And I haven't even broached *Ulysses*. There are many things to like about Joyce. One of which was his lack of disgust, his relish, his anti-Puritanism which means that he's not a man at all. He's just not a bloke. I've said in the past that Joyce was the first Irish woman writer and I stand by that. He has all the faults that are ascribed to women writers.

And the opening section of *The Pleasure of Eliza Lynch* is very reminiscent of the Molly Bloom soliloquy.

Well thanks. I actually haven't read Molly Bloom in decades but of course there is a lot of it in Eliza in that first chapter. That was just fun. But it was kind of deliberate fun actually, because in a way I set myself against contemporary male writers who write about sex like it's the worst thing that could happen to anyone. So I very much deliberately set out to write a sex scene that was really good. Because it was a sexual relationship I thought that probably the sex was very important, it probably meant a lot, and it fact in some ways it meant everything, as she says, everything, at the time. I did a lot of research, again in the ephemera. I read, in Trinity library, sex advice for young married couples in America in the 1890s, so I was trying to look at how these things were discussed at the time. Then I realized that there was a huge difference from culture to culture. I read about a survey of French prostitutes in the nineteenth century, which was actually useful. But there's very little hard information about what actually went on and how people felt about it. So I was really going — what is it for this woman to have sex with this man? How do they consider it themselves? One thing I discovered was that it was generally assumed that it was better to be very fast, that was good. Whether it was not to disturb the woman too much [Laughs], or not to get anyone stirred up, fast was good! Fast was considered to be more hygienic and more reproductive. It's one of the reasons that it is quite a short episode [Laughs]. So I went through all this material and it was fascinating, of course. But I was no further on. So I arrived at the first line and I thought, well, at least I know this is true. So that's why I wrote it that way. And then I was free, which was good. But, you think in terms of you know, swooning, I don't know why/when women stopped swooning. But that was what they were supposed to do. In *Pamela*, the episode in *Pamela*, she's unconscious. So this is how difficult it is to go back to 1854, I mean that was a century after Pamela, but it is still hard to say what women thought sex was. So that's why I wrote that first line. I just said, what happened? It seemed to be the only way through. And that was good fun.

Your work seems to consistently deal with the themes of connection and disconnection. For example, in the short story 'Natalie' from *Taking Pictures*, the narrator is concerned that Natalie thinks 'we are not connected'. Could you comment on this?

Yeah, the exact same thing happens in 'Shaft' [*Taking Pictures*] where the woman says 'We're all just stuck together'. The girl in Natalie is only a dote. She's highly connected, you know. She's highly connected and obviously Natalie isn't and that is a problem and a question for her. The possibility that we are not connected is a shock to her. It always must be a shock, perhaps, for my characters to realize these things. I don't know. It's a kind of childhood experience, isn't it — it's not that you think everything is lovely, but it's part of the process of individuation, that requires some sort of — I was going to say cauterization — isn't that a very strong word. But it must require some sense of removal, of separation and loss.

Is that the issue in *The Pleasure of Eliza Lynch* — the question of subjectivity and loss?

These are not adolescent concerns, these are infantile concerns if you think about it — the idea of becoming an individual, of losing that kind of huge subjectivity. It's a kind of megalomania to be a baby. Your subjectivity extends to everything around you and then you lose that and the world becomes peopled by other subjects or objects, so that kind of process must be very shocking, and all these ideas of yearning and desire are also infantile. They're about the desire for the mother as well. So perhaps most of the things that provoke writers' work are very primal, very early. These are things that happen in the first year of your life. Who knows? They're endlessly problematic and interesting. The thing about 'Shaft,' this is a woman in a machine. She is in a lift, and I really love the idea of this pregnant woman in this box, it's umbilical really — the rope. So that floated my boat really and the same with Eliza — the pregnant woman on the boat, in a hammock. It was a kind of gyroscope. She herself is a kind of gravity machine, that she was a gyroscope for the child. But the woman in 'The Bed Department' is concerned about escalators, and the machine — there's an awful lot of it really, of putting the organic against the inorganic.

And why this interest in the machine?

In 'The House of the Architect's Love Story', the house is a kind of machine, although it's a very creative one. Apart from machines I'm also very interested in the difference between being inside a space and outside a space. And that would be a kind of feminist aesthetic about the internal and the external, which informs my own looking at my work, whether it informs the way I actually produce the work or not, I don't know. But 'Men and Angels' and an awful lot of the early stuff is about systems and machines. He tries to put love into a box. He kind of succeeds as well.

It's a very sad story

It is a very sad story but it's not a terribly good story! It's a bit derivative. What I like about it is the description of the kaleidoscope, which is,

I think, really sexy. I actually think it's somehow quite sexy to have the twist of the kaleidoscope as a description of sex.

Does that link then with the scene in *The Wig My Father Wore* where Grace and Stephen's lovemaking is described in terms of alphabet shapes?

Oh the alphabet! Well you see, that was in my high metaphorical stage. Yeah, the alphabet was just a bit of fun. There's something even further to be said about this, which is, in a story like 'Historical Letters' where the past, and the telling of the past, is a kind of machine, or language could be seen as a kind of mechanism as well. Language is a machine. Quite a good one, actually.

Could you consider that in relation to Eliza Lynch as well – that history is a mechanism that obscures her?

Eliza is a much more social and public novel really. She becomes a national object very quickly in the book. We have her journal going all the way through the book, but it is only a description of her journey and we have no idea how she feels about anything from the time she lands in Asunción. I don't have a huge amount of sympathy for her, except as somebody trapped in the gaze of the other, or of the crowd, which is what she is. Eliza isn't one of those women characters that I want to liberate. She wouldn't be burdened with a huge amount of self-knowledge. It would have been difficult to put her at the centre of a book in a different way, in a more realistic way. There's nothing to be gained from moving close to her subjectivity because there's not much going on in there.

So, in the sections with Eliza's voice …

Well, they are sympathetic – she's interesting as a fresh adventurous person. She does not know what she will become.

Eliza's representation oscillates between 'Angel of Mercy' and 'Angel of Death'.[3] Does this refer to a fear of the feminine and the female body, as well as an objectification and idealization?

Well, yes it's the mythologizing of women and I think it's to do with how the crowd sees her, it's not how an individual sees her. So it's an archetype. She is an icon, it's a crowd phenomenon. I don't think I would write an individual seeing that happen – that shift between 'angel of mercy' and 'angel of death'. It just wouldn't work for me. A male writer might do that – I don't know. I'm very interested, or I was very interested, in a book by Elias Canetti called *Crowds and Power*. He writes about different kinds of crowds, like the mass of the dead, for example. But Eliza is a greedy girl. I did think that Eliza was about the boom, when I was writing it, but nobody else noticed that. Stewart at one stage says that he thinks that her real talent was for shipping. You know, that she could do this amazing consumer thing in the middle of all the mould and this very organic, semi-tropical place, I made up. She could do that – I mean it's not Manaus [city in Brazil] but it was tropical enough – so she was better at it than all the girls these days with their Louis Vuitton.

Because she is a consumer ...

Completely, but also when you're looking in terms of consumption, when Eliza comes into the theatre, this is her apotheosis, she becomes this object. What you're looking at is a Worth gown. I mean Charles Worth started later in Paris, he was a tiny bit too late, but if you looked at the price of the clothes, it would be certainly more than the price of a dwelling, or of a horse. It was as different as the bankers and their cleaners. It was an amazing difference of proportion and scale. It's the difference between Abramovich and somebody in the street. So that was interesting to me as well.

And all those stories about her being cannibalistic ...

There's many stories about Idi Amin, and his guests finding bits of people in the fridge. I did a general sweep of dictators, great dictators we have known. I read, in order to prepare for Eliza or research Eliza, Imelda Marcos's biography certainly, and Svetlana Stalin's biography of her father, which has the most glorious line in it, which is 'My father was a Sagittarius. He was an archer, a seeker.' [Laughs] I wanted to put this at the beginning of Eliza. My publisher said no, nobody would get it. The seed of that book came many years ago when I was talking to a Filipino friend and he said Ferdinand [Marcos] was OK but she's just completely evil. This was in the 1980s. Or in Romania, myself and Colm [Tóibín] and Hugo Hamilton, were on the Black Sea, Constanza, where Ovid was exiled. On the Black Sea, which has no life in it whatsoever, and on the left was Elena's petrochemical's factory, and on the right Nicolae's nuclear power plant, just up the road [Elena and Nicolae Ceauşescu]. And they all said, he was OK, the honourable dictator who has the interests of his country at heart, you know, tired, worn out, two o'clock in the morning, papers falling on the floor, 'oh dear sorry another death warrant', just trying to keep it all together! But she was evil. So Eliza is, as I say, a very social public sort of book about icons and crowds and not about anyone learning anything. If you look at a lot of fiction, it's about someone learning something. Eliza doesn't exactly learn anything. In fact you could say she loses her ability to learn. And though she is quite brave, she is also wrongheaded. She just makes more and more mistakes. And I couldn't tell it otherwise. I killed her son, mind you – though that was also historically true – so she certainly does, you might say, see what her path has led her to.

One of the major concerns of The Gathering is remembering and forgetting, and the relationship between storytelling and memory – the unreliability of the past as it is uncovered. Could you comment on this?

Yes, I was writing recently about Alice Munro for The Globe and Mail in Canada and I realized how important memory is for her fiction. Her memory is good, her characters' memory is good. And their memory refreshes the past. The past changes because of events in the present; the past becomes more apparent. And the characters learn about their own pasts by the good functioning of their memory. So you could also say, that they don't remember things properly, even though they have really good solid memories, even though this is the scaffolding of the work. I was at one stage interested in hysteria and the history of hysteria. Also the whole alien abduction thing really charmed me completely. But in the eighties, when I was starting out – alien abduction was kind of more the nineties – in the eighties it was all recovered and false memories of child abuse, and group abuse, what might have been called in the old-fashioned terms as mass hysterias, but very, very serious. Not in Ireland. Ireland has a different kind of thing going on. But in Britain. And I was there 1985–86, at the University of East Anglia, which is when it was all going on. I see how important my reading in psychoanalysis is to my work. I read all of Freud when I was in college and sort of loved Freud's work and laughed at it as well. But it's a great way to think about things and he's also a wonderful writer and stylist. A wonderful stylist. I like Adam Phillips' work, I am also quite interested in Melanie Klein. So the process of recovering memories – that's already an interesting phrase – the process of remembering and forgetting and undoing the forgetting and re-remembering and all of those, these are great, and also very modernist, questions. Modernism is often concerned with a kind of ever-expanding present, a moment. Realism, you might say, is about continuity, about cause and effect, about change, about growth, all these. It's almost like there are two axes in my work, one of which spreads, which is the moment, a sort of infinite moment that is somehow very difficult to get over or beyond – very pleasurable too. And then this other axis, where I try to construct, or refuse to construct, a linear self that is connected moment by moment through a life. The connections are where it gets interesting. That is part of what I'm working on at the moment, though nobody, with a bit of luck, will notice [Laughs]. This is part of it. So I've always been interested in that because I'm interested in the construction of a self. And the word 'construction' is also interesting and relates to what we were talking about machinery and systems and connections, as opposed to an organic self which relates very closely to the body and the inescapability of the body. So the subject matter of abuse is very keenly connected to issues about memory. I mean, *The Gathering* is interested in the edges between, certainly fantasy or imagination and memory, between memory and history and where we let go of memory, where it ossifies and turns into history, where it becomes static, when people die. You kind of think of history as what happens after people are dead, it is the story that is told when there is no one left who remembers, no one there to contradict it. And yet history is something that has to be broken open again and again and retold, even though officially it's something that has stopped. But as we continue, history shifts and changes all the time. We see different things. It is on the scale of a society that this happens. In Alice Munro's work it happens on the scale of a life, that a life is rediscovered because of what's happening in the present. These are great themes. And child abuse fits in with all of these problems and concerns. So The Gathering was the book that is most like one of my books really. Someone said to me that it made my other work more clear. So that's what a writer really wants. If you're writing a book that will make their other books more legible, then you know you're getting somewhere.

You mention in an interview with Hedwig Schwall that you are very impatient with the real.

I am very impatient with the real. I'm very impatient with the claim to be real, okay, because I just don't think it's possible. There are many ways of writing about life itself. Language is already an act of translation from the real. So I think that once you've made that leap anything goes. And I think of people who claim to be real as people in denial of that first act of translation into words. Words are not reality, broadly speaking. The description of an act is not the act. I think, once you're through that barrier and you're into language, then you can do whatever the hell you like and if you're going to get very pious about it and say, no I'm going to write the truth and everyone else is just making it up, that particular kind of piety bores me. I shouldn't say this because it is the kind of dominant discourse, or morality. So many writers do this that I can't afford to insult them all actually! [Laughs] For myself I feel I can't do that particular sleight of hand, that trick that says 'all this is real'. Or I don't claim that trick.

Has this any connection to influences you've mentioned like *Alice in Wonderland*, or fairy tales and myth and legends in terms of the fantastic?

Yes, you see I'm sort of moving away from it and I'm moving towards the real which makes many of my statements a nonsense! In my twenties I would have been hugely interested in all of the above. I mean the fairy tales and the myths and legends. I was never interested in stereotypes, I was going to say archetypes, but if you're interested in stereotypes then you're a satirist and I'm absolutely the furthest thing away from a satirist. I don't write satire at all. What I'm finally interested in is in work that keeps moving. I'm interested in things that are not static. I'm interested in writing that is alive and has a life independent of me as well. Anything that tries to nail things down annoys me, within a book, or when talking about books. The thing about fairy tales, legends whatever, or metaphors, all of these are fun, this is colour, this is excitement and adventure, it's good fun. I suppose it's also escape. If you bring all the concerns down to the level of the sentence, which is where it all happens – how much are you going to limit your sentence? How small is your sentence going to be? Is it going to be just as big as it is or is it going to have value added in terms of metaphor? Metaphor can be spooky. Flaubert said that metaphors are like vermin, he was picking them out of his work all the time. What I like to do if I can is to get the sense of opening and possibility you get with metaphor under the sentence and not in the sentence. I like to bury my effects and keep it fairly real on the surface, or real is shorthand, but keep it kind of small on the surface, and have the resonance, the potential, underneath it without stating it. But then, that's all bullshit, that would be a very posh way to proceed but actually I'm very involved in the character who is narrating the book and they have a whole other way of describing the world from that. I would like to go into third person next time around and do exactly what I'm describing there. That's what I want to be, right. I'm very bad at describing what I actually have been in the past, but I do sort of know what I want to be in the future, maybe, as a writer.

NOTES

1. Quoted in P. Freyne, 'We're Back to Normal Service', *Sunday Tribune*, 26 April 2009.
2. A. Enright, 'Muscular Metaphors in Anne Enright: An Interview by Hedwig Schwall', *The European English Messenger*, 17, 1 (2008), pp.16–22.
3. A. Enright, *The Pleasure of Eliza Lynch* (New York: Grove Press, 2002), p.122.

CHAPTER THREE

Distorting Mirrors and Unsettling Snapshots: Anne Enright's Short Fiction

ELKE D'HOKER

Seventeen years and four novels separate Enright's first collection of short stories, *The Portable Virgin* (1991), from *Taking Pictures* (2008), her second one. Moreover, there are nineteen years between Enright's first published stories, 'Felix' and 'Seascape' in Faber's *First Fictions: Introduction 10* (1989), and the publication of her collected stories, *Yesterday's Weather*, in 2008.[1] With her recent return to short fiction in *Taking Pictures* and *Yesterday's Weather*, Anne Enright shows that she does not belong to that considerable group of novelists to whom a collection of stories is but an apprentice work, a first and easier outing in print.[2] Her stories thus merit a place in the rich tradition of the Irish short story and deserve the attention of literary critics as much as her novels. To the literary critic, the considerable gap between the two collections is, of course, an interesting one, prompting questions about the evolution of Enright's art. How did Enright's short fiction change in the course of these two decades? What developments can be noted in terms of narrative form, style, or subject matter? And do these changes reflect other national and international trends in fiction in general and the short story in particular? These are some of the questions that I propose to address in this essay, hoping to gain insight into both Enright's development as a writer and her place within the Irish literary tradition.

FROM DESIRE TO DEATH

Reviewers of Enright's fiction have often noted how the twin themes of sex and death dominate her fiction.[3] Viewed comparatively, however, a shift of focus from desire to death seems to take place from The Portable Virgin to Taking Pictures. In the first collection, women's bodies and desires are at the forefront of most stories. In 'The Portable Virgin', 'Revenge' and 'Historical Letters', this desire is the frustrated, yearning desire of a woman for her adulterous husband or departed lover. In order to regain their lover's desire, the protagonists of these stories are prepared to take extreme measures. In 'Revenge', the first-person narrator decides to 'be unfaithful *with* my husband, rather than *against* him' and chooses the 'suburban solution' of advertising for 'other couples who may be interested in some discreet fun'.[4] After all, she points out, 'I had my needs too: a need to be held in, to be filled, a need for sensation. I wanted revenge and balance. I wanted an awfulness of my own.'[5] Yet the occasion does not bring the hoped for reconciliation with her husband. Finding herself in the spare room with the other husband, she is reminded of wetting the bed as a child: 'First it is warm then it gets cold. I would go into my parents' bedroom, with its smell, and start to cry.'[6]

In several other stories, however, female desire is an active and even destructive force, as the classic adultery story is reversed with a vengeance. In 'Luck be a Lady', Mrs Hanratty's desire for a stranger she meets in the local pub upsets the ordered world of numbers she has created for herself: 'That night, for the first time in her life, Maeve Hanratty lost count of the vodkas she drank ... She wanted him. It was as simple as that.'[7] In '(She Owns) Every Thing', Cathy's predictable life behind the handbag counter of a department store is disturbed when she 'fell in love one day with a loose, rangy woman who came to her counter and to her smile and seemed to pick her up with the same ease as she did an Argentinian calf-skin shoulder bag'. As a result, 'Cathy began to slip. She made mistakes' and ultimately 'started to sleep around'.[8] 'Indifference' also turns the tables on the traditional seduction story, when the female protagonist picks up a young man in a bar and enjoys a one-night stand which robs him of his virginity. And in an even more self-conscious literary parody, 'Felix' goes back to countless 'Lolita-stories' by focusing on an older woman's affair with a young boy. In her 'suicide note', the narrator tackles the taboo subject of female desire:

> Old women are never perverts. They may be 'dotty' or 'strange', poor things, they may, and often do, 'suffer from depression'; but they emphatically do not feel up boys in public parks ... I want I want I want. I am not an hysteric. I am a woman of ten and a half stone with a very superior brain. I do not know what the word 'maternal' was ever supposed to mean.[9]

Enright's foregrounding, in these early stories, of women's bodies and desires brings to bear a theme she would continue to develop in her novels.[10] At the same time, this emphasis on women's powerful sensuality is also reflective of feminist developments in late-twentieth-century literature in general. Enright's critique of what has been a traditionally powerless feminine identity and her insistence on the reality of female desire seem in particular indebted to Angela Carter's focus on women's identity and desire in the short stories collected in The Bloody Chamber and Black Venus.[11] Through the use of parody, metafiction and postmodern play, both writers draw attention to the performative dimension of feminine identity, as captured in Enright's title image of the 'portable virgin' which can be appropriated and discarded at will.

Although desire is certainly not absent in Taking Pictures, the objects of desire have changed. More than sex and men, the female protagonists in this second collection want love, happiness and children. The story 'What You Want' seems to be an answer of sorts to the narrator's very explicit sexual desire in 'Felix': 'I want I want I want.' After lengthy deliberations, the narrator – a middle-aged Irish cleaning lady in London – decides, 'I want grandchildren. More than anything, I want grandchildren. Because grandchildren are simple. You wish for them and you have them. And I don't care if they are ashamed of me.'[12] As the protagonist rejects the wishes she would have made earlier in her life – for beauty, men and passion – it becomes clear that she has come to value love, and, in particular, a mother's love for her (grand)children, as the most important thing in her life. Moreover, the narrator's frequent references to ageing suggest a strong link between these modified desires and the awareness of mortality. This connection between death and desire can in fact be traced throughout the whole collection. Mortality, or the intimation of it, appears in every story of Taking Pictures. Examples include Kitty's miscarriage in 'In the Bed Department', the death of an anorexic sister in 'Little Sister', and the (impending) death of a parent in 'Natalie', 'Honey' and 'The Cruise'. In 'Pillow', the protagonist is almost smothered by one of her roommates and, in 'Here's to Love', the protagonist is held at gunpoint by a rooftop sniper. Death makes its appearance as a ghost – an 'extra corpse'[13] – in 'Caravan', as 'Old Nick' in 'What You Want', and as a woman with a slit throat in 'Wife'. The reality of death permeates these stories, just as the reality of desire pervades The Portable Virgin.

Several of the middle-aged protagonists of the stories in Taking Pictures are trying to come to terms with ageing. In 'Until the Girl Died', the narrator finds her husband crying on the sofa after the sudden death of one of his euphemistically called 'lapses': '[He was] staring mortality in the face', the narrator notes wryly, 'And what else? His own smallness.'[14] In 'The Cruise', Kate watches her elderly parents 'go through the departure gate at Dublin airport – her mother in a powder-blue track-suit and her father in white running shoes' and she realizes 'that they would die. It was the tracksuit that did it.'[15] These 'intimations of mortality' are typically rendered in brief moments which both puncture the story and hold it together. In these instants, the protagonists become aware of the finiteness of life, or by implication, of its limits and inevitable disappointments. In 'Natalie', for instance, the young narrator is trying to figure out in retrospect what it was that 'broke' on the night of the debs' dance.[16] She finally comes to the following conclusion, 'It was the sheets. When I lay down, just for a second, on Mr and Mrs Casey's moss-green sheets. Before the dance, when I was all dolled up in my silk skirt ... It was the smell of those sheets – cool, unwashed; like something I really wanted, going stale.'[17] The stale smell of this marriage/sick bed – Mrs Casey has cancer – confronts the narrator with the futility of her youthful desire for love and passion, crystallized in the long-awaited dance, as she recognizes that the reality of life and marriage may be nothing like her dreams of it.

Such moments of insight, which structure several of the stories in Taking Pictures, are reminiscent of a characteristic feature of the modern short story. In her theory of the short story, Valerie Shaw notes that 'short stories often work towards a single moment of revelation ... suddenly the fundamental secret of things is made accessible and ordinary circumstances are transfused with significance',[18] while Clare Hanson has pointed out that in the modern short story 'a moment of heightened awareness acts as a focus, a structural equivalent for conventional resolution of plot'.[19] Joyce, of course, called these moments 'epiphanies', for Woolf they were 'moments of being', and for Frank O'Connor they were the 'moment[s] of change in a person's life ... and anything that happens to that person afterwards, they never feel the same about again'.[20]

Yet several stories of *Taking Pictures* also offer a sense of life going on in spite of – or even in defiance of – the sudden insights or intimations of mortality. In 'Yesterday's Weather', for instance, a couple with a small baby returns home after an exhausting family weekend and a violent row, and though 'The whole world seemed as tender as they were', the protagonist realizes that life goes on, for 'No one ever stopped to describe yesterday's weather'.[21] In 'Honey', the insistence of life in the face of death is even more powerfully realized in the protagonist's sudden surge of desire at her mother's funeral:

> She was ashamed of what she had felt as she stepped away from her mother's grave. That lightness – it was desire ... It was like she could fuck anything: the Killarney lakes and the sky that ran over them, and posh hotels with waffle-cloth robes, and the pink scent of a rose that showed grey in the darkness, and the whole lovely month of May. She could swim in it, and swallow it, and cram it into her in each and every possible way.[22]

Catherine's desire is deepened, rather than annulled, by the awareness of death in this instance, which becomes much more than a mere sexual drive. This expansion of desire in the face of death is characteristic of the collection as a whole: instead of the rather narrow focus on sexual desire in *The Portable Virgin*, desire in *Taking Pictures* encompasses nature and children, love and friendship, life and death.

FROM EXPERIMENT TO TRADITION

The frequency of moments of insight as structuring elements in Taking Pictures is characteristic of a second development in Enright's art of the short story: a move from experiment to tradition. The experimental quality of Enright's writing in The Portable Virgin has often been remarked upon. The stories have been called 'postmodern'[23] and 'unconventional'[24] and Enright was heralded as 'a new voice in Irish fiction'.[25] A number of stylistic features signal Enright's break with tradition in this collection. First, there is the fragmented quality of her short stories. While the modern short story traditionally presents a certain storyline or is centred on the psychological drama of the main character, Enright's stories consist of a sequence of separate scenes. These scenes are sometimes taken from the life of one protagonist, as in 'Indifference', 'Revenge' or 'Juggling', where they cover a period from childhood to middle age. Yet, in other stories, the fragments or scenes are much more disparate. 'Men and Angels', 'Historical Letters', 'Liking' and 'What are Cicadas?' juxtapose different characters and stories, brought together around a common theme. In 'Men and Angels' this is the historical sacrificing of women to male ambition, while 'Liking' seems to consist of a number of disparate conversations in a pub. The lack of explicit connection between the separate scenes that make up the stories in The Portable Virgin is highlighted typographically by the unconventionally large white spaces in between these scenes.[26]

As Patricia Coughlan has argued with regard to The Wig My Father Wore, this postmodernist suppression of connections between the elements of the story constitutes a challenge to the reader, who is invited to provide connections and to actively make sense of the story.[27] Still, the stories of The Portable Virgin often possess an alternative form of unity, conferred not through plot or causality but through a common topic or an overriding metaphorical scheme. In 'The House of the Architect's Love Story', the house provides a central metaphor for the condition of the protagonist's marriage. Between the first sentence – 'I used to drink to bring the house down' – and the last – 'the house is inside my head, as well as around it, and so are the cracks in the wall.'[28] Enright builds an elaborate metaphorical structure which explores many different aspects of the central image of the house. The house is likened to the narrator's marriage, but also to her life and to the story she is telling: 'From outside, the house of the architect's love story is a neo-Palladian villa, but inside, there are corners, cellars, attics, toilets, a room full of books with an empty socket in the lamp.'[29] In a gesture that will prove to be quite typical for Enright's fiction, the metaphor acquires body and substance, assumes a life of its own. Similar fleshed-out metaphors can be found in several other stories in The Portable Virgin: there is rubber in 'Revenge', numbers in 'Luck be a Lady', film in 'Mr Snip Snip Snip', and acting in 'Juggling Oranges'.

A third experimental and clearly postmodern feature of this first collection is its metafictional dimension. Many of the stories reflect on the process of telling stories: the power of storytelling, the necessity of lies and the role of the imagination. In 'Indifference', for instance, the omnisciently narrated story of a one-night stand is interrupted by stories the lovers tell each other and by the girl's written account of the affair in a letter to her friend. 'What are Cicadas?' and 'Liking' are almost completely made up of the act of telling: the stories may be real or imagined, tall tales or lived experiences; they are always embellished, self-consciously so. And in the early story, 'Seascape', the 'reality' of a young couple's holiday at the seaside is mediated and subverted by the way in which the woman writes about it on a postcard to her friend. The first-person narrators in The Portable Virgin are also highly conscious of the echoes and effects of the story they are telling: 'This is the usual betrayal story, as you have already guessed – the word "sofa" gave it away', notes the narrator of 'The Portable Virgin', and she goes on to make references to other betrayal stories, whether in film ('BBC mini-series where Judi Dench plays the furniture and has a little sad fun'); literature ('Mrs Rochester punched a hole in the ceiling'); or TV commercials ('Mary's soap is all whiffy, but Mary uses X – so mild her husband will never leave').[30]

In many other stories too, intertextual allusions abound. The popular media of TV, film, and music frequently determine the voices and perceptions of characters and narrators alike. 'He had the thin Saturday-matinée face of a villain; of the man who might kidnap the young girl and end up in a duel with Errol Flynn',[31] notes the narrator of 'Indifference' and in '(She Owns) Every Thing', Cathy 'heard herself say

"DIVE RIGHT IN HONEY, THE WATER'S JUST FINE"' in response to a question about handbags – 'a phrase she must have picked up from the television set'.[32] Two of the stories echo another literary text even more explicitly. Critics have already noted how 'The Brat' is stylistically Joycean in its mock-heroic portrait of the alcoholic patriarch O'Donnell, 'making his way from the Customs House to O'Beirne's on the Quays, so sited as to add to the distance between the two buildings a length of nearly three hundred yards'.[33] Yet, as Heather Ingman also notes, Enright's patriarch no longer inspires fear and the protagonist instead turns her back on her pathetic father and takes up study in order to get out of this life. The early story 'Felix' announces its main intertext quite plainly in the opening lines: 'Felix, my secret, my angel boy, my dark felicity. Felix: the sibilant hiss of the final x a teasing breath on the tip of my tongue', but the story also contains ironic references to Poe, Proust and Thomas Mann.[34]

In short, in both theme and form *The Portable Virgin* constitutes a deliberate rejection of tradition. Thematically, Enright's stories criticize the patriarchal myths of passive and asexual femininity in focusing on women's bodies and desires. Formally, her experimental stories break away both from the realist, plot-bound stories of a writer like Frank O'Connor and from the psychological, mood-dependent stories of Elizabeth Bowen.[35] In doing so, Enright crafts her own, postmodern, voice characterized by a cinematographic juxtaposition of scenes, a high degree of metafictionality and self-consciousness, and an insistence on the materiality of metaphors.

Compared to the experimental quality of *The Portable Virgin* then, *Taking Pictures* constitutes in many ways a return to tradition. Most of the stories of this second collection have, to a large extent, abandoned the celebrated postmodern elements of *The Portable Virgin*. Gone are the metafictional remarks about stories and storytelling.[36] Gone too are the frequent references to literature and popular culture. As the far more conventional lay-out of *Taking Pictures* makes clear, the fragmented, cinematographic quality of earlier stories has also been abandoned in favour of a smoother and more unified storyline. This is not to say that the stories have the event-based plots of the short stories of Somerville and Ross, Frank O'Connor or Benedict Kiely. In fact, one of the reviewers of *Taking*

Pictures bemoaned the fact that, 'These are largely static, situational pieces, and, by the end of the collection, one yearns for something to happen.'[37] Rather, as I indicated before, Enright's stories are constructed around a central event or crucial moment which the story either leads up to or circles around. Far more than in *The Portable Virgin*, moreover, the stories are governed by the thoughts and perceptions of a single consciousness as it moves back and forth between past and present, trying to decide where the crisis – or insight – occurred. In 'Little Sister', for instance, the narrator tells of the gradual decline and death of her rebellious, anorexic little sister. The narrative starts from the moment her sister disappeared for the first time and, after many excursions to events prior to and following that event, returns to this turning-point again:

> I keep thinking, not about Brian, but about those ninety-one days, my mother half crazed, my father feigning boredom, with my own bedroom for the first time in years. I think of Serena's absence, how astonishing it was, and all of us sitting looking at each other, until the door opened and she walked in, half-dead, with an ordinary, living man in tow.[38]

In 'Here's to Love', the defining scene seems to be the protagonist's confrontation with mortality in the form of a gun on a Parisian boulevard: 'I still walk down the street most evenings. And every time I do this, I think about a bullet in the back – about the fact that most of the time, it does not happen to me.'[39] In other stories, the defining moment is a dream, as in 'Green' and 'The Bad Sex Weekend', or a recurring day-dream, as in 'Della'. Yet common to most stories in *Taking Pictures* is that unity is conferred not through metaphorical constructs or metafictional frames, but rather through the consciousness of the protagonist, whose thoughts, feelings, hopes and memories constitute the main interest of the story. In this way, Enright returns, to a certain extent, to the tradition of the so-called plotless short story with such well-known Irish representatives as James Joyce, Elizabeth Bowen or John McGahern. While this 'return' to tradition could be seen as evidence of Enright's personal development as a writer, involving a moderation of her attacks on (patriarchal) tradition and a reconsideration of the influence of that tradition, it is also in tune with international developments in fiction since the 1990s, as postmodern experiment has made way for a new form of realism.[40]

The greater focus on individual consciousness in the stories from Taking Pictures can also be linked to the different narrative tone of this collection. Although third-person and first-person narratives alternate in both collections, the properties of these narrative structures differ considerably. Compare, for example, the opening lines of '(She Owns) Every Thing' and 'Honey', respectively:

> Cathy was often wrong, she found it more interesting ... She was wrong about where her life ended up. She loved corners, surprises, changes of light.
>
> Of all the fates that could have been hers (spinster, murderer, savant, saint), she chose to work behind a handbag counter in Dublin and take her holidays in the sun.[41]

> When she tried to think what they looked like, the women who stood in front of him at wine receptions, or at his desk, or at the door of his office, the nearest she could come up with was 'drenched'.[42]

In the first instance, the narrator keeps a distant, external perspective, as the protagonist's life and character are summed up in a few lines. In 'Honey', on the other hand, the narrator focalizes through the main character, entering her thoughts and rendering her perspective on the events. Although focalization does occasionally occur in the third-person narratives of The Portable Virgin, it is nowhere as insistent as in Taking Pictures, where it is usually kept up throughout the entire story. A similar difference characterizes the first-person narrators of both collections. As I have pointed out before, the first-person narrators in The Portable Virgin and the earlier story, 'Felix', are extremely self-conscious. They are artists, crafting a story, complete with elaborate metaphors, literary references and precocious wit. The literary skill of the narrator of 'The House of the Architect's Love Story' has already been demonstrated, but similar examples can be found in other stories. The narrator of

'Revenge', for instance, observes her own feelings quite distantly: 'I realised in myself a slow, physical excitement, a kind of pornographic panic. It felt like the house was full of balloons pressing gently against the ceiling.'[43] The narrator of 'Felix' takes this artistic self-consciousness to an almost parodic level when she comments on the act of writing itself: 'Believe me, I write for no one but myself. Mine is not the kind of crime to be spoken out loud. This, then, is the last, or the penultimate, motion of the fingers that burned alive on the cool desert of his skin. You can always count on a suicide for a clichéd prose style.'[44]

How different then are the first-person narrators of *Taking Pictures* who seem to be surprised in the act of telling the story. They use colloquial idiom, address their listeners, and are generally very straightforward in their telling. Moreover, if the voices of the first-person narrators of 'The House', 'Revenge' or 'The Portable Virgin' sounded more or less alike, in *Taking Pictures*, Enright has individualized the different voices so that they reflect the character of the person speaking. Take, for example, the following passage from 'Natalie':

> I wake up in the middle of the night I am so upset. I mean, when I put down the phone I didn't know what to think – Natalie is so polite, you could hardly call what we had a fight – and then I'm lying there with my eyes wide open; looking at what turns out to be the ceiling (duh!), wondering what terrible thought just woke me up.[45]

The narrator's idiom quite accurately catches the character of this 17-year-old, who tries to make sense of certain experiences. And the same can be said of the narration of the middle-aged owner of an organic farm in 'Green', the elderly cleaning lady in 'What You Want', or the pregnant woman in 'Shaft'.

It is clear that the narrative mode in *Taking Pictures* thus contributes to the greater emphasis on individual consciousness in this collection. The reader is given more direct access to the central character's thoughts and feelings, whether through focalization or first-person narration. In this way, the reader's engagement with, or sympathy for, the characters also increases. In *The Portable Virgin*, on the contrary, both sympathy and closeness are held at bay by the greater artificiality and distance of the narratives which are governed by a single idea or metaphor rather than a primary consciousness. In this way, *Taking Pictures* bears witness to a third development in Enright's fiction, a development which can be characterized, somewhat schematically, as a shift from ideas to people, from distance to sympathy, and from form to feeling.

Let me make this development somewhat more concrete by comparing two stories with a similar theme, a wife's reaction to the husband's unfaithfulness: 'The Portable Virgin' and 'Until the Girl Died'. In both stories, the initial conflict is one between wife and mistress, 'I' and 'she'. Both narrators try to conjure up images of their rival. To the narrator of 'The Portable Virgin', her husband's mistress is a walking cliché: 'She was one of those women who hold their skin like a smile, as if she was afraid her face might fall off if the tension went out of her eyes.'[46] Yet when the woman's name turns out to be Mary, just like hers, the opposition between them slowly dissolves. The narrator has her hair dyed in a fancy hairdresser, with 'Mary sitting to my left and to my right. She is blue from the back down ... Her skin is pulled into a smile by the rubber tonsure on her head.'[47] She steals the handbag of one of these Marys and applies the woman's make-up to her face. This interchangeability is further underscored by the 'small, portable Virgin' (with blue cloak) she finds at the bottom of the bag: 'Down by the water's edge I set her sailing on her back, off to Ben, who is sentimental that way. Then I follow her into his story, with its doves and prostitutes and railway stations and marks on the skin. I have nowhere else to go. I love that man.'[48] In spite of her earlier proclamation that this 'is not a story about hand-jobs in toilets, at parties where everyone is in the van-rental business ... There are no doves, no prostitutes, no railway stations, no marks on the skin',[49] the narrator now abandons her own original story – of sofas, knitting and sex – for that of her husband. She abandons her own daring 'dowdiness' for the artificial beauty of 'Marys' who pander to men's desires and bow down to an impossible ideal of desirable femininity.

'The Portable Virgin' has received more critical attention than any other of Enright's stories. Jeannett Shumaker has read it is as a critique of the patriarchal virgin/whore dichtomy (compare the 'doves' and 'prostitutes' in the husband's story);[50] for Heather Ingman, the story demonstrates 'the idea of gender as performance',[51] and Caitriona Moloney notes how the story juxtaposes the two 'radical theoretical constructs' of 'virginity and portability'.[52] These readings confirm that the story's main interest is on an abstract or theoretical level. The characters in the stories remain – like their names – oddly anonymous and the events are calculated to bring home certain points. The images and ideas are more compelling than the characters and the story suggests archetypal situations rather than an actual reality.

Quite the opposite is the case in 'Until the Girl Died', where the narrator tells her story in a welter of domestic detail. She describes her children, the grilled salmon she prepares for her husband, and the Richard Allan coat she receives to make up for his unfaithfulness. Her husband's lover – initially just 'the girl' – becomes slowly more individualized as the narrator seeks out her name, the street where she lived, the year she graduated and, finally, the place where she lies buried. If in 'The Portable Virgin', wife and mistress seemed to lose their individuality to the extent of becoming interchangeable, in 'Until the Girl Died' they gradually gain in personality. As a result, the conflict shifts from a clash between rivals to a silent war between the narrator and her husband: 'This is the last real thing I say to him, for a long while. *Where's the gas bill gone when will you be home would you pick up Shauna from her ballet?* We could do this forever. After a few weeks of it, my husband gets a nervous cough.'[53] Finally, the narrator decides to 'call him back home' – back, as it were, to her story. She visits the grave of her husband's dead lover – 'I put lilies on the ground under which she lay, and I told her that she mattered'[54] – then she goes home and picks up their life again.

In this second story, Enright does not offer a general critique on patriarchy or feminine identity, but rather provides a concrete, conventional, and convincing picture of a middle-class marriage. The domesticity of the narrator's life is flaunted rather than denied, yet in the end it is the woman of 'Until the Girl Died' who comes out stronger. Her very honest narrative admirably catches her inner struggles as she manages to keep her pride and save her marriage. The Virgin-metaphors, the metafictionality, and the feminist dimension certainly make 'The Portable Virgin' more interesting from a theoretical perspective; yet the domestic details, the sympathetic narrator, and the convincingly dramatized feelings make 'Until the Girl Died' perhaps more powerful as a story. Enright herself seems to have recognized something of this movement from form and ideas to feelings and characters in her stories, when, in her introduction to *Yesterday's Weather*, she expressed her surprise at the 'innocence and affectation' of the early stories and noted that what she seemed to remember most about them was not their content, but their 'shape'.[55]

ESTRANGEMENT

Along with the developments I have sketched, there are also some features of Enright's short fiction which remain constant throughout both collections. By way of conclusion, I will focus on two of these aspects which align Enright with trends in Irish short fiction in general. The most noticeable similarity between both collections, first of all, is the insistent focus on women. In *Taking Pictures*, all but one of the focalizers and narrators are women and in *The Portable Virgin* too, women make up the central characters of the majority of stories. Although one might again be tempted to outline a development here – from a more general or abstract concern with the representation of women's bodies and desires in *The Portable Virgin* to an interest in concrete women's lives in *Taking Pictures* – it is clear that Enright continues her attempt to re-imagine women's lives in the face of patriarchal constructs of femininity. In doing so, she places herself in the remarkably rich tradition of Irish short fiction by women writers which has been particularly concerned with the changing nature of women's roles and identities in Ireland.

Another typical feature of Enright's fiction in both collections is her use of the technique of defamiliarization or estrangement. In *The Portable Virgin*, as we have seen, Enright effects this defamiliarization primarily through the postmodern form of her stories: the distant, apparently indifferent narrators, the juxtaposition of scenes, and the embodied metaphors which dominate her stories. By turning women into interchangeable Marys in 'The Portable Virgin', by judging the effects of adulterous desire through handbags ('(She Owns) Every Thing'), houses ('The House of the Architect's Love Story'), or numbers ('Luck be a Lady'), or by likening the effects of memory to the editing of a film in 'Mr Snip Snip Snip', Enright is able to cast ordinary reality in a surprising new light.

In *Taking Pictures*, these unsettling metaphors have not disappeared, but they no longer structure the story in the same overarching way.

Instead they mostly appear as disturbing pictures which puncture the narrative and question its ordinariness. In 'Honey', Catherine pictures her mother's cancer as 'bees in a swarm; the cancer being smoked out of her mother's body to settle in the space under her arm, a drowsy mass. If she could just scoop them up as a beekeeper might, and carry them away, and leave not a single one behind.'[56] And in 'Yesterday's Weather', the strangeness of being a new mother is aptly captured in the following image: 'The baby buried his face in her shoulder and wiped his nose on her T-shirt. He had a summer cold, so Hazel's navy top was criss-crossed with what looked like slug trails. There was something utterly depressing about being covered in snot.'[57] 'It's the little things that get to you', notes the narrator of 'Green'[58] and that remark neatly captures the small, but powerful, instances of defamiliarization that affect Enright's characters in this second collection. Unlike in The Portable Virgin, where the defamiliarizing effect primarily prevails on the reader, in Taking Pictures the estrangement is more often experienced by the characters themselves.[59] Seeing a woman whose 'throat had been slit', when buying a newspaper, throws Noel's day in 'Wife' momentarily off kilter; glimpsing a 'ghost sitting at the table' in their rented caravan gives an edge to Michelle's family holiday in 'Caravan'; Della's recurring dream of naked boys playing with sticks in a river runs as an unsettling undercurrent to her dealings with her blind neighbour in 'Della'; and similarly, in 'The Bad Sex Weekend', a dream of a boy in Wellingtons haunts the protagonist all through her weekend of (bad) sex with a backpack tourist.

With defamiliarization as one of the most constant and insistent features of her short fiction, Enright fits in a strand of Irish short story writing which moves from the haunting tales of Sheridan Le Fanu over the anxious short fiction of Elizabeth Bowen to the fantastic stories of Éilís Ní Dhuibhne. In A History of the Irish Short Story, Heather Ingman has drawn attention to this alternative strand of Irish short fiction, which has often been obscured by the dominant association of the Irish short story with mid-twentieth-century realism. She recognizes in this tradition a preoccupation with alienation and anxiety, with fragmentation and dissolution. Of course, defamiliarization and alienation can also be observed in the work of many other short story writers and are in no way exclusive to an Irish tradition.[60]

More generally, I would argue that one cannot do justice to Enright's short fiction by confining it to only one tradition or trend. Instead, the changes, as well as the constant features, of her stories can be attributed to a combination of Irish and international influences and to a mixture of personal, social and aesthetic factors. Thus, the thematic developments in the stories can be viewed in the light of Enright's personal experiences (becoming a mother, growing older), but also in the context of the changing face of international feminism, with the attack on patriarchy giving way to an attention to otherness and difference. Similarly, the move from postmodern experiment 'back' to tradition may reflect an international trend in fiction, as well as suggest Enright's reconciliation with the rich Irish tradition of the short story. It is, in any case, testimony to her greatness as a writer that she can bring together and transform all these influences into original, compelling and ever-changing short stories.

NOTES

1. *Yesterday's Weather* contains all the stories from *Taking Pictures*, eleven of the seventeen stories from *The Portable Virgin* and Enright's two earliest stories, 'Felix' and 'Seascape'.

2. John Banville, Ian McEwan, Neil Jordan, Thomas Pynchon and Graham Swift are some examples of writers who published a single short story collection early in their career and then moved on to writing novels.

3. See S. Merritt, 'Sex and Death and Caravans', *Observer*, 6 April 2008; K. Guest, 'Review of *Taking Pictures*, by Anne Enright', *Independent* (UK), 28 March 2008; and R. Scurr, 'Novel of the Week: *What Are You Like*, by Anne Enright', *New Statesman*, 10 April 2000.

4. A. Enright, 'Revenge', in *The Portable Virgin* (London: Vintage, 1998 [1991]), pp.38–9.

5. Ibid., p.39.

6. Ibid., p.46.

7. Enright, 'Luck be a Lady', in *The Portable Virgin*, p.74.

8. Enright, '(She Owns) Every Thing', in *The Portable Virgin*, pp.6, 7, 8.

9. A. Enright, *Yesterday's Weather* (London: Vintage, 2009), p.298.

10. See Coughlan's detailed analysis of the imagery of food, sex and bodies in *The Pleasure of Eliza Lynch*, P. Coughlan, '"Without a Blink of her Lovely Eye":The Pleasure of Eliza Lynch and Visionary Scepticism', *Irish University Review*, 35, 2 (2005), pp.349–73.

11. A. Carter, *The Bloody Chamber* (London:Vintage, 1979) and *Black Venus* (London: Chatto and Windus, 1985). Enright was taught by Angela Carter when she studied creative writing in the University of East Anglia.

12. A. Enright, 'What You Want', in *Taking Pictures* (London: Jonathan Cape, 2008), p.158.

13. Enright, 'Caravan', in *Taking Pictures*, p.185.

14. Enright, 'Until the Girl Died', in *Taking Pictures*, pp.189, 193.

15. Enright, 'The Cruise', in *Taking Pictures*, p.209.

16. Enright, 'Natalie', in *Taking Pictures*, p.49.

17. Ibid., p.51.

18. V. Shaw, *The Short Story: A Critical Introduction* (London: Longman, 1983), p.193.

19. C. Hanson, *Short Stories and Short Fictions, 1880–1980* (London: Macmillan, 1985), p.9.

20. Quoted in H. Ingman, *A History of the Irish Short Story* (Cambridge: Cambridge University Press, 2009), p.147.

21. Enright, 'Yesterday's Weather', in *Taking Pictures*, pp.147–8.

22. Enright, 'Honey', in *Taking Pictures*, p.90.

23. C. Moloney, 'Anne Enright', in *Twenty-first-Century British and Irish Novelists*, ed. Michael R. Molino (Detroit, MI: Gale, 2003).

24. 'Anne Enright', in A.O. Weekes, *Unveiling Treasures: The Attic Guide to the Published Works of Irish Women Literary Writers* (Dublin: Attic Press, 1993), p.120.

25. E. Battersby, Review of *The Portable Virgin*, *The Irish Times*, 25 February 1991.

26. Interestingly, when the stories were collected again in *Yesterday's Weather*, several of these breaks have disappeared altogether, while those that remain have been reduced to a more conventional width, which gives the stories a more traditional appearance.

27. P. Coughlan, 'Irish Literature and Feminism in Postmodernity', *Hungarian Journal of English and American Studies*, 10, 1–2 (2004), p.182.

28. Enright, 'The House of the Architect's Love Story', in *The Portable Virgin*, pp.55, 63.

29. Ibid., p.56.

30. Enright, 'The Portable Virgin', in *The Portable Virgin*, pp.81, 83, 84.

31. Enright, 'Indifference', in *The Portable Virgin*, p.11.

32. Enright, '(She Owns) Every Thing', in *The Portable Virgin*, p.6.

33. Enright, 'The Brat', in *The Portable Virgin*, p.160. See Moloney, 'Anne Enright'; Ingman, *A History of the Irish Short Story*, p.256.

34. Enright, 'Felix', in *Yesterday's Weather*, p.295.

35. In histories of the short story, a distinction is often made between two 'types' of stories. Clare Hanson succinctly describes the difference as follows: 'In the short story the primary distinction which can be made is between those works in which the major emphasis is on plot and those in which plot is subordinate to psychology and mood', Hanson, *Short Stories and Short Fictions*, p.5. Although the difference is relative rather than absolute, it can be traced in the Irish short story as well. William Carleton, Somerville and Ross, Daniel Corkery, Frank O'Connor and Benedict Kiely would be examples of the first tradition, while George Moore, James Joyce, Elizabeth Bowen and Mary Lavin could be said to represent the second kind.

36. I should point out that some of the stories of *Taking Pictures* – viz. 'Switzerland', 'The Bad Sex Weekend', 'Pale Hands I Loved beside the Shalimar', and 'Taking Pictures' – resemble more closely those of the first collection in the juxtaposition of separate scenes, the wry, deadpan humour and the strangely elliptic conversations. Still in the reverse chronological ordering of the two collections as they are combined in

Yesterday's Weather, these stories occur in the second half of the collection, thus perhaps confirming rather than gainsaying Enright's development.

37. L. Shriver, 'Still Life with Thumb on Lens'. Review of *Taking Pictures*. *Telegraph*, 15 March 2008.
38. Enright, 'Little Sister', in *Taking Pictures*, pp.64–5.
39. Enright, 'Here's to Love', in *Taking Pictures*, p.171.
40. In the œuvre of writers like Ian McEwan, John Banville and J.M. Coetzee one can also note how postmodern experimentation has made way for a more straightforward and 'realistic' mode of writing.
41. Enright, '(She Owns) Every Thing', in *The Portable Virgin*, p.3.
42. Enright, 'Honey', *Taking Pictures*, p.81.
43. Enright, 'Revenge', in *The Portable Virgin*, p.43.
44. Enright, 'Felix', in *Yesterday's Weather*, p.295.
45. Enright, 'Natalie', in *Taking Pictures*, p.41.
46. Enright, 'The Portable Virgin', in *The Portable Virgin*, p.81.
47. Ibid., p.86.
48. Ibid., p.88.
49. Ibid., p.82.
50. J. Shumaker, 'Uncanny Doubles: The Fiction of Anne Enright', *New Hibernia Review*, 9, 3 (2005), pp.108–10.
51. Ingman, *A History of the Irish Short Story*, p.249.
52. Moloney, 'Anne Enright'.
53. Enright, 'Until the Girl Died', in *Taking Pictures*, p.196.
54. Ibid., pp.197–8.
55. Enright, *Yesterday's Weather*, pp.ix–x.
56. Enright, 'Honey', in *Taking Pictures*, p.83.
57. Enright, 'Yesterday's Weather', in *Taking Pictures*, p.137.
58. Enright, 'Green', in *Taking Pictures*, p.117.
59. This ties in with the greater emphasis on the character's consciousness in *Taking Pictures* in general.
60. Consider, for example, the short fiction of such writers as Franz Kafka, Jorge Luis Borges, Robert Louis Stevenson or Flannery O'Connor.

CHAPTER FOUR

Beyond Local Ireland in
The Wig My Father Wore

HEIDI HANSSON

In the autumn of 2008 I had the privilege of teaching a course in Irish women's writing at Davidson College, North Carolina.[1] One of the works studied was Anne Enright's first novel, *The Wig My Father Wore*, a fast-paced commentary on love, death, sex, family, religion, the media and Dublin in the mid-1990s.[2] The story centres on Grace, one of the team at the TV-show, *LoveQuiz*, and her relationships with her parents, co-workers, and the angel Stephen, who unexpectedly comes into her life. There is no linear plot, but instead the narrative traces a kind of reverse development where Grace regresses from cynical experience to hopeful innocence and a promise of a new beginning at the end. The absurdities of modern life are frequently exposed through the deployment of magical realism.

Introducing the text to the students, I suggested that Enright was, in fact, not Irish but Canadian. They believed me only briefly, and we began working with the text by determining what aspects made it Irish. The Dublin setting, some Irish place names, and names of characters, such as Aoife, Mrs O'Dwyer and the protagonist Grainne/Grace were selected as signs of Irishness, together with a number of Irish phrases and expressions. A fragmented instruction for how to use a scapular medal was also considered to signal an Irish context, as well as the fact that the snake that turns up at the TV-station towards the end of the story is called Patrick.[3] It soon became obvious that the list contained only characteristics that corresponded to our preconceptions of Irishness, particularly in terms of religion. However, Catholicism, although immensely important in Irish history, is not an exclusively Irish topic. Alongside characters with traditional Irish names, there are also characters called Frank, Jo and Marcus, and the names used in the novel do not function as labels of a certain ideological outlook or carry any particular political importance. With neither character nor setting invested with a deep, cultural significance, the Irishness of the novel can be attributed to a number of exterior characteristics that might have been exchanged for, say, Scottish or South African features to give the text a different flavour. Although the story is located in Ireland, there is nothing in plot, theme or style that must be regarded as intrinsically Irish and the novel's national origin is not necessary for the production of meaning. At a time when culture is becoming increasingly global, it seems reductionist to insist on an exclusively or even predominantly national framework for Irish works. As Mads Rosendahl Thomsen points out, however, there is 'no tradition of thinking of authors as belonging to a subsystem within the literary world which is independent of nations'.[4] This tendency to privilege national concerns is particularly insistent when the nation in question is characterized as postcolonial and, as a result, The Wig My Father Wore is primarily discussed as an Irish novel, whereas a work published in England in 1995 is not automatically expected to be about current English issues.

According to Gerry Smyth, Irish novelists towards the end of the last century no longer felt 'constrained to locate their work in terms of self-conscious "Irish" concerns', but were beginning to 'deal instead with a broad spectrum of human experience, and with themes which, perhaps possessing local significance, also have a wider resonance'.[5] Nevertheless, the way in which an Irish text represents Irishness has long been a central concern in Irish literary criticism and a main criterion for categorization. In spite of writers' thematic reorientation, critics seem reluctant to give up the national context. Discussing Enright, Patrick McCabe and Dermot Healy a few years later, Glenda Norquay and Smyth conclude that 'the condition of Ireland' is still the main focus of the Irish novel:

> Despite new times, (Irish) novel and (Irish) nation still appear to be caught in a bind of mutual fascination. For all these writers, even when the action is set elsewhere, or when the subject matter appears overtly non-national, the national narrative is still there, hovering in the background, still exercising influence at a deep structural and/or conceptual level.[6]

The national tale is a prominent category in Irish literature, but if the critical purpose is not to identify the author's influences or place her in literary history, a national categorization is unnecessarily restricting. When the nationality of the writer is made central, it is easy to disregard other traditions and influences. For Irish works of an experimental nature, for example, it is tempting to establish a Joycean genealogy, as in the *New York Times* review of *The Wig My Father Wore* where 'echoes of the Joyce of "Dubliners"' are detected in the text.[7] Enright herself is less inclined to admit such a heritage, however, and argues for a tradition of her own:

> Male writers sometimes refer to Joyce as father/competitor, thereby somehow flattering themselves as being in the same league. As the 'old father, old artificer', he smothers them, and renders them powerless. As far as I am concerned, this is a false conversation that takes part entirely between men … I don't compare myself to the dead. I hardly compare myself to the living. I would hope my writing is my own.[8]

Rüdiger Imhof also disregards the Joycean tradition and compares Enright to American writers like Ronald Sukenick and Raymond Federman, but with a 'humorous touch'.[9] There are a few exceptions like these, but otherwise the expectation of a national connection remains strong. It is perhaps symptomatic that Enright received her hitherto most prestigious recognition when she was awarded the Man Booker Prize in 2007 for *The Gathering*, a novel organized around the well-known Irish literary theme of the wake and dealing with the familiar topic of the dysfunctional Irish family.[10] Although Irish writers may be looking beyond Irish subjects in their works, it seems that canonization processes, national as well global, have a different logic and still favour literature that can be connected to questions of cultural identity. As far as a national literature is a part of nation-building, identity matters are indeed crucial, but in an age of globalization, other questions should also receive attention. Commenting on Irish reviewing practices, Enright says she prefers the 'simplicity of the reception' that she gets outside Ireland: 'You get a fresh look elsewhere with no baggage'.[11]1 To access and assess new literary visions of Ireland, the frames of interpretation may need to be changed.

An often quoted comment on Enright's fiction is Colm Tóibín's declaration that the Dublin represented in her works is 'post-Freudian, post-feminist and ... post-nationalist'.[12] Insofar as Enright's works can be seen as theoretical interventions, a questioning of current taxonomical systems seems to be an important concern in the texts. If this is the case, it would seem worthwhile to place her works in a selection of different critical contexts to see what aspects of the texts are highlighted in the process. A number of categories appear to be relevant, such as women's literature, postmodern literature, historical literature and postnationalist literature, while the category Irish literature seems to be problematized in several of her novels. In *The Pleasure of Eliza Lynch*,[13] for example, Enright's use of a South American setting can be taken as a reaction to the preoccupation with inquiries into what it means to be Irish based on a connection with the land. The postnationalist themes present in the earlier novel *What Are You Like?*,[14] likewise, deny national borders of Irishness and, for slightly different reasons, 'Irish literature' may be too narrow as a description of *The Wig My Father Wore*. In all these cases, world literature emerges as a possible alternative to an Irish categorization.

According to one of the current definitions, world literature should be understood as both 'locally inflected and translocally mobile'.[15] *The Wig My Father Wore* can certainly be related to an Irish tradition in several ways. Enright's narrative technique harks back to ancient Irish story structures, like the winding place name stories or *dindsenchas* where one version of 'truth' is immediately replaced by another, and to myth and folklore where magical creatures are an obvious, unquestioned presence. The same strategies, however, may also be understood as examples of the kind of magical realism most prominently found in South American literature from the late-twentieth century and may be related to a post-modern aesthetic. Enright thus combines a long-established Irish story-telling tradition with postmodernist literary strategies, and the novel is firmly grounded in Irish culture at the same time as it presages the postnationalist ideas that come to the fore in her later works. The literary traditions that are fused together originate in different cultures, but their original context is not necessary for the production of meaning. On the grounds of language and plot structure, it could therefore be argued that *The Wig My Father Wore* represents the idea that Ireland is not an island, but part of global culture. It carries a double heritage, as both locally Irish and global at the same time: world literature, in Cooppan's definition of the term.

The term 'world literature' is usually traced to Goethe's declaration in 1827 that a new, universal world literature, or *Weltliteratur*, was in the process of being formed,[16] or to the slightly different notion of literature as common, intellectual property, free from national biases, expressed in *The Communist Manifesto* in 1848.[17] Meanings of the term vary from ideas of a canon of world classics to 'a mode of circulation and of reading',[18] but a basic prerequisite is that the works in question circulate and have an impact 'beyond their culture of origin'.[19] Although there has been a tendency to privilege an already established canon of 'great works', the term world literature has expanded in recent years to refer to non-Western literature and it can also be understood as analogous to world music or the fusion of different cultural expressions. There is some debate about the question of how and on what terms literature can travel, however. The sinologist Steven Owen, for example, distinguishes between Chinese literature and literature that began in the Chinese language to show how translation and the influence of Western literary traditions may lead to a homogenization that causes a literary work to lose its cultural connection.[20] David Damrosch, on the other hand, suggests that Owen's distinction can be used in a positive sense to illustrate the difference between literature that communicates only within its cultural context and literature that communicates across cultural and national boundaries.[21] A work of world literature begins in a particular language, at a particular time and place, and the reader needs to be aware of this original context, but the work is engaged with themes and ideas that reach beyond the specifics of the cultural and national history where it was produced. In the case of *The Wig My Father Wore*, themes that transcend the local might be the possibilities of love, the limits of communication, and media's misrepresentations of reality. Although they are presented against an Irish background, they do not require specific knowledge of Irish history or culture to be understood.

A contrasting meaning of world literature is that it refers to works that function as windows on their parts of the world and contribute to cross-cultural understanding.[22] The 'window' definition returns the focus to a national context, and primarily interests itself with the works' representative qualities. *The Wig My Father Wore* might, for example, represent Celtic Tiger Ireland, 1990's Dublin, or the situation for Irish women in the workplace. There are limits, however, to how culturally specific 'windows on the world' are allowed to be, and unless they conform to the current images of the culture they are thought to represent, such works will probably not circulate particularly widely. Received as representations of their cultures of origin, works of world literature are vulnerable to the opposing dangers of exoticism and assimilation, as David Damrosch cautions.[23] The Man Booker Prize effect aside, *The Gathering* is the only Enright novel translated into Swedish so far, possibly because it is felt to be more 'typically Irish' than her other works. Frank McCourt's *Angela's Ashes* (1996), on the other hand, has sold in great numbers across the world, since its depiction of Ireland conforms to readers' expectations and the story fits comfortably in the genre of rags-to-riches literature. At least in Enright's view, the success of McCourt's novel has more to do with confirming the readers' self-images than with a believable representation of Ireland: 'I thought of the phenomenon of *Angela's Ashes*; Americans wanted to feel that they all came from some peasant European hell. It wasn't a story about Ireland; it was a story about getting out, of being successful in America.'[24] Apart from encouraging the circulation of preconceived ideas of foreign cultures, the expectation that literature should represent and convey images of its place of production may reduce works of art to vehicles for information. The episodic and impressionistic narration of *The Wig My Father Wore*, however, undermines the representative function of the text, and the novel offers no coherent picture that readers can accept or reject, nor does it perform a sustained critique of images of Irishness. Although the novel might still function as a window on the world, it challenges rather than confirms received ideas about Ireland.

The threat of assimilation means that readers are likely to interpret foreign literature according to their own domestic paradigms because they lack sufficient knowledge of the cultural context of the piece.[25] A similar danger is that works that reach beyond the representative level are constantly brought back to their cultural context and only allowed to make sense in the domestic critical climate. Magical realism in Irish literature is, for example, often understood as a postcolonial strategy that undermines colonial cultural and social power by breaking with the confines of realism.[26] Although this is a viable interpretation of the technique, regarding magical realism as a predominantly postcolonial strategy reinstates a colonial discourse against which the magical realist text must necessarily be read and leads to an interpretative model where non-representational elements are insistently brought back to the representational fold. The national context becomes central, overshadowing other potential meanings, and there is a danger that qualities beyond the representational are lost. While valuing the insights into foreign cultures offered by literature, Anders Pettersson argues for a reading position that acknowledges and engages with many different dimensions of a literary work:

> The fact that a text is written by a foreign author in a foreign language, responding to specific concerns of a foreign culture and history, does mark it out for special attention as articulation of a different perspective, but we should engage it in a dialogue just as we engage many others, and regard it as an individual utterance rather than some representative specimen of an entire culture.[27]

Looking only for the Irishness of a novel like *The Wig My Father Wore* is to give prominence to its representational and informational features, at the expense of other qualities. The value of political and national critical perspectives is not in question, and should be brought in alongside 'world literature readings', but interpreting the magical realism in the novel as a postcolonial strategy, for instance, immediately brings in the oppressive force of canonized English literature and imposes a number of themes like resistance, identity and Irish Orientalism that may not always be of importance. Opening up the national context may shift the critical perspective from aspects of representation to aspects of communication, which brings to the fore questions that can have universal application. Enright's magical realism could then be understood as a strategy that attempts to transcend the local by building bridges to other cultures and literatures, and not only as a postcolonial strategy with particular relevance against the background of Irish history.

The Wig My Father Wore is told in the first person, with most events seen from the perspective of the narrator Grace. Although the protagonist's name could have been used to establish connections with the female pirate Gráinne Ní Mháille or Grace O'Malley, or to create a Celtic heritage by suggesting a link to the Diarmuid and Gráinne tale, such connotations are not directly invoked. Neither is her decision to change her name from Grainne to the Anglicized Grace described as politically or religiously significant, but as a schoolgirl's strategy to avoid being called 'groin'.[28] Names with spiritual, political or social overtones become constraints, as Enright explains:

> Though John means nothing and Paul means very little, John Paul will be a Catholic ... born in the early 1980s; he will also possibly be working class. The more socially legible the name, the more satirical the book (or proud, sometimes), and the less the name is of use to me. Contempt or pride are not emotions I have about the people I create. That is not what I create them for. I create them to see what they will do.[29]

Grace's Irishness is consequently not made central to the novel's meaning. Instead, she is placed in the nowhere of the media world where geographical places are interchangeable. The rootlessness created by this unstable environment frames Grace's search for a personal history and a sense of attachment in the novel.

The story opens with the angel Stephen appearing on Grace's doorstep, asking for a cup of tea. The conventions of realist narration are cancelled from the very beginning, but so are those of myth and legend. Stephen became an angel after he committed suicide in Ontario in 1934, and Enright counters the tradition of representing suicide as a sin by describing angels as 'ordinary men who killed themselves once when times were bad'.[30] Despite his supernatural status, Stephen is given historical presence, with a professional background as a bridge-builder. As an earthly, Canadian angel who used to build bridges, he becomes a mediator between real and unreal, physical and spiritual, Irish and non-Irish, and his in-between nature is a symbolic representation of the interrogation of various sense-making systems that is a major concern in the text. His hybridity is not an illustration of an identity category beyond nation, gender or humanity, however, but a dramatization of the possibilities of communication, contrasted with the non-communication that characterizes Grace's relations to her family, her colleagues and the TV show where she works. Through Stephen, the rest of the world –

even the heavens – are brought into the story, but via a bridge that also acknowledges the centrality of Dublin and Irish history, as when Grace has to support him through 'all the pain between the GPO and O'Connell Bridge'.[31] The local and the translocal exist side by side.

Throughout the narrative, Stephen functions as an overarching metaphor that encapsulates the main themes of the novel. In particular, he becomes a reminder that the ways we use to organize and regulate reality fall short. It is not only the boundaries between real and surreal that are shown to be permeable, but also the categories of real and fake, true and false, image and reality. These themes are paralleled on the metalevel through the collapse of the differences between literary genres, as Caitriona Moloney indicates: 'All of Enright's fiction ... challenges traditional belief systems and epistemologies, often conflating the genres of journalism, history and fiction to problematize our sense of the past'.[32] In *The Wig My Father Wore*, even different media are conflated, since the story is arranged like a series of brief episodes from different TV shows in channel-surfing manner.[33] Narrative logic is thus one of the sense-making systems questioned in the novel, through Enright's equilibristic use of language and lack of a coherent plot structure, as well as through the frequent one-liners that stop narrative flow and turn common ideas and phrases upside-down.

If the novel is received as an example of world literature, rather than as a representation of Irish culture, its representative function is downplayed. An indication that it might benefit from a mode of reading that focuses on non-representational aspects is that one of its central themes is the limits of representation. The relationship between various forms of visual representation and memory, especially, is scrutinized and found lacking. Photographs are shown not to reflect reality, but create a version of reality that never existed, as Grace realizes:

> There is a picture of us on our last Christmas, the one before the camera died ... I am going to cut my knee, you cannot see this in the photograph. But first I will throw my plate against the wall, you cannot see that either. You cannot see the plate flying, the shove in the back from Phil, the grazed leg, the split hand, the simple way Brenda drops the camera on the floor. Look closely at our smiles. That picture is a black and white suicide. It is an accident waiting to happen.[34]

The episode can be connected to Susan Sontag's insight that the information-value of a photograph is 'of the same order as fiction' and that although the camera 'makes reality ... manageable', it produces a 'view of the world which denies interconnectedness, continuity'.[35] The Christmas dinner in the photograph never took place, while the important events and emotions of the evening remain undocumented. Documents intended to preserve the past are shown to misrepresent instead. The idea is further developed in the description of Grace's co-worker Frank who 'never developed most of his photos, in case they turned out different to what he remembered'.[36] His wife suspects that one of his undeveloped rolls of film contains photos of another woman, but instead of developing the film to find out, she keeps it in her bedside drawer pulled out of its casing.[37] Whatever evidence the pictures contained is lost, and the roll of film represents nothing. Instead of functioning as an aid to memory, photographs are shown to distort memory and falsify the past:

> I look at the photograph. My mother is beautiful. She is in love. She looks like the sort of mother you are supposed to remember. It looks like the picture you grow up with. My mother was beautiful and laughing and kind. I cannot fit it inside my head ... The photo is a lie.[38]

There is a difference between the falseness of the Christmas photo and that of Grace's mother, however. The Christmas photo fails to accurately depict the situation it represents, but the photo of Grace's mother becomes false because it does not correspond to Grace's expectations. There was once a moment of beauty that the camera captured, and Grace's inability to accept the image may also be interpreted as an effect of her fraught relationship with her mother. Although photos fail to communicate reality, the viewer is also shown to resist responding. In this way, the questioning of visual representations in the novel becomes intertwined with the theme of communication and its lack.

Mirrors, on the other hand, reflect only the instant, and Grace's father who hated cameras, 'put a mirror in every room, because they forget you when you walk away'.[39] Nevertheless, the mirror image cannot represent reality any more correctly than the photograph:

> My jumper in the mirror was a pinker shade of pink, but the jumper in the mirror had no smell. In the mirror it all looked the same,

except that it could not feel. Perhaps that was why the mirror was there, to witness the act without pain. Whether or not I felt pain was another matter. Perhaps I did not. Perhaps the pain was in the mirror.[40]

The idea that reality cannot be represented in anything but skewed fashion is emphasized by the intertextual relationship with Lewis Carroll's *Through the Looking-Glass* (1871) where nonsense and chaos rule. After his stroke, Grace's father 'lives on the wrong side of the mirror and says table instead of chair'.[41] As in Carroll's classic, his comments make an odd kind of sense, however: "'Anything good on the telly?" "There were some flowers on it, but they've gone."'[42] Grace's father's literal replies, like the one-liners scattered through the text, function as defamiliarization strategies that force the reader to consider the actual meanings of the words, drawing further attention to the limits of representation. Double meanings, stock phrases used in unexpected ways and creative word combinations foreground the non-representative levels of language in a corresponding way.

The wig Grace's father wears is the primary symbol of falsehood in the novel, linked to the insincerity of the media world by its arrival in Grace's childhood home simultaneously with the TV set.[43] The wig hides her father's baldness and allows him to appear as a man with hair, and in a similar manner television changes real people into something false and delivers this as truth. The main example is the show *LoveQuiz*, which presents a dating game as true love. On the show, constructed reality becomes more real than the world outside, and the game show host even fashions his own identity through film:

> Damien stumbles in wearing a trench coat, a cigarette clamped in his teeth. What movie is he in today? *Columbo*? *The Big Sleep*? He looks out at us through his hangover and twitches, as if every move were a jump cut from *A Bout de Souffle*.[44]

In contrast to photographs and mirrors that simply fail to give an accurate reflection of reality, the TV show actively deceives, as when Grace films one of the participants in the show in Killarney instead of Crete, as had been planned.[45] The change of location meant that the programme had to be dubbed afterwards so that in the final version not even the place name bears reference to the real:

We just spent two hours cutting out the word 'Crete' and trying to stick 'Killarney' in instead, but of course it wouldn't fit ... So we tried saying it very very fast, then we tried saying it very, very fast, then we tried saying 'Kerry' instead and it ended up sounding like 'Kree' which is neither Crete nor Kerry and there was nothing we could do, so we all went home.[46]

Mass culture as a totalizing force is an issue scrutinized in postmodern art, and Enright's descriptions of the deceptions and insincerities characterizing the TV world can be seen as an example of a postmodern philosophical position in the novel. At the same time, the programme is subject to the viewers' interpretation so that different viewers experience different shows,[47] and in the end it does not matter that people's lives and places are both misrepresented. Since television fails to represent reality, it becomes unimportant who or what is shown on the screen.

In apparent contradiction to its failure to represent, television seemingly organizes and gives coherence to reality. Despite its constructedness, the fake reality governs individual memories, with Grace's colleague Marcus inventing a childhood for himself by watching old movies,[48] and Grace trying to re-create her memories with the help of a TV guide from the night of the moon landing on 20 July 1969. Her mother claims that they listened to the touchdown on radio, however,[49] and the programmes Grace believes herself to have watched turn out not to have been broadcast in Ireland.[50] Other documents from the past are equally unreliable, and the scraps of newspaper, theatre bills, recipes, poems and old letters she finds when she strips the wallpaper in her house provide no historical information, only a confused jumble of images.[51] This distrust of 'the archive' connects The Wig My Father Wore to historiographic metafiction, a genre frequently described as a key example of postmodern literature.[52] Works of historiographic metafiction are self-reflexive and foreground their fictional nature, use multiple points of view, unreliable narration, unresolved contradictions in plot or theme, and acknowledged uncertainty to emphasize the inaccessibility of the past.[53] The central idea that it is impossible to gain access to the past as past, since only fragmentary narratives have survived, is present also in Enright's novel, but her focus is rather the impossibility of any kind of representation and, as a logical corollary, the uselessness of documentation.

Attempts to understand reality through processes of categorization are shown to be equally ineffective. Before he is to appear on the *LoveQuiz* show, Stephen puts together a list of fears, including entries like 'eisoptrophobia' – fear of mirrors; 'pteronophobia' – fear of feathers; and 'gephyrophobia' – fear of bridges.[54] Although it is possible to give names to all the different fears, and later, to give names to a number of manias,[55] it is a futile exercise, which is underscored by the fact that the list also includes the fear of names, 'onomatophobia'.[56] The deceptively stable list is followed by Grace's request that Stephen tell her something he knows, and he explains that 'Tum Tum [...] is the talmudic word for an angel whose sex cannot be easily determined'.[57] The information is shown to be worthless, however, because, 'They only knew about two sexes. And women can't be angels.'[58] The term 'Tum Tum' has no application, since it refers to an entity that does not exist, and so the category established is meaningless. In a similar manner, gender, as well as age, are shown to be empty categories, with Stephen and Grace leaking into each other's bodies so that he acquires body hair whereas she goes through the changes of a woman's life in reverse and loses her adult body.[59] But, despite her regained virginity, she becomes pregnant. Therefore, while all the visual signs indicate that she is a young girl, she is still also a woman, like a modern Virgin Mary. The foundations for forming categories are undermined so that categorization becomes both impossible and pointless.

Apart from signalling the possibility of rebirth and a new beginning for Grace, the bodies of Stephen and Grace leaking into each other can be regarded as a symbol of communication in the text. The dystopian images of a media world where nothing is real and a family life characterized by either non-communication or accidental communication are off-set at the end by the promise of new life. In the idea of the child, all categories come together and collapse, and the baby becomes the physical result of communion between angel and human, man and woman, non-Irish and Irish. It could be interpreted as the Second Coming, but in line with postmodern thought, no new systems or categories are constructed, nor is any resolution offered to the problem of representation. This indeterminacy seems to be something Enright values and seeks to attain:

> I can't be Irish all day; it's too much of an effort. I can't be a woman all day; the work of it is far too strenuous ... as a writer, I

don't want to use language that has become ideological because that's a deadener for a writer of fiction. So, I like to keep my politics fluid so that it won't hem in the work.[60]

To place The Wig My Father Wore in the category 'world literature' is one way to achieve readings that manage to accommodate the fluidity of Enright's novel. It acknowledges the local origin of the work at the same time as it allows the text to produce meanings independent of its cultural background. Literary works are at home in a number of different contexts, inside and outside national boundaries. From a feminist perspective, the rejection of categorical thinking could be understood as parallel to the splintered female subjectivity Grace is made to display.[61] The failure of representational systems, and historical documents in particular, could be connected to the activities within revisionist history in the past few decades in Ireland. The questioning of communication and its limits could be understood as a metafictional comment on Enright's own linguistic and stylistic strategies. As David Damrosch sees it, a phenomenology of the work of art is more necessary than an ontology of the work of art, since 'a literary work manifests differently abroad than it does at home'.[62] The local Irish background of The Wig My Father Wore should not be disregarded, but neither should it be exclusively enforced. For an Irish critic, the situation in 1990's Dublin, the influence of Catholicism or the changing conditions for Irish women may be the most relevant issues to explore in the novel. For a critic from abroad, the text manifests differently, which means that some un-Irish, or perhaps universal, questions may instead become central. As an instance of world literature, the novel can travel and generate meanings that go beyond the local.

NOTES

1. I would like to thank the Swedish Foundation for International Cooperation in Higher Education and Research and Davidson College for the opportunity to teach at an American Liberal Arts College. I would also like to thank my wonderful students Marina Coma, Emily Copeland, Sarah Beth Keyser, Kimberly Larkin, Jessica Malordy and Ellen Thomas for their fresh insights and wise comments throughout the course. Our class discussions were of crucial importance for the ideas in this chapter.

2. A. Enright, The Wig My Father Wore (London: Minerva, 1996). The novel was first published in 1995.

3. Ibid., p.196.
4. M. Rosendahl Thomsen, *Mapping World Literature: International Canonization and Transnational Literature* (London: Continuum, 2008), p.23.
5. G. Smyth, *The Novel and the Nation: Studies in the New Irish Fiction* (London and Chicago, IL: Pluto Press, 1997), p.47.
6. G. Norquay and G. Smyth, 'Waking Up in a Different Place: Contemporary Irish and Scottish Fiction', in *Across the Margins: Cultural Identity and Change in the Atlantic Archipelago*, ed. G. Norquay and G. Smyth (Manchester: Manchester University Press, 2002), p.167.
7. T. Gilling, 'Earth Angel', *New York Times*, 18 November 2001.
8. A. Enright, 'Anne Enright Interview by Caitriona Moloney', in *Irish Women Speak Out: Voices from the Field*, ed. C. Moloney and H. Thompson (Syracuse, NY: Syracuse University Press, 2003), p.57.
9. R. Imhof, Review of *The Wig My Father Wore*, by Anne Enright, *The Linen Hall Review* 12, 2 (1995/96), p.13.
10. A. Enright, *The Gathering* (London: Jonathan Cape, 2007).
11. Enright, 'Interview by Caitriona Moloney', p.54.
12. C. Tóibín, 'Introduction', in *The Penguin Book of Irish Fiction*, ed. C. Tóibín (Harmondsworth: Viking, 1999), p.xxxiii.
13. A. Enright, *The Pleasure of Eliza Lynch* (London: Jonathan Cape, 2002).
14. A. Enright, *What Are You Like?* (London: Jonathan Cape, 2000). See H. Hansson, 'Anne Enright and Postnationalism in the Contemporary Irish Novel', in *Irish Literature since 1990: Diverse Voices*, ed. M. Parker and S. Brewster (Manchester: Manchester University Press, 2009), pp.216–31 for a discussion of *What Are You Like?* and postnationalism.
15. V. Cooppan, 'World Literature and Global Theory: Comparative Literature for the New Millennium', *symplokē*, 9, 1–2 (2001), p.33. Cooppan's definition is also quoted in D. Damrosch, *What is World Literature?* (Princeton, NJ: Princeton University Press, 2003), p.22.
16. Damrosch, *What is World Literature?*, p.7; A. Pettersson, 'Transcultural Literary History: Beyond Constricting Notions of World Literature', *New Literary History*, 39 (2008), p.469; Thomsen, *Mapping World Literature*, p.11.
17. K. Marx, *The Communist Manifesto*, ed. M. Cowling and trans. T. Carver (Edinburgh: Edinburgh University Press, 1998), p.17.
18. Damrosch, *What is World Literature?*, p.5.
19. Ibid., p.4.
20. Ibid., p.22.
21. Ibid.
22. Ibid., p.24.
23. D. Damrosch, *How to Read World Literature* (Chichester: Wiley-Blackwell, 2009), p.13.
24. Enright, 'Interview by Caitriona Moloney', p.58.
25. Damrosch, *How to Read World Literature*, p.13.
26. See, for example, D.L. Potts, '"When Ireland was Still Under a Spell": The Poetry of Nuala Ní Dhomnaill', *New Hibernia Review* 7, 2 (2003), pp.52–3.

27. Pettersson, 'Transcultural Literary History', p.469.

28. Enright, The Wig My Father Wore, p.37.

29. A. Enright, 'Author, Author: Name that Plume', Guardian, 9 August 2008.

30. Enright, The Wig My Father Wore, p.1.

31. Ibid., p.6.

32. C. Moloney, 'Re-Imagining Women's History in the Fiction of Éilís Ní Dhuibhne, Anne Enright, and Kate O'Riordan', Postcolonial Text, 3, 3 (2007), p.8.

33. See H. Hansson, 'To Say "I": Female Identity in The Maid's Tale and The Wig My Father Wore', in Irish Fiction since the 1960s: A Collection of Critical Essay, ed. Elmer Kennedy-Andrews (Gerrards Cross: Colin Smythe, 2006), p.145; Enright, 'Interview by Caitriona Moloney', p.52.

34. Enright, The Wig My Father Wore, p.110.

35. S. Sontag, On Photography (New York: Picador, 1977), pp.22–3.

36. Enright, The Wig My Father Wore, p.104.

37. Ibid., p.105.

38. Ibid., p.171.

39. Ibid., p.109.

40. Ibid., p.111.

41. Ibid., p.51.

42. Ibid., p.75.

43. Ibid., p.28.

44. Ibid., p.120.

45. Ibid., p.23.

46. Ibid., p.79.

47. Ibid., pp.47, 187–96.

48. Ibid., p.33.

49. Ibid., p.36.

50. Ibid., p.34.

51. Ibid., pp.87–9.

52. L. Hutcheon, A Poetics of Postmodernism: History, Theory, Fiction (New York: Routledge, 1992), pp.105–40.

53. S. Onega, 'British Historiographic Metafiction in the 1980s', in British Postmodern Fiction, ed. T. D'haen and H. Bertens (Amsterdam: Rodopi, 1993), pp.47–61.

54. Enright, The Wig My Father Wore, p.175.

55. Ibid., pp.211–12.

56. Ibid., p.176.

57. Ibid.

58. Ibid.

59. Ibid., pp.126–8.

60. Enright, 'Interview by Caitriona Moloney', p.63.

61. Hansson, 'To Say "I"', pp.148–9.

62. Damrosch, What is World Literature?, p.6, original emphasis.

CHAPTER FIVE

'Now the blood is in the room': The spectral feminine in the work of Anne Enright

ANNE MULHALL

Enright's work is full of ghosts. In it, the dead persist: they return, they speak, they even fall in love. Besides these more flamboyant sorts of revenants, there are the other 'banal, living ghosts' – spectral parents who emerge eerily from the faces of their children, dead siblings whose presence insists in the living.[1] Even seemingly inanimate objects are saturated with the spectral. Things become, in Enright's work, ghostly palimpsests of past, present and future, artefacts that hold the sedimented interconnections across the generations, on whose surfaces the past can rise up suddenly again in the gap gouged out of the wallpaper, the worn pattern of an old carpet, or the chipped paint of a much-used cot. For Jacques Derrida, spectrality, the time of the ghost, involves '*the non-contemporaneity with itself of the living present*', an untimeliness that is the condition for an openness to the other that cannot be achieved within the dialectic of the either/or: 'this responsibility and this respect for justice concerning those who *are not there*, of those who are no longer or who are not yet *present and living*'.[2] Such untimely hauntings are at the core of Enright's work. The spectral feminine is a particular mode of untimeliness that recurs in her work, whether in the traumatized ghosts of dead mothers, the repressed feminine of a representational and literary tradition, or in the re-emergence of an occluded substratum of being that Bracha Ettinger calls the matrixal borderspace – a feminine stratum that punctuates the hygienic discreteness of the identified subject and its stratified temporal horizons.[3] In keeping with the irruptions that besiege her female protagonists, the aesthetic developed across Enright's body of work is one of fragmentation. Enright's 'fragmented books', as she describes her work in *Making Babies*, disrupt illusions of a governable world, a knowable self, or a transparent language.[4] The 'insides' of the shattered self and the fragmented text are indissociable from the 'outside' that gives them their shape: 'Ireland broke apart in the eighties, and I sometimes think that the crack happened in my own head'.[5] The 'incoherence' of her writing, as Enright would have it, is the representational inscription of the outside enclaved on the inside: a peculiarly Irish mode of hysteria that manifests in cultural and social prohibitions around the gendered body. As she observes:

> [the novels] were slightly surreal, because Ireland was unreal. They dealt with ideas of purity, because the chastity of Irish women was one of the founding myths of the Nation State (well that was my excuse). But they were also full of corpses … it is the past that lies down but will not shut up, the elephant in the national living-room.[6]

For Enright, the 'awful hole in the text', the 'unsayable thing in the center of a book', the 'silences … illusions and the slippages … the jumps, and the uncertain way of making sense' are 'part of a feminist aesthetic'.[7] As such, the elaboration of these gaps and holes in Enright's work reaches toward an enigmatic truth that is covered over by the nervous verisimilitude Enright ascribes to an archetypal post-Joyce Irish prose writing, and the phantoms that body forth such gaps speak to a specifically feminine spectrality.[8] Transgenerational transmissions are one recurring trajectory through which this spectral feminine is communicated in Enright's work. Enright's insistent focus on pregnancy, motherhood, the mother and the complexity of mother-daughter relations performs a conscious restitution of a definitively shaping gap within the Irish literary tradition. In place of the real mother, Enright has observed that Irish writing has traditionally either appointed 'the iconised mother figure', or posited an absence: 'They are very often dead, or left out of the narrative. The mother gets half a sentence and there is an awful lot about fathers.'[9] The mother is the unspeakable phantom, the gap enclaved within the novel's geneaology. Enright works to make this absence present, to answer to its uncanny insistence, and, in some cases literally, to enable the ghost to speak.

The hole in the Irish literary tradition where the mother is buried, alive or dead, is the effect in representation of the repudiation of the mother and the repression of the feminine that subtend a phallic symbolic order, where the oedipal relation between father and son is preserved at the cost of the dereliction of the feminine and mother-daughter connectedness, as Moynagh Sullivan has argued in relation to the Irish poetic tradition.[10] In place of the reverential and rivalrous identifications structuring the male line, in The Wig My Father Wore Grace reaches toward another lineage, one that passes between generations of women, an inheritance that, while certainly no less troubled, resolutely confirms the significance of the body – that which language functionally obscures – and articulates a spectral feminine stratum of being that, by dint of being specifically feminine rather than phallic, eludes conventional symbolic articulation. The gendered dichotomy of mind and body is played out in the novel in the interactions between Stephen and Grace. Stephen, the living corpse who is all spirit, all mind, progressively manifests bodily signs of his masculinity – the hair that rushes to fill in the blank canvas of his skin, a re-awakened tumescence – inscriptions on his body of his sexual desire for Grace. The maturity of Grace's woman's body, the engravings in the flesh of time and experience, are, conversely, undone and erased through her desiring relation with Stephen, and her body becomes increasingly spectral and strangely disembodied as it reverts to an unearthly girlish purity. Helpless to her desire for Stephen, Grace weakly protests the disappearance of her body's enfleshed history, which she intuits as an erasure of female intergenerational connection and a specifically feminine stratum of being: 'I missed the lines and the markings and the moles ticking away like timebombs. I missed my mother's knees and my Granny's hammer toes.'[11] Grace realizes with a shock that Stephen's touch will erase her navel – a temporal punctuation in the flesh, the point that situates the 'before' and 'after' of the cut, marking on the body the enfleshed memory of her first home, her mother's womb, and her separation from that originary body: '"What's a navel after all?" I say to myself … but I feel a pang … I think of what it has been tied to – a dead piece of my mother and me they hadn't bothered to bury.'[12]

'The wound we can never heal, never cure, opens up when the umbilical cord is severed.'[13] Such is the analysis of Luce Irigaray. This wound, the mark of our severance from the mother, opens a gap that is covered over, Irigaray contends, by language and by the proper name of the father. Symbolic language cuts us off from the body in its foundational denial of where we all begin – the mother's womb, 'that first body, that first home, that first love'.[14] For the Lacanian tradition, we do not 'begin' in utero, but rather first, embryonically, in the imaginary Ego, and then, fully, in language as the speaking subject, as being in such a schema is conflated with the Subject that emerges in relation to an Other in the specular and linguistic orders. For Irigaray, this equates to the negation of our relation to the mother, which is carved into the subject as lack. This lack opens up a gap, an 'awful hole', to echo Enright's words, 'in the texture of language'.[15] Language and the speaking subject are *ghosted*, we could say, by what is thus entombed within us by this severance or primary structural trauma: the foreclosure of the mother's body and our experience of co-emergence with her. To recover the negated maternal body and our relation to it – in particular the mother-daughter relationship that is fatally cut and mutilated by this severance from the feminine – a new language and a new form of representation have to be reached toward. Such a language needs to remain close to the truth of the body: to speak with it, rather than act as the body's substitute, 'clothing it in words that do not erase the body but speak the body'.[16] The mother is not a solitary subject, but is rather connected through the body to past and future generations of women. Umbilically connected, the maternal body cannot be isolated from the 'genealogy of women' – the spectral feminine line – which must also be made manifest and tangible.

Bracha Ettinger's elaboration of what she calls the 'matrixial border-space' speaks to this call for the restitution of the feminine. The matrixial is a feminine stratum of subjectivization that is other than the plane on which the speaking subject is constituted. According to Ettinger, we do not 'begin', as Lacan would have it, with the coming-into-being of the subject via the alienation and separation entailed by our installation within language. Before this, our experience in utero of co-becoming with the mother-to-be – before language, before 'the cut' – lays down within us a sub-subjective, transsubjective stratum of being, which she designates as feminine rather than masculine, the matrixial substratum as distinct from the phallic Symbolic order of language posited by Lacan. For Ettinger, this stratum does not represent an early stage of the phallic subject; it is not pre-oedipal or pre-symbolic, but *non-oedipal*, an entirely other stratum of subjectivization, one that precedes the phallic subject and that persists 'beneath' that subject, a stratum of partial subjects or transjects sharing traces in a threshold space, the matrixial borderspace.[17] The matrix is not coextensive with the womb, but is a *psychic structure*, although this stratum of being is first transcribed in the womb. The non-recognition of this other stratum – which is difference itself – effects a warping of the feminine and the maternal, which in Lacan and Freud become associated with the 'Other' – death, dissolution, the death-drive, psychosis, madness: irruptions from the Real – in Lacanian terms the inchoate formlessness of the presymbolic that is inevitably associated with the woman and the mother – and the repressed contents of the unconscious that disarticulate the speaking and oedipal subject. For Ettinger, the matrixial feminine stratum is itself thereby rendered a kind of corpse. The repressed, spectral feminine is fatally subject to interminable mutilation, misrepresented as the abject, the monstrous, the death-drive: the whole concatenation of the uncanny that 'sticks' to the mother and thus to the woman and to the feminine via the structural process of repression within a phallic symbolic order.

'He was looking for death, but I did not want to give him mine': Grace feels that the loss of her navel, the cost of ceding to Stephen's desire, will constitute a kind of death.[18] Stephen's desire to erase this 'piece of old rope' is a manifestation of the death-drive, displaced onto the feminine and effected in the erasure of the traces of a feminine transgenerational connectedness. Grace's 'body's infinity' contrasts with Stephen's lack of a navel. Given the transconnectivity on the feminine stratum that the navel represents, Stephen's lack signifies the founding illusion of the Symbolic: the self-birthing, self-sufficient phallic subject, born of a repudiation of the feminine and the connection to the mother. Such self-sufficiency is illusory, however, as Stephen's lack signifies a kind of castration: the submission of the subject to the Law, and the 'cut' from the maternal and, with it, the feminine. As Andrew Donnelly has observed, Grace's sense of a 'women's time' embodied in the navel reworks the *omphalos* as it is figured in *Ulysses*, and Stephen himself is inhabited, seriously and hilariously, by the ghost of Stephen Dedalus.[19] The *omphalos* in *Ulysses* signifies a 'navel-gazing' insularity in its connections to Buck Mulligan's nationalist posturing, but it also signifies the umbilical connection across time and generation that Kristeva describes as 'monumental time', and that I associate with Irigaray's umbilical feminine and Etttinger's matrixial.[20] The *omphalos* is the fleshly yet spectral cord that transconnects all humanity, and binds all generations back to Eve, the first mother. Stephen Dedalus describes it: 'cords of all link back, strandentwining cable of all flesh', the 'successive anastomosis of navel-cords'.[21] However, Joyce's Stephen also muses on the umbilical cord as the record in the flesh of our fall from grace into mortality and history. Like Enright's Stephen, Eve 'had no navel', her belly was 'without blemish', but she was also the 'womb of sin', whose transgression humanity pays for with relentless death, so that the sign on the body of our connection to the life-giving mother is also, simultaneously, the sign of the death to which her line has consigned us.[22] In *The Wig My Father Wore*, Stephen's lack of a navel and his desire to erase Grace's can, like many of his symbolic associations, accommodate contradictory readings. On the one hand, Stephen is the untimely spectre, coming from outside history to unmake and remake Grace, removing sin and shame. He remakes Grace's belly 'without blemish', undoing the wounds of history and the mark of the Fall. On the other hand, Stephen's urge speaks of the phobic association of woman with sin and death. His dead mother ghosts the Joycean Stephen's preoccupation with the *omphalos* in *Ulysses*: she is the 'corpsechewer', the 'ghostwoman with ashes on her breath', dripping decay and reeking of the grave.[23] While it is at least partially true that, as Maud Ellmann observes, 'In Joyce, the phallus is supplanted by the *omphalos*', his figuring of the *omphalos* is saturated with ambivalence, with dread of the devouring mother and the female body in its death-bringing aspect.[24]

In this light, Stephen's erasure of Grace's navel attempts a definitive cut from the mother; it is a castration that threatens to simultaneously submit Grace to the phallic law and render the maternal and the spectral feminine as abject. From one perspective, the 'unmaking' of Grace's body and its connection to an embodied feminine lineage is a process of becoming-statue: her body becomes increasingly iconized as the signs of messy, threatening female embodiment are smoothed over by a flawless, marble patina. The process is a parodic literal rendition of the iconizing of woman and mother within the Irish cultural, political and literary traditions. As Enright puts it: 'the politics of women's bodies involves an uneasy and damaging relationship with ideas of the sacred. The less physical we are, the more we are admired, this is why we turn ourselves into images, icons, transparencies.'[25] To reify the woman as a flawless icon is to deny and render abject the embodied reality of women and the particular transsubjective transitivity that originates in the relation between the becoming-mother and becoming-infant. It substitutes a bachelor transcendence for the infinity of an immanent transgenerational connectedness. It is not Grace, however, who is emblematic of mortality in Enright's novel, but rather Stephen, emissary of heaven and angel of death. Stephen has a direct, literal proximity to death. He is shot through with its intimations: he is a 'little piece of the real', in Lacan's sense, an apparition in reality of that which lies beyond representation.[26] He has an affinity with the unrepresentable: he is nothing but waves and particles, made of the same non-substantial substance as television transmission signals; he is a little piece of nothing; as he tells Grace, he 'could get lost ... in that little bit of nothing-at-all' in the television, because he is made of the same 'little bit of nothing'.[27]

Rather than marking a break from the uncanny temporalities held within the body and psyche, Grace's involvement with Stephen catalyzes their return as she becomes increasingly possessed by the ghosts of her former selves, who show themselves on the surface of the body itself. The nature of time has shifted, its uncanny warps and foldings exposed; it 'leaks', it 'drips', the metaphors of fluidity emphasizing the emergence of an uncanny feminine stratum of temporality that, for Freud as well as Ettinger, is associated with the known and unknown unheimlich of the first home, the womb.[28] In the chapter following 'The Mark', Grace's relation to the normal order of things becomes distinctly slanted, 'lopsided' as she describes herself. Things slip from her hands, Freudian slips trip from her mouth, she takes wrong turns and cannot make sense of phone numbers. 'I sit and yearn, mutely, for my mother', she tells us.[29]

After taking a shower at work, she looks at her self in the mirror and, 'The body that looks back at me is nine years old, or fourteen mixed with nine, or my own, mixed with all the bodies I used to have. I wonder if I am a virgin again.'[30] Her two-year-old self emerges, 'the childhood body, its milk white parting', emphasizing her return to a liminal position on the borders of the separation from the mother and the emergence of the child as fully a subject in and of language.[31] Grace goes back further yet, remembering her own birth: whether by her piss or her tears, she 'poisoned my mother, nearly killed my mother', leaving behind her an uncanny double, a monstrous twin who was but a clot of skin, hair and teeth.[32] She imagines that it was her father's wig that planted this horrible thing in her mother. Later in the same chapter, lying in the bath in her parent's house, she recalls her father at work under the bathroom sink, pulling a clot of hair from the blocked pipes, assisted by a wire hanger, like some gruesome abortionist. The hair clot is contiguously related to the ball of hair and teeth removed from her mother's womb, and to Grace's evisceration of her sitting room earlier in the narrative, through tropes of eviscerated wombs, recalcitrant birth canals and still and monstrous births. The deliberate layering of figures of monstrosity and abjection with images of the reproductive female body captures the revulsion against the feminine that saturates the social, cultural and historical imaginary, emphasizing the moment of the cut from the mother's body that renders that body abject and unspeakable from the perspective of a dominant phallic symbolic.

Alongside the horrors that ghost the feminine within a phallic imaginary, we can posit the matrixial stratum that can be glimpsed in Grace's relations with Stephen and that is intimated by the uncanny warpings and leakings of the temporal tissue outlined above and in the contradictory meanings of the navel in 'The Mark'. In reworking these associations, Enright recovers the woman's body, the mother and the feminine within a literary geneaology that has taken their abjection as a given. The phobic understanding of the feminine and the maternal as the Real – as Žižek puts it, 'the pulsing of the presymbolic substance in its abhorrent vitality' that threatens the subject with dissolution – is radically rearticulated in Ettinger's matrixial theory.[33] It is also significantly countered in Enright's work, where the weakening of the threshold between self and other, inside and outside, opens up a space of potentiality that can be generative as well as traumatizing. Grace and Stephen connect in a space that is other than that of the identified phallic subject. Due to her intimacy with Stephen, the edges of Grace's body and psyche have a rediscovered porousness, bringing into dim apprehension a threshold where the subject ends and something else, something more partial, enigmatic and transsubjective begins. 'The alphabet abandons me as his hand reaches the top of my legs', Grace submits when they finally have sex, before describing the conjunctions of their bodies as an alphabet newly wrought in the transitivity opened up by exchanges of the flesh: 'M was one of them, a touching O, an informal kind of R'.[34] The language that gives rise to the identified subject is undone during sex, as the threshold of the subject temporarily dissolves. Their merging and separating bodies supplant and rewrite the letter, bringing into view an other level of co-becoming that language and the *logos* obscure. The *logos*, the word made flesh, is significantly reworked as here it is the flesh that makes the word, signifying a level of being that precedes and persists beneath and beside the word.

Patricia Coughlan has noted the association between Stephen and the colour white, an association that underlines his connection to a spectral matrixial stratum.[35] On the one hand white, with its associations of purity, transcendence, things of the spirit, entails a denial of the putative impurity and immanence of the body. On the other, white is also the colour of milk – one of Enright's recurring motifs – which Hélène Cixous limns as the 'white ink' that comes from the mother.[36] Grace eviscerates her sitting room at one point, gouging through the layers of wallpaper and newspaper that line it – a 'menstrual image' Enright has said, a sloughing away of the sedimented history of exclusions and distortions effected on the body and the woman in Irish culture and history.[37] Following her frenzy, Stephen paints over the tattered walls: the white of whitewash, of the blank page and of milk. Again, Stephen's actions and associations can be read in two different registers: on the one hand, the white paint covers over, denies and occludes, and on the other, it opens up a space of potentiality that pulses with the whiteness of the milk that is a kind of channel or hinge between mother and infant: the whiteness of a feminine transconnectivity.

As we can see in Enright's playful rearticulation of the 'word made flesh' above, language and its relation to subjectivity, embodiment and the physical world is an enduring preoccupation in her work. The ability of signification to keep the world in place is weakened where the threshold between subjects grows thin. Metaphor sheds its substitutive function and wrecks havoc on reality; in a sense, it reverts to a prior state, where the distance between word and thing is effaced. On one occasion, for instance, as Grace and her colleagues break into a drunken sing-song, Grace observes that

> we sat in the rising tide of friendship like milk was slowly filling the room while we sat up to our oxters in it, not knowing if the gathering clots were inside us or outside ... small milk mermen with mouths like guppies and fins like wings, grazed their way politely through the wet sweet sea lettuce of our pubic hair.[38]

This collapsing of the gap between the world and the language that, like metaphor, functionally displaces and substitutes for the world, is ascribed to Stephen – 'You're giving me hallucinations', Grace tells him.[39] The temporary emergence of a porousness between inside and outside, between words and reality, rather than signalling an intrusion of the Real into reality, is from another perspective the matrixial making itself felt: defined edges blur, and the transitivity between selves, language and things subverts the language that would keep things in their proper, discrete positions. The recurrence of the milk motif again 'reclaims' whiteness from its metaphorical relation to purity and transcendence, as the milk of human kindness divests itself of the metaphorical displacement that keeps its occluded meaning at arm's length to become, literally, itself again. The trope recurs at the close of the novel where a dreamily pregnant Grace imagines Stephen as a diffusely dispersed substance watching from the skies while the milk in her bicycle basket spills from its burst container. The existence of another kind of Eros in the matrixial is articulated in the closing lines – an Eros that does not demand someone's death: 'For a woman, nothing has to die'.[40]

Milk signifies our attachment to the mother, but this attachment is shot through with ambivalence. In her function as *container*, is the mother the nurturing facilitator who sustains and holds us, or the threatening crypt that paralyzes, haunting us from within? In *Making Babies*, Enright wryly connects this function of the mother as container to the woman as 'old bag': 'that "Mother" thing ... The container (the old bag, my dear, the old bag)'.[41] Elsewhere, she discusses the textual origins of certain enigmatic repetitions in her writing. One of these is a 'dangling bag with something horrible in it. A corpse or skeleton or something worse'.[42] Such things, Enright tells us, 'pose a question to which I do not know the answer, or answer a question that remains obscure'. 'What is in the bag?' Enright asks, and the contiguity with the 'old bag' suggests one answer.[43] Enright's question again echoes Joyce: Stephen Dedalus, on Sandymount Strand, watching a midwife swinging her bag as she comes down the beach, asks: 'What has she in the bag? A misbirth with a trailing navel-cord.'[44] The thing enclosed in both bags conjures up a dark entombment rather than nurturing containment. These bags have the shapeless yet shaping form of the crypt: a secret that has been forgotten, that perhaps was never known, but that is the unrecognized centre of the psychic and family dramas explored in Enright's novels, many of which involve the encrypted phantom of the dead or absent mother. The bag contains something of the old bag – the death-bringing mother, the maternal corpse, or rather, in Enright's work, the corpse of the maternal phantom, the spectral feminine that is rendered as death within a phallic symbolic. The inflection is important, as it recognizes the significant rearticulation of the feminine and the maternal that is one of Enright's major achievements in the Irish literary context.

The neo-Freudian psychoanalyst Nicolas Abraham describes the phantom thus: 'the phantom is meant to objectify, even if under the guise of individual or collective hallucination, the gap that the concealment of some part of a loved one's life produced in us ... [w]hat haunts are not the dead, but the gaps left within us by the secrets of others.'[45] The phantom is the secret of the other, the other's other, buried alive within. The unspeakable secret, the unsymbolized event that the parent cannot articulate is 'passed down' intrapsychically and intergenerationally to the child as an experience of some inexplicable, inaccessible gap or absence in the parent or object that the child cannot metabolize. Thus, the parent's crypt is an enclave – a gap, a kind of nothing – carved into the subject and inhabited by the other's secret: the phantom. The phantom makes its presence known, according to Abraham, within *language* as the anaseme, or the unspeakable word hidden within or adjacent to the words that are spoken. It is the haunting absence that ghosts the presence of the word. The anaseme disrupts order and coherence, fragments reason and reality, impelling 'surrealistic flights of fancy or of *oulipo*-like verbal feats'.[46]

Abraham thus articulates transmissible trauma beyond representation as a toxic crypt. Ettinger perceives something that is missed in this articulation, however: the transitivity that impels the phantom, evidence that psychic traces can be *shared*, and that, therefore, there must be some space in which supposedly singular, bachelor subjects transconnect. Otherwise, how can the subject carry the traces of another's trauma? Such traces are transmissible and sharable, according to Ettinger, because of the universal transsubjective capacity for co-affectivity. The psychic conditions that result, for Abraham, in the toxic entombment of the other's other in the subject's crypt are, for Ettinger, potentially generative (but also traumatic and traumatizing) transsubjective webs that resonate with the psychic structure first laid down in the embodied experience of intrauterine existence and the traumatic 'cut' from this stratum that is installed by the intervention of the Symbolic law. Ettinger's reformulation of the crypt as *transcryptum* is an important aspect of her rehabilitation of the feminine, as the crypt, with its resonances of death, the corpse and the abject, seems, like Lacan's Real, a threatening space, a 'hole' or gap in reality and the subject that is implicated with the feminine and maternal, auguring breakdown and psychosis.[47] Furthermore, all traumatic events, resonating with this primary structural trauma, are likewise associated with this black hole of Woman as Other.[48] Ettinger proposes to read such gaps and crypts otherwise, as the manifestations both of wounds to the feminine matrixial, and as signposts to the existence of another trans- and sub-subjective stratum of being – the matrixial feminine – that appears 'mad' or toxic because it is not of the order of phallic meaning and signification. Ettinger's reformulation of the crypt as *transcryptum* affords us another way of understanding such 'gaps', offering another way of answering the question of 'what is in the bag' that is posed by Enright and Joyce's Stephen. The *transcryptum* is the space where traces of an other's trauma transconnect and vibrate within several partial subjects across time and generation. What appears from Abraham's perspective, then, as the toxic crypt of the other's other installed as a gap within the self becomes, instead, the manifestation of the transconnectedness and transmissablity of trauma: this transmissibility hurts, but it speaks to our capacity to carry the trauma of an other, to its shareability, however painful that might be.

Enright's fiction is punctuated by subjects on the edge of dissolution. Such dissolutions manifest in the breakdown of 'normal' conventions of signification. This breakdown of language is sometimes a symptom of extreme bodily malfunctionings: Grace's father becomes aphasic after suffering a second stroke, while in *What Are You Like?*, Anna's fatal brain tumour compromises her ability to follow linguistic and social conventions. While these symptoms should be confined, physiologically, to the subjects who suffer them, they prove to be *transmissible*. In transmission, such malfunctions behave like psychosis: like Lacan's unsymbolizable Real that disarticulates the chain of signification and bleeds into the world as hallucination, or Abraham's phantom that ruptures language and the functioning of the subject. In light of the repeated emergence in Enright's work of a spectral feminine stratum that is a transsubjective, transgenerational space, it is possible to interpret such apparently psychotic intrusions of the Real and toxic emissions from the crypt otherwise: as signalling events and capacities that belong to an unsymbolized matrixial feminine borderspace that enables transsubjective transmissions and the potential for the sharing of an other's traces and 'carrying' of an other's trauma. There is always, in Enright's work, 'a place ... where words and actions are mangled'.[49] This place is often associated with trauma; it is also often the space of the pregnant body and the transsubjective relation between mother and child, 'this peculiar, mutant double self – motherandchild'.[50]

The relation between language and trauma, the masculine symbolic and the feminine matrixial, is illuminated by a 'slanted' reading of Enright's second novel, *What Are You Like?*. In the opening chapter, Berts at first mistakes the symptoms of his wife's brain tumour for a kind of feminine 'madness' unleashed by her pregnancy. At first, the doctor agrees with this diagnosis: a surfeit of hormones have made her already skittish female constitution excessively flighty. However, turning her coat inside out before putting it on, Anna wishes him 'Hello' as she and her husband turn to leave; the doctor re-evaluates. In compliance with the law, the pregnant Anna's disease is not treated. And so, as her babies grow inside her, Anna slowly dies. We meet Anna in her own right in the seventh section of the novel, where she speaks from beyond the grave in a chapter that interrupts the main narrative – the 'crypt' of the novel, the return of the repressed and unspeakable, the reanimated sacrificial mother. For Žižek, the dead return because 'they cannot find their proper place in the text of tradition'.[51] The spectre has been improperly buried, consigned to the realm of the dead without the correct symbolic rites, and returns to claim 'some unpaid symbolic debt'.[52] Looked at from another perspective, however, any unpaid debt here is due to the matrixial rather than the symbolic, as the matrixial web has been catastrophically torn by the sacrifice of the mother to the law, by Anna's premature death while her daughters were still in utero, and again by Berts's abandonment of their daughter Rose to adoption. It is not the lack of symbolic integration within the tradition but rather the rending and repression of a female transgenerational connectedness that deny Anna any rest or peace. In that sense, Anna's death and the premature 'cut' between her and her daughters is symbolic of the mutilation of mother-daughter relationality and female transconnectedness within an oedipal economy. Her death is, at the same time, representative of the sacrifice of mother and woman to a reproductive religio-social law, as pregnancy renders Anna's body an incubator for future subjects, rather than a body deserving of care and treatment in its own right.

The complexity of Anna's fraught relationship with conventional signification becomes increasingly evident in her narrative. Rather than being solely ascribable to the disease warping her brain's machinery, Anna's aphasia appears to be a maternal inheritance that she deploys in response to her situation. She recalls her mother's lists:

> things that she shifted around the kitchen; the tea cosy placed on the table for more tea, the lid of the bread bin propped open for flour, the cat's saucer upside down beside the door when we needed polish for our Sunday shoes.[53]

This obdurately material sign-system is transmitted to a young Anna, who translates between two systems of meaning-making:

> She would sit at the table and check the room and I would hold the list of things translated in my head as I ran down the road … a twist of baking soda, sugar, a wick, two wicks, a bar of soap cut down the middle so it leaves itself on the knife.[54]

This 'language', refusing words and relying instead on idiosyncratic and arbitrary conjunctions between household objects for its meaning, serves as a muted feminine refusal of a social, symbolic and representational system that circumscribes and limits the position and meaning of woman, the feminine and the mother. What could be seen as a symptom of madness, of psychosis, becomes a meaning-making system with its own integrity. It resignifies the place that circumscribes the mother and woman – the kitchen, with its objects of nurture and care – in a silent parody of the representational system that so defines and delimits her. Anna intuits this in her affective connection to her mother's strange object-language: 'moving things from place to place, and knowing what they meant, not just a string of words – the shopping list bouncing in my head, my own breath cutting it short at every step'.[55]

Anna is haunted by language. Words torment her; they stalk her, they will not let her be. Words, and the identified subjects and phallic self-other relations that they regulate, are what come to terrify her beyond death's threshold: 'I am terrified, here in my grave, by words and what they might want. Mother. Father. Brother. Sister. Home.'[56] And yet the emptiness of the signifier is fully revealed, its non-coincidence with reality unveiled: '[words] were just themselves, and did not join with anything else'.[57] Anna's frenzied attempts to wrest some meaning from the darkness within her and without her, 'a gap in the middle of a hole'[58] as she describes herself, might be read as a symptom of her illness, or as an inherited psychosis:

> I wrote words down and I buried them in the garden, the names of flowers: wallflower, phlox, peony rose, dog rose, tea rose. A twist of baking soda, sugar, a wick, two wicks, a bar of soap cut down the middle so it leaves itself on the knife.
>
> I knew I was pregnant now. I knew the words would never

grow. There was something wrong with me, but I could not stop myself. I wrote words down and I ate them, but I knew they would not keep me alive.[59]

Words are what holds reality and the subject in place, but words, as Anna finds, cannot create or prolong life, cannot fend off the void. It is not Anna who is mad; rather, the belief in the omnipotence of signification is itself figured as a kind of psychosis. This perspective on signification is, for Žižek, aligned with an anamorphic looking: 'a detail of a picture that "gaz'd rightly", i.e., straightforwardly, appears as a blurred spot, assumes clear, distinguished shapes once we look at it "awry", at an angle'.[60] As Valerie Rohy observes, this anamorphic spot announces the 'gaping hole in symbolic reality and the intolerable lack around which our own subjectivity is structured'.[61] Viewed from another angle again, however, the anamorphic spot comes into focus as a spectral feminine space that is other than the Real. It is to her mother's muted, fugitive system that Anna turns when her own approaching death drains the 'normal' order of things of all meaning: 'There is no story to living, and having a child, and dying ... So I put vegetables in the wardrobe and buried my clothes. I turned the hoover on itself, all the way up the flex. I rolled along the wallpaper, like Cleopatra coming out of a carpet, and I wrote lists on the floor.'[62] This persistence of the strange grammar of the mother's object-language could, from Abraham's perspective, be diagnosed as the phantom of the other encrypted as a traumatizing gap in the subject. Looked at from the anamorphic spectral feminine perspective, however, what is transmitted transgenerationally between mother and daughter is the spectral matrixial feminine: something in me carries and shares in the unknown trauma of an other, even as I am traumatized by this too. The trauma is transmitted in an alternative grammar and a slanted, 'lop-sided' relation to signification – an enigmatic articulation of the displacement of the feminine within symbolic representation. The transmission of the mother's language to the daughter indicates the presence of some other stratum of being and meaning that is occluded and 'garbled' by the Symbolic, that cannot be 'translated' directly into a phallic representational system because it is other than that system, even while it continues to be wounded by it.

The repressed but persistent feminine stratum is figured in the passing on between women of an anamorphic, slanted take on signification. While both Rose and Maria are shaped by the void left by the absence of their mother, who died before they even reached term – a particularly terrible tearing of 'the matrixial web'[63] – their mother's line seems to persist in them in this uncanny disruptive relation to the grammars of visible, ordered reality. Rose, who was given up for adoption and so was cut off from her birth family, nonetheless carries traces of her unknown mother Anna. She is 'too full of things', and 'was born with a hole in her head, a hole in her life. Everything fell into it.'[64] The right words will not come, gestures and directions get lost in transit: 'When she opened her mouth, the wrong words hopped out of it. Everything she tried to do came out backwards. She drank from the hot tap. She said things like, *He is the kind of woman who.*'[65] These parapraxes are the verbal and gestural inscriptions of a relation to the mother and grandmother that Rose has never known, the enigmatic residue of their transconnectedness. The spectral transitivities between female generations in *What Are You Like?* are the grammar of that relation: the traces of known and unknown 'I's and non-'I's that are shared, transmitted, and carried in a threshold matrixial borderspace. Whether we view such ruptures in language and reality as traumatizing or generative, it is the very fact that they are transmitted and shared between subjects that suggests the space of the transcryptum. These are the traces of the spectral feminine: traces that transmit trauma, allow for the carrying of another's trauma, and that attest to a feminine spectral time and space of transconnectivity across the thresholds of generations, of subject and object, life and death.

ACKNOWLEDGEMENTS

Many thanks to Jody Allen Randolph for generously sharing the fruits of her bibliographical work on Anne Enright with me. Thanks as ever to Noreen Giffney for her astute, precise and illuminating comments on this essay. Particular thanks to Linda Mach and Andrew Donnelly who took the undergraduate seminar 'Readings in Irish Culture: Tradition and Modernity' with me in 2008 and 2009, for insightful and stimulating conversations about *The Wig My Father Wore.*

NOTES

ANNE ENRIGHT

1. A. Enright, *What Are You Like?* (London: Vintage, 2001), p.126.
2. J. Derrida, *Specters of Marx*, trans. P. Kamuf (New York and London: Routledge, 1994), p.xix.
3. B. Ettinger, *The Matrixial Borderspace* (Minneapolis, MN and London: University of Minnesota Press, 2006).
4. A. Enright, *Making Babies: Stumbling into Motherhood* (London: Vintage, 2005), p.193.
5. Ibid., p.186.
6. Ibid., p.193.
7. A. Enright, 'Anne Enright Interview by Catriona Moloney', in *Irish Women Speak Out: Voices from the Field*, ed. C. Moloney and H. Thompson (Syracuse, NY: Syracuse University Press, 2003), p.63.
8. Enright discusses this in ibid., p.55.
9. Ibid., p.61.
10. See L. Irigaray, *Speculum of the Other Woman*, trans. G.C. Gill (Ithaca, NY: Cornell University Press, 1985) and *This Sex Which Is Not One*, trans C. Porter (Ithaca, NY: Cornell University Press, 1985); M. Sullivan, 'The Treachery of Wetness: Irish Studies, Seamus Heaney and the politics of parturition', *Irish Studies Review*, 13, 4 (2005), pp.451–68.
11. A. Enright, *The Wig My Father Wore* (London: Jonathan Cape, 1995), pp.126–7.
12. Ibid., pp.129–30.
13. L. Irigaray, *Sexes and Genealogies*, trans G.C. Gill (New York: Columbia University Press, 1993), p.14.
14. Ibid.
15. Ibid., p.16.
16. Ibid., p.19.
17. See Ettinger, *The Matrixial Borderspace*, passim.
18. Enright, *The Wig My Father Wore*, p.130.
19. Andrew Donnelly has made this point in discussion and in his essay for my seminar, 'Reading Irish Culture: Tradition and Modernity'. I am grateful to Mr Donnelly for permission to cite his key insight here, and my analysis here is indebted to this observation.
20. See J. Kristeva, 'Women's Time', in T. Moi (ed.), *The Kristeva Reader* (Oxford: Blackwell: 1986), pp.187-213.
21. J. Joyce, *Ulysses*, intro. D. Kiberd (Harmondsworth: Penguin, 1992), pp.46; 511.
22. Ibid., p.46.
23. Ibid., pp.46; 682.
24. M. Ellmann, 'Skinscapes in "Lotus-Eaters"', in *Ulysses: En-Gendered Perspectives – Eighteen New Essays on the Episodes*, ed. K.J. Devlin and M. Reisbaum (Columbia, SC: University of South Carolina Press, 1999), p.66.
25. A. Enright, 'The Body Royal', *The Irish Times*, 18 November 1995.
26. S. Žižek, *Looking Awry: An Introduction to Jacques Lacan through Popular Culture* (Cambridge, MA and London: The MIT Press, 1992), p.31.

27. Enright, *The Wig My Father Wore*, pp.141–2.
28. See S. Freud, *The Uncanny*, trans. D. McLintock and H. Haughton (London: Penguin, 2003), p.150; and Ettinger, 'The Heimlich', in *The Matrixial Borderspace*, pp.157–61.
29. Enright, *The Wig My Father Wore*, p.132.
30. Ibid., p.137.
31. Ibid., p.163.
32. Ibid., p.170.
33. Žižek, *Looking Awry*, pp.14–15.
34. Enright, *The Wig My Father Wore*, pp.178, 180.
35. See P. Coughlan's insightful analysis in 'Irish Literature and Feminism in Postmodernity', *Hungarian Journal of English and American Studies*, 10, 1–2 (2004), pp.184–5.
36. H. Cixous, 'Sorties', in *The Newly Born Woman*, H. Cixous and C. Clément (Minneapolis, MN: University of Minnesota Press, 1985 [1975]), pp.93–4.
37. See Enright, 'Anne Enright Interview', p.64.
38. Enright, *The Wig My Father Wore*, pp.72–3.
39. Ibid., p.73.
40. Ibid., p.215.
41. Enright, *Making Babies*, p.51.
42. A. Enright, 'Author, Author: A Writer's Treasure Trove', *Guardian*, 7 February 2009.
43. Ibid.
44. Joyce, *Ulysses*, p.46.
45. N. Abraham, 'Notes on the Phantom: A Complement to Freud's Metapsychology', trans. Nicholas Rand, *Critical Inquiry*, 13 (1987), p.287.
46. Ibid., pp.290, 291.
47. See G. Pollock, 'Art/Trauma/Representation', *Parallax*, 15, 1 (2009), p.47.
48. See Ettinger, 'Transcryptum: Memory Tracing In/For/With the Other', in *The Matrixial Borderspace*, p.163.
49. A. Enright, *The Gathering* (London: Jonathan Cape, 2007), p.221.
50. Enright, *Making Babies*, p.20.
51. Žižek, *Looking Awry*, p.23.
52. Ibid.
53. Enright, *What Are You Like?*, p.234.
54. Ibid.
55. Ibid.
56. Ibid., p.235.
57. Ibid., p.246.
58. Ibid.
59. Ibid., p.247.
60. Žižek, *Looking Awry*, p.11.
61. V. Rohy, 'Ahistorical', *GLQ: A Journal of Lesbian and Gay Studies*, 12, 1 (2006), p.73.
62. Enright, *What Are You Like?*, p.235.

63. See Ettinger, 'Neighbourhood and Schechina', in 'Seduction into Life: Co-responding with Bracha L Ettinger', ed. N. Giffney, A. Mulhall and M. O'Rourke, *Studies in the Maternal*, 1, 2 (2009), http://www.mamsie.bbk.ac.uk/back_issues/issue_two/bracha_ettinger.html, accessed 5 January 2010.
64. Enright, *What Are You Like?*, p.140.
65. Ibid., pp.153–4.

CHAPTER SIX

'Dreaming of upholstered breasts', or, How to Find your Way Back Home: Dislocation in *What Are You Like?* [1]

SUSAN CAHILL

What Are You Like? is a novel palpable with a sense of absence. It is a novel of the lost, the displaced and the missing; a novel populated with abandoned children, dead mothers, missing siblings, uncanny doubles and separated twins. A general sentiment of dislocation unites the many characters, and their relation to the environment in which they find themselves varies from feelings of confusion and disorientation to more complicated interconnections between corporeality and architecture, between the body and the material world that surrounds it. The novel charts the complex relationships made between subjectivities and the material world in order to negotiate feelings of loss, alienation, as well as a desire for connection; the characters variously experience 'a place with no proper map and no way home' (the 'place with no proper map' is the decision made at the beginning of the novel to allow Berts's pregnant wife to die of her brain tumour in order that her twins be born).[2] The impulse to navigate difficult emotions through recourse to the material world and the spatial environment runs throughout the novel; the mapping metaphor is one means by which characters attempt to make sense of the world.

The novel tells the story of identical twin girls, Maria and Rose, separated at birth following the death of their mother, Anna, whose brain tumour goes untreated so as to protect the unborn babies (a decision she does not make and is unaware of). Their father, Berts, insists that he can only cope with one child, so Maria is raised in Ireland with Berts and his second wife, Evelyn, while Rose is adopted by a couple in England (who also share their house with boys that they foster for short periods). The novel operates by means of multiple viewpoints and alternates between Berts's life, Maria's childhood and early adulthood in New York, Rose's childhood and early adulthood in England, a brief insight into the life of the nun who was present at Rose's adoption, Evelyn's married life with Berts, as well as the voice of the twins' dead mother, Anna, which is the only instance of a first-person narrative voice in the novel. The girls finally meet towards the end of the novel when Rose accidentally walks into the changing room of the shop in which Maria works. Enright contends that this novel is 'a book about how things get buried'.³ *What Are You Like?* charts the traumatic effects of these buried things on the lives of its protagonists, the hauntings they suffer on account of 'a place with no proper map and no way home', manifested in the off-kilter ways that the characters relate to their environment.

Most significantly, that which gets buried in the novel is Berts's wife Anna, who is dead before the twins are even born, kept 'alive' by a life support machine in order that the babies grow along with the tumour that will kill her: 'What kind of a child comes out of a dead woman?' Berts asks, 'A child with no brain? A child with two heads?', gesturing towards the fact that Maria is one of twins. Maria and Rose are haunted by each other's loss though they are unaware of the fact that they are one half of twins; Rose 'was born with a hole in her head, a hole in her life. Everything fell into it.'⁴ Maria unconsciously experiences her lost double: 'Her chest starts to go all stupid and so do her eyes. She has a feeling like there is someone always coming around the corner, who never arrives.'⁵ Berts's refusal to acknowledge Rose's existence is his second symbolic act of 'burial'. In a vain attempt to erase the presence of two children, Berts only proffers one name, Maria. When registering the abandoned twin, the nun, Sr Misericordia, alters the last letter of Maria to 'e' – Marie – in remembrance of the loss of the letter from her own adopted name Misericordiæ: 'What she liked best was the way the

A and the E stuck together. She was ten at the time. Of course, when it came to it, she had to lose the "e" – it wasn't grammatical, apparently.'[6] Thus, the twins' registered names signal simultaneously their similarity and difference and the conjoined 'æ' in the Latin term for compassion highlights their connectivity; their separation is mirrored in the loss of the letter 'e' from Sr Misericordia's name and also ironically indicates Berts's lack of compassion.

Enright's narrative explores the twins' unconscious intersubjective relationship, interconnections between self and environment, and the traumas experienced by efforts to preserve definite borders between self and other.[7] The erasure of the maternal is at the heart of this trauma and the absence of the mother resonates through the narrative both in her haunting monologue from beyond the grave and in the constant imagery of gaps and holes that all characters experience, most often in terms of the landscape that they inhabit.[8] However, the persistence of the gap is experienced differently by Berts and the twins: throughout the narrative Berts attempts to eliminate the haunting absence of his dead wife, whereas Maria and Rose attempt to find the gaps in their life and to locate the missing origin.[9] This difference between Berts's and the twins' relations to the buried maternal body maps onto Luce Irigaray's work in which she details the ways in which masculine subjectivity is achieved through the separation from and complete erasure of the maternal body, an erasure which returns to haunt: 'once the man-god-father kills the mother so as to take power, he is assailed by ghosts and anxieties'.[10] Irigaray argues that all knowledge production is underpinned and inherently influenced and produced by corporeality. In Western culture and philosophy the point of reference has been masculine and phallocentric, thus effacing the importance of the maternal body, resulting, in fact, in a symbolic matricide. In contrast, Irigaray's model for feminine subjectivity is based on the desire for connection, for intersubjective relations: 'the feminine universe's relationship between two'.[11] Enright is passionate about engaging with the traditional silencing and erasure of the mother figure in much of Irish literature. Speaking about *What Are You Like?*, she noted that she had 'split that big iconic mother presence' into two, Anna and Evelyn.[12] The mother is both the living person, epitomized in Evelyn, 'a perfectly likable person who is friends with her children, rears the child who is left', as well as 'the omnipresent dead mother in Irish fiction, never explained, never made manifest or real', with whom the living mother must contend.[13]

The novel's sustained motifs of twins and doubling gesture towards Irigaray's model of intersubjectivity and also highlight displacements of self, inconsistencies in subjectivity, and lack of coherent identities. Maria's first words are ghosted by the distressing events of her birth: 'What could be more monstrous than her birth? Only this: that the first word to bubble up in her throat was her own name – twice.'[14] Maria's first words are actually '"Ma Ma". It was enough to break your heart, said the aunts, but Berts understood. "Maria", he said. "Maria."'[15] Her sense of an embodied self is similarly troubled:

> She lies in bed and tries to tell what size she is. When she closes her eyes her tongue is huge and her hands are big, but the bits in between are any size at all. When she opens her eyes she is the size of the dress. Or she might be.[16]

Maria's vexed relationship with the mirror registers her difficulties with her sense of self ('Maria wanted to take the mirror and throw it across the room'),[17] and both she and Rose at various points fail to recognize themselves in it. Her subjectivity is troubled on two levels – a longing for an engagement with someone other than herself as well as an inability to form adequate connections to location, something which I will come back to below.

Juliana de Nooy, in her study of twins in literature and culture, notes that imbricated in stories concerning twins is a difficulty concerning ways of thinking about such a pair: 'at stake is the question of the viability of a certain understanding of coupledom, a coupledom not defined by dialectical opposition'.[18] De Nooy points out that literary representations of twins most often depict separated twins or resolve the difficulty by dispatching either one or both halves of the duo. Twins are commonly figured in terms of a dualistic opposition, the good twin versus the bad twin, and difference and otherness are either negated in order to stress ultimate sameness, or are 'magnified into opposition'.[19] She suggests that the reason for these common narrative trajectories in stories concerning twins is that 'twins threaten our notions of discrete bodies and indivisible individuals ... they disturb the opposition between same and different, and between self and other'.[20] Twins upset rigid definitions between self and other. In *What Are You Like?*, the unconscious experience of separation, the perceived lack of interconnection between self and other, underpins the psychic trauma of Maria and Rose. Maria's realization that '*We are on our own*', which she repeats twice, leads to her suicide attempt, yet the novel foregrounds the extent to which Maria and Rose are actually intimately connected.[21] Maria's '*We are on our own*' finds later echoes in Enright's short story 'Natalie' whose narrator despairs that 'We are not connected', though again this belies her empathetic and intersubjective responses to those she encounters.[22] In 'Shaft' the pregnant narrator laments that, 'We are all just stuck together'.[23] This concern surrounding our connectivity to other people, our intersubjective relations, is a refrain that runs throughout Enright's work. While Maria is attempting to commit suicide, Rose mistakes a lampshade in the house opposite her for a woman hanging herself, 'At two in the morning, her eye was caught by a lampshade hanging over an archway in a flat across the road. For a second it looked like a body hanging there', and Rose shouts, '"NO!"'[24] The novel also sets itself up as a gothic novel, but without a gothic ending, and the challenges to the autonomous self that the twins highlight are bound up in this gothic aspect. While Berts is haunted by the dead mother, the twins are ghosted by their living others.

Maria's childhood is inscribed with absence, marking out the space of her lost twin and of her mother, absences which become particularly potent during significant rites-of-passage such as her Communion: 'In the photographs you see her [Maria], the extra inch between her and the world', and her eyes 'don't belong to anyone'.[25] Maria colours in the photos with crayons to create 'the other girl'.[26] The measurements for her communion dress begin at Maria's bellybutton, a corporeal signifier of the mother's present absence but past connection, possibly echoed in Berts's joke, 'Where's it [the bellybutton] gone? Oh, she's lost it.'[27] Evelyn's comments hint at Maria's doubleness: 'Like there's a mirror down through her middle'.[28] Her neighbour's house is experienced as a mirror image of her own:

The kitchen goes to the left instead of the right and when you try to go into the dining room there is a massive blank wall. Maria lifts her hand as though there might be a handle in the wallpaper, then turns around in fright, because there is a door open behind her back, like a room in a dream.

Upstairs someone comes out of her bedroom, but it is the wrong bedroom and it is not even a girl who comes out of it, but stupid Ben Quinlan.[29]

The emphasis on the mirror works to underline the absence of Maria's twin and her own experience of herself as inchoate and dislocated. Maria appears to have had an altered 'mirror stage', during which, according to Lacan, we misrecognize in our mirror image a whole and coherent subject in contrast to the fragmented body and self-identity that we actually experience.[30] For Maria, the mirror instead reflects back and reinforces her feelings of loss and incompleteness. Her discovery in New York of an uncanny photograph of 'herself' (actually Rose), at twelve years of age, in the wallet of her lover Anton (who had been fostered by Rose's adoptive parents in his childhood) heightens this relationship with the mirror: 'She went over to the mirror to check if it was still there. She had been completely robbed.'[31] Furthermore, the girl in the photograph appears as her mirror image: 'Her hair was the same, but the parting was on the other side'.[32] The mirror reflects absence and her 'robbed' subjectivity.[33] Irigaray argues that the mirror stage is predicated on the position of the mother as infrastructure, as support to the formation of the subject: 'The mother supports the processes of the male imaginary but is not herself represented, a neglect equivalent to matricide.'[34] The twins' difficulties with the mirror image, their inability to recognize themselves in its surface, register the problems for feminine subjectivity inherent in this paradigm that seeks to erase the mother. For them, this is further exacerbated by the actual death of their mother, the state-sanctified matricide which privileges the unborn child's life over that of the mother, though they are, as yet, unaware of the particulars surrounding their birth. Significantly though, Rose's dislocation and experiences of an incoherent subjectivity heighten after she learns of her mother's death from the adoption agency: 'Rose sat on the tube, and watched her shattered reflection in the opposite window, the two faces juddering apart.'[35]

Irigaray further argues that 'women as body/matter are the material of which the mirror is made, that part of the mirror which cannot be reflected, the tain of the mirror for example, and so never see reflections of themselves'.[36] Anna, the twins' mother, imagines her name as a reflection of itself and operates in the novel as a mirror that fails to reflect: 'I looked at Anna, who was the same, any way you looked at her. And when I died the mirror went blank.'[37] The blankness of the mirror is an explicit comment on the position accorded women, particularly mothers, in the symbolic economy – her pregnant body becomes a 'blank body in the centre of it [her house], like a gap in the middle of a hole'.[38] Anna fails to register herself as anything other than a gap, the lack that she is reflected as in the Western philosophical tradition and it is the persistence of this gap that the characters experience throughout the novel, which is often projected onto, or experienced most profoundly, through their environment. Enright is, she says, 'really interested in the gap, but I see it as part of a feminist aesthetic. When women have been silent so long, you have to read the silences really urgently ... the gaps, and the slippages, and the jumps, and the uncertain way of making sense.'[39] Re-writing Lacan's Mirror Stage, Irigaray shows that this flat mirror merely represents female embodiment as lack. Furthermore, women themselves form the basis of this mirror. They cannot be reflected within it.[40] The failure of the mirror stage for Maria is an effect of the complicated position of the woman in the symbolic order. Anna's death, the failure of the state to treat her as a proper subject, exemplifies her role as foundation for the subject and underlines the erasure of her own subjectivity. Her dead body merely houses the twins and as foundation, as the 'tain of the mirror', she is not reflected in the mirror that guarantees subjectivity. Maria and Rose find themselves reflected as only partial subjects due to this complete erasure of the mother's subjectivity which means that the mirror/mother into which they look in order to secure a 'coherent' (though necessarily illusory) subjectivity is a blank one. The severance of the mother-daughter relationship enacted in order to form the ego is shown here to profoundly affect female subjectivity. This is further exacerbated for the twins by their unconscious sense of each other's loss – another missing mirror image.

Maria's discovery of the photograph of Rose precipitates her nervous breakdown; her feelings of dislocation become heightened and expressed through imagery of the mirror, as if she has travelled to the other side of the looking glass:

> Maria was in the country of the lost. They were everywhere ... It was a parallel world. It was just over the other side. Maria had always known it was there, but, now she was in it, she did not know how to get back out again.[41]

Maria experiences the city as its own mirror image; the city is, like her body, inscribed with doubleness and absence. The geographical manifestation of psychic disturbance continues through Maria's compulsive meandering through the streets of New York City until she

> passed a sad-looking woman who ignored her, and recognized, too late, her own reflection. Even she did not know what she looked like any more.
> Finally.
> She had wiped herself off the map.[42]

Rose similarly reacts to the revelation that her biological mother is dead and father unknown:

> She started to wind through the street for no reason at all. She started to wind through the street, like a ball of string, trying to confuse herself with turns and changes of mind. She crossed from one side of the road to the other ... She had been running on a long leash. All her life, she had been attached by an invisible rope and when, finally, she got around to tugging on it there was no one holding the other end.[43]

Rose merely discovers that she is linked to nothing. This umbilical rope reveals an absence at its origin – the dead body of the mother. Maria too, following her suicide attempt experiences this absence, this 'nothing': 'she lay there untangling herself, the monster and the ball of string. She waited for her life to unravel in the dark, so she could follow the string and slay the monster – which was nothing at all.'[44] The labyrinth allusions are worth noting here as Irigaray connects this space with the dislocations of the female subject: 'She is your labyrinth, you are hers. A path from you to yourself is lost in her, and from her to herself is lost in you. And if one looks only for a play of mirrors in all this, does one not create the abyss?'[45] This disorientation here is linked to the complex positioning of women in the symbolic order which becomes an abyss of mirrors, reflecting nothing back.

Maria's impulse, while slitting her wrists, to put her blood on a mirror, to 'see the sheet of glass between the real blood and the reflected blood. It is very thick. It is very clean and calm',[46] highlights her desire for the cold, clean separation imposed between the messiness of the blood.[47] But it also makes the mirror itself visible – 'the tain of the mirror',[48] the unacknowledged infrastructure that supports the subject which is the body of the mother – in this novel an already dead body. Maria and Rose both attempt to reveal the absence that motivates their psychic trauma. This is what they are searching for.

In contrast, Berts's desire is to eliminate this gap completely, to make the absence of his wife fully absent. Following the death of his wife he continuously imagines a voyage around Ireland's coastline. Berts's anxiety concerning the potential accuracy of the cartographic process – 'He worried about piers. Should he travel the length of them, going up the near side and coming back by the far?'[49] – expresses, for Claire Connolly, a 'sharp contrast to the unmapped emotional spaces that the novel charts: adoption, childlessness, sexual loneliness'.[50] Berts imagines his journey on two levels, as a physical expedition and, in more abstract terms, as an imaginary mapping: 'He took an imaginary piece of red wool and wove it around an imaginary map, curling it into coves and wriggling around headlands, then stretching it out along a ruler for miles per inch.'[51] The imaginary journey functions as Berts's means of controlling the memory of his wife. The anxiety expressed about the boundaries of Ireland also translates into a concomitant concern about his dead wife's presence in his life:

> The house would be the same when he got back, but it would be better the second time around, or at least different. His wife would be dead, but he would be alive, with a circle inscribed around that life. She would leave him alone.[52]

His imagined cartographies attempt to demarcate boundaries to manage his wife's death but her absence, which becomes in the process a powerful presence, can attach itself to his body and is capable of obliterating the map by inscribing it completely:

> But, as he rolled over the hollow she had left in the mattress, he might catch the edge of her absence like an elastic band on his foot, he might drag it with him around the entire country, until his wife's death had filled the map, emptied the map ... He would have to cross her last, or even not cross her at all, skirting the bed at the end of his trip, leave her outside the circle, on the side of the sea.[53]

His only option is to expel his wife beyond the boundaries of his map and of Ireland (much like he has with Rose). The borders, however, remain too complicated for him to trace and neither the exorcism of his wife nor of Rose is fully secure.

Instead, Berts realizes that a gap exists inside his own head. It is 'the place where he had put his wife'[54] which finally disappears when he confronts the embodied return of his actions when both daughters walk through his door:

> For years he had allowed a gap in his head where she could live undisturbed, and now it was not even she who was disturbed, but nothing at all. It was not even she who fled, as the gap closed, but no one at all ... How long had he lived here, in the dead self of his wife?
>
> *I have been living in a grave,* he thought, *I have been living nowhere at all.*[55]

Berts's final exorcism of his wife, following his first sight of the reunited twins, is configured in terms of an effective rebirthing from the grave, from a vacuum, from '*nowhere at all*':

> The doorbell rang. And the hoover of his wife turned around and sucked itself up. The house of his wife turned itself inside out for him. The house of his wife flipped over in space; with the wallpaper showing on the outside and the furniture drifting into the garden, and the lampshades floating off the roof; vomiting Berts out on to the road.[56]

Berts imagines a second exorcism of his wife, closing the 'gap in his head', pronouncing her dead, and his rebirth is achieved through the erasure of his wife as she vacuums herself up. However, Anna's voice has directly preceded this in a lengthy narrative speaking from beyond the grave, insisting that 'I am not dead. I am in hell. And I blame the feet that walk over me.'[57] Thus, Berts's attempted erasure remains troubling and Enright explicitly draws attention here to the degree to which the maternal body forms an unacknowledged basis of phantasies of the coherent masculine subject.

The aimless journeys and incessant recourse to mapping of Berts and his two daughters operate in sharp contrast to the proscribed spatial possibilities for Anna who is explicitly connected with the domestic space. Berts notes that he has not seen her outside the house since they got married, and when she is taken to the hospital, 'The carpets seemed emptied of pattern, the cushions made no sense'.[58] His wife and the domestic space become so inextricably connected that he dreams of 'upholstered breasts'.[59] Domestic spaces are again linked to the pregnant body when his second wife, Evelyn, conceives. Her pregnancy manifests itself in an obsession with the redecoration of the house, although Berts refuses to change the carpets, associated as they are with his dead wife. In an Irigarayan moment, Berts's first wife, Anna, is relegated to the space of the ground:

> 'I want my own carpet', she [Evelyn] said, finally, as he knew she would say, now that she had her own child.
>
> And Berts said, 'my wife chose this carpet. You know that. My dead wife.'[60]

Later, when we encounter Anna's voice for the first time from beyond the grave, she articulates her anger.[61] In *Making Babies*, Enright also links the experience of motherhood to a foundational positioning: 'Not just mother, also platform and prosthesis. I'm not sure I feel like a person, any more. I think I feel a little used.'[62]

For Irigaray, the concept of woman is the condition for and foundation upon which Western philosophy is based:

> The culture, the language, the imaginary and the mythology in which we live at the moment ... let's see what ground it is built

on ... The substratum is the woman who reproduces the social order, who is made this order's infrastructure: the whole of our western culture is based upon the murder of the mother.[63]

Furthermore, this idea of the female is the maternal. The body of the woman is the unacknowledged ground upon which Western philosophy and formations of the subject are built. In psychoanalysis, separation from the mother's body is the condition upon which subjectivity is structured. Given the positioning of woman as foundation, combined with her lack of place within a morphologically male philosophical tradition, it follows that women metaphorically and literally possess a fraught relationship to space: 'She is never here and now because it is she who sets up that eternal elsewhere from which the "subject" continues to draw his reserves, his re-sources, though without being able to recognize them/her.'[64] The woman's positioning, which nurtures and reinforces constructions of the subject as whole, unified and coherent, results in a need to contain and restrict female movement by confinement to the home or status as guarantor of the future of the nation in Irish culture.[65] To break up such ontologies, what is required is a 'movement of revolt and refusal, a desire for/of the living mother who would be more than a reproductive body in the pay of the polis'.[66] Although they cannot articulate it, it is this desire for the living mother that mobilizes Maria and Rose's journeys, journeys, however, which manifest their psychic trauma and dislocations due to the fact that their mother is inaccessible and unrepresentable to them precisely because she is 'a reproductive body in the pay of the polis'.

This unrepresentability of the maternal in the patriarchal cultural economy is experienced by Anna herself in her difficulties in articulating her own subjectivity, idiosyncrasies relating to inscription that she has inherited from her own mother.[67] Domestic spaces are used by Anna's mother as a writable surface upon which she can inscribe reminders by rearranging objects in the kitchen: 'The whole room was a reminder to her. There was no telling, when you touched something, what it might mean. "Who moved the sweeping brush?" she would say. "When we haven't a sausage in the house?"'[68] Anna, in her narrative, articulates her desire for this kind of inscription: words trouble her. Language and writing, for her, are a source of particular anxiety:

> There is no story to living, and having a child, and dying. Not for
> me. No matter what order I put them in. So I put vegetables in the
> wardrobe and buried my clothes. I turned the hoover on itself, all
> the way up the flex. I rolled along the wallpaper, like Cleopatra
> coming out of a carpet, and I wrote lists on the floor … I am
> terrified, here in my grave, by words and what they might want.[69]

Anna's anxiety concerning language also translates to her relationship
with her own body. Looking at her naked self for the first time in a
cracked eighteenth-century mirror she 'could not find the words for it.
Pink. White. Hill. Cunt. Move. You move the tea cosy from the pot to
the table, you move it to the side of the range, you turn the cosy inside
out.'[70] The inability to attach language to the body is deflected onto the
house, onto a rearrangement of space that becomes the only means of
communication, though unintelligible to everyone else. Anna's hell is
the incessant re-emergence of the repressed body as furniture to be
moved around a room:

> I am in hell. This is what I see, this is what I see, I see the turd, I
> see the rope, I see my own private parts that I never saw and Berts'
> private parts that I never saw, I see them clearly. I shift them
> around the room. I give my husband breasts. I am not ashamed. I
> shit through the noose and I cry through my backside. I am in
> hell.[71]

Elizabeth Grosz, in her analysis of Irigaray, claims that 'this appropriation of the right to a place or a space correlates with men's seizure of
the right to define and utilize a spatiality that reflects their own self-
representations'.[72] Irigaray explicitly connects the female body to the
domestic space: 'I was your house. And, when you leave, abandoning
this dwelling place, I do not know what to do with these walls of
mine.'[73] Anna's voice from beyond the grave represents the attempt of
the repressed and effaced body to speak from what Irigaray terms 'that
decorative sepulchre, where even her breath is lost'.[74] She speaks from
the place of death, from beyond the symbolic order, and from the
position of the abject, attacking the processes by which subjecthood is
achieved through repression and abjection.[75] Enright brings the psychosis and violence of this space into focus in a way that is missing

from Irigaray's account. Enright's novel illustrates that women's relationship to space has been configured in a way that makes their engagement
with it seem pathological. The depressions and attempted suicides of
Maria and Rose exacerbate an already troubled experience of spatial
relations: 'Space had flattened for her, she does not so much cross the
room as crawl up the face of the floor.'[76] Enright in this novel makes
explicit the symbolic murder of the mother – these twins are born
from a dead body. The mother here is nothing but a womb, a body to
house the twins until born. She is a grave in Berts's imaginary and a
vacuum, the gap inside his head, and the constant imagery of holes,
gaps, blankness and loss in the novel make this erasure of the mother
explicit. The twins' dislocations, both psychically and geographically,
are propelled by this erasure at their origin – the dead body of the
mother that births them and Berts's refusal to detail the circumstances
of their birth.

The reconciliation between the girls, their connection following
dislocation, initiates a sense of possibility: 'Anything was possible, even
then.'[77] Despite the sense of potentiality that the twins' encounter with
each other produces, the narrative highlights the troubling place of the
mother in the Irish cultural imaginary and the relation between the
female/maternal body and space. Rose expresses her wish to visit her
mother's grave, yet Berts's response is merely to mention a tree that
Rose's mother had liked, evading questions concerning where Anna is
buried. For Enright, narrative itself is bound up in absence:

> Novel narrative is involved in revelation; it's the gap, the awful
> hole in the text, through which the characters fall. I do think that
> there is an unsayable thing in the centre of a book, and that if you
> fill it with something too obvious, then you are lost. You have to
> fill it with something archetypal that has the possibility of being
> at least two things at once – that energy has to be maintained.[78]

In *What Are You Like?* the 'unsayable thing' is the erasure of the maternal
body, her disconnection from place. Anna later recognizes and articulates
her dislocation:

> I was always pregnant. I was never pregnant. I walked from room
> to room, ambushed by all these things. The past and the future

were as big as they ever were, with nothing in the middle, except this empty, waiting house, my blank body in the centre of it, like a gap in the middle of a hole. I was bothered by memories, I was bothered by things that had not happened yet. I was squashed between two unshiftable things and I started to rearrange the house, moving the furniture from room to room.[79]

In Irigaray's words: 'The mother may signify only a silent ground, a scarcely representable mystery.'[80] The novel charts the trauma incurred by this silencing of the mother, the relegation of the maternal to the space of the ground, and the mother as infrastructure for the formation of the ego. But the 'unsayable thing' is also everything that is projected onto the mother, the repressed and abjected body. Enright makes the position of the mother within this cultural economy explicit and also gives her a voice, she is not simply 'a silent ground'.

Enright's use of twin and double motifs in the novel initiates an engagement with questions of sameness and difference that refuses to privilege ultimate similarity or opposition, or autonomous selfhood. In *What Are You Like?* this is epitomized in its final sentence concerning Rose's adoptive father's feelings towards the girls: 'he loved them both equally, though he preferred his own'.[81] Enright's interest in this type of couple may suggest potential ways of thinking about the positioning of mother and daughter in relation to each other. Irigaray argues that there is inadequate representation for the mother-daughter relationship due to the sole concentration on woman as mother. The connection between mothers and daughters is under-symbolized and therefore does not offer women the facility to negotiate this relation in positive and potential terms. Because of this lack of symbolization a maternal genealogy is invisible; as Whitford argues, 'the major and most significant absence in the symbolic' is that of 'representations of a maternal line or genealogy'.[82] Enright's fiction contains repeated images of such interconnection: Grace and her mother swimming while pregnant in *The Wig My Father Wore* (subtly highlighting connections between mother and foetus in terms of their surroundings, both floating in liquid), the pregnant Eliza on the boat in *The Pleasure of Eliza Lynch*, the pregnant woman in the lift in 'Shaft'. As Enright says of the images,

She is in a lift, and I really love the idea of this pregnant woman in this box, it's umbilical really – the rope. So that floated my boat really and the same with Eliza – the pregnant woman on the boat, in a hammock. It was a kind of gyroscope. She herself is a kind of gravity machine, that she was a gyroscope for the child.[83]

These images of interconnectivity are paramount to Enright's literary project and the gyroscope is an interesting metaphor, given its interlocking rings that freely rotate. Neither ring is merely infrastructure, both are mobile and move freely. The gyroscope as mechanism is used to 'provide a horizontal or vertical reference direction', to orient.[84] *What Are You Like?* explores the consequences of relegating the maternal to a foundational function – without this interconnecting, mobilized relationship everyone is disorientated, most particularly the mother, Anna, who at the end of the novel remains dislocated – though she is given a voice within the novel, she does not have a narrative, and the ending of the novel leaves her immanent, a 'nothing at all'[85] which haunts.

ACKNOWLEDGEMENTS

Many thanks to Claire Bracken, Gerardine Meaney, and John O'Neill for their careful reading of this essay and their insightful, instructive and illuminating comments.

NOTES

1. This is a revised and lengthened version of an article which first appeared under the title, 'Doubles and Dislocations: The Body and Place in Anne Enright's *What Are You Like?*', in *Global Ireland: Irish Literatures for the New Millennium*, ed. O. Pilný and C. Wallace (Prague: Litteraria Pragensia, 2005), pp.133–46. I thank the editors for permission to reprint this.
2. A. Enright, *What Are You Like?* (London: Vintage, 2001), p.7.
3. R. Padel, 'Twin Tracks and Double Visions', *Independent* (UK), 26 February 2000.
4. Enright, *What Are You Like?*, p.140.
5. Ibid., p.54.

6. Ibid., p.82.

7. Enright's privileging of connectivity mirrors her narrative style and form. Reviewers have remarked on Enright's ability to create innovative connections; for James Wood of the *Guardian* 'she speeds up the connections between thoughts', whereas for Justine Ettler of the *Observer*, the detachment that accompanies the multiple viewpoints, 'leaves the reader free to move backwards and forwards between plot and subplots, making the various associations and connections and observing the novel's numerous parallels'. See J. Wood, 'To Thrill – A Mockingbird', *Guardian*, 11 March 2000; J. Ettler, 'The Twins of the Father', *Observer*, 16 April 2000.

8. For example, 'Rose looked at the carpet, a swirl of green on brown. She felt that if she took one step away from him she would fall into its gaps and holes.' Enright, *What Are You Like?*, p.194. We will see later that in the novel the carpet becomes intimately connected to the mother, to the place of the maternal. For Berts, 'the city was a subsidence, a slow-stirring trap. The city was full of holes.' Ibid., p.72.

9. Rose decides that, 'She would write to her father and ask him where he was, or where was her mother's grave. And when he wrote back to her, she would fly to Dublin and rent a car, and leave the car at a cemetery gate, and walk through the confused rows of the dead, until she found the right stone and the name it held.' Ibid., pp.196–7.

10. L. Irigaray, 'Women-Mothers, the Silent Substratum of the Social Order', in *The Irigaray Reader*, ed. M. Whitford (Oxford: Blackwell, 1991), p.49.

11. L. Irigaray, 'The Wedding Between the Body and Language', in *Luce Irigaray: Key Writings*, ed. L. Irigaray (London and New York: Continuum, 2004), p.13.

12. A. Enright, 'Anne Enright interview by Caitriona Moloney', in *Irish Women Speak Out: Voices from the Field*, ed. C. Moloney and H. Thompson (Syracuse, NY: Syracuse University Press, 2003), p.61.

13. Ibid.

14. Enright, *What Are You Like?*, p.9. Berts's refusal to acknowledge that Maria's first utterance most likely refers to her mother, illustrates his constant attempts to erase the maternal.

15. Ibid.

16. Ibid., p.28.

17. Ibid., p.24.

18. J. De Nooy, 'Reconfiguring the Gemini: Surviving Sameness in Twin Stories', *AUMLA – Journal of the Australasian Universities Language and Literature Association*, 97 (2002), p.75.

19. Ibid., p.76.

20. Ibid.

21. Enright, *What Are You Like?*, p.152

22. A. Enright, 'Natalie', in *Taking Pictures* (London: Jonathan Cape, 2008), p.50.

23. Enright, 'Shaft', in *Taking Pictures*, p.131.

24. Ibid., pp.154, 156.
25. Ibid., p.26.
26. Ibid., p.35.
27. Ibid., p.27.
28. Ibid.
29. Ibid., p.34.
30. See J. Lacan, 'The Mirror Stage as Formative of the Function of the I as Revealed in Psychoanalytic Experience', in Écrits: A Selection, trans. Alan Sheridan (London and New York: Routledge, 2001), pp.1–8.
31. Enright, What Are You Like?, p.25.
32. Ibid., p.37. Enright plays with the word 'parting' here to underline the twins' separation.
33. Rose 'was startled by her own reflection in the coatstand mirror'. Ibid., p.167.
34. M. Whitford, Luce Irigaray: Philosophy in the Feminine (London: Routledge, 1991), p.34.
35. Enright, What Are You Like?, p.191.
36. Whitford, Luce Irigaray, p.34.
37. Enright, What Are You Like?, p.247.
38. Ibid., p.246.
39. Enright, 'Interview by Caitriona Moloney', p.63.
40. See L. Irigaray, This Sex Which Is Not One, trans. C. Porter and C. Burke (Ithaca, NY: Cornell University Press, 1985), p.151.
41. Enright, What Are You Like?, p.57.
42. Ibid., p.145.
43. Ibid., p.166.
44. Ibid., p.163.
45. L. Irigaray, Marine Lover of Friedrich Nietzsche, trans. G.C. Gill (New York: Columbia University Press, 1991), p.73.
46. Enright, What Are You Like?, p.158.
47. Effectively this separation is what Berts attempts when he refuses to accommodate twin daughters and takes only Maria home.
48. Whitford, Luce Irigaray, p.34.
49. Enright, What Are You Like?, p.10.
50. C. Connolly, 'The Turn to the Map: Cartographic Fictions in Irish Culture', in Éire-Land, ed. Vera Kreilkamp (Chicago, IL: McMullen Museum of Art and University of Chicago Press, 2003), pp.32–3.
51. Enright, What Are You Like?, p.10.
52. Ibid., p.11.
53. Ibid.
54. Ibid., p.251.
55. Ibid., pp.251–2.

56. Ibid., p.252.

57. Ibid., p.248.

58. Ibid., p.8.

59. Ibid.

60. Ibid., p.14.

61. Ibid., p.248.

62. A. Enright, *Making Babies: Stumbling into Motherhood* (London: Jonathan Cape, 2004), p.60.

63. Irigaray, 'Women-Mothers', p.47.

64. L. Irigaray, *Speculum of the Other Woman*, trans. G.C. Gill (Ithaca, NY: Cornell University Press, 1985), p.227.

65. See M. Sullivan, 'I am, therefore I'm not (Woman)', *International Journal of English Studies*, 2, 2 (2002), pp.123–34; M. Sullivan, 'The Treachery Of Wetness: Irish Studies, Seamus Heaney and the Politics of Parturition', *Irish Studies Review*, 13, 4 (2005), pp.451–68; M. Sullivan, 'Feminism, Postmodernism and the Subjects of Irish and Women's Studies', in *New Voices in Irish Criticism*, ed. P.J. Mathews (Dublin: Four Courts Press, 2000), pp.243–50; G. Meaney, 'Race, Sex and Nation', *The Irish Review*, 35, 1 (2007), pp.46–63.

66. Irigaray, 'Women-Mothers', p.47.

67. See Anne Mulhall's essay in this volume for a detailed discussion of these issues in relation to the erasure of the maternal.

68. Enright, *What Are You Like?*, p.234.

69. Enright, *What Are You Like?*, p.235.

70. Ibid., p.247.

71. Ibid.

72. E. Grosz, *Space, Time, and Perversion: Essays on the Politics of Bodies* (New York: Routledge, 1995), p.121.

73. L. Irigaray, *Elemental Passions*, trans. J. Collie and J. Still (New York: Routledge, 1992), p.49.

74. Irigaray, *Speculum of the Other Woman*, p.143.

75. See Gerardine Meaney's essay in this collection for a detailed discussion of attempts to speak from the space of death, psychosis and madness.

76. Enright, *What Are You Like?*, p.155.

77. Ibid., p.253.

78. Enright, 'Interview by Caitriona Moloney', p.63.

79. Enright, *What Are You Like?*, p.246.

80. L. Irigaray, 'Volume Without Contours', in *The Irigaray Reader*, ed. M. Whitford (Oxford: Blackwell, 1991), p.54.

81. Enright, *What Are You Like?*, p.257.

82. Whitford, *Luce Irigaray*, p.76.

83. A. Enright, 'Interview by Claire Bracken and Susan Cahill', this volume, p.26.

84. 'Gyroscope', in *Oxford English Dictionary*, 1989, http://www.oed.com, accessed 20 June 2010.

85. Enright, *What Are You Like?*, pp.163, 251.

CHAPTER SEVEN

'Without a blink of her lovely eye': The Pleasure of Eliza Lynch and Visionary Scepticism[1]

PATRICIA COUGHLAN

The *Pleasure of Eliza Lynch* is a historical novel with a female figure at its centre, set in nineteenth-century Paris and Paraguay.[2] It is a remarkable achievement which deserves further critical attention.[3] In this, her third novel, Enright realizes a fictional milieu in which she can allow her anarchic imagination full creative play. Far from a costume drama, as it was partly marketed and partly received, *Pleasure* is a searching analysis, with postcolonialist overtones, of feminine and masculine ways of being in the nineteenth-century world. The surreal character of Enright's vision comes into its own in this representation of European values and order being tested to destruction in Latin America. A certain deliberate excess of linguistic effect over fictional cause creatively disturbs the surfaces of her previous works, set in quotidian Dublin: this was already evident in *The Portable Virgin*, and, in the anarchic comedy of *The Wig My Father Wore*, postmodernist games with language help to generate a coruscating account of 1990s Irish postmodernity just before the boom.[4] In *Pleasure*, dark political and ethical ironies supplant the ultimately comic vision of *Wig*. But her characteristic sardonic insight produces a brilliant staging of Paraguay as outlandish milieu for the freakish genius of her central character Eliza, who moves from 'Angel of Mercy to Angel of Death, without a blink of her lovely eye'.[5]

To choose a nineteenth-century Latin American setting, and to place a female character at the centre of the narrative, is already to perform an

implicit rejection of those narratives of masculine identity-formation –
within a primarily local, often rural, context – which had dominated Irish
literary tradition. This may help to account for the failure in Ireland to take
much notice of the book, and to understand it as an Irish novel. But *Pleasure*
cannot readily be pigeon-holed under 'women's writing' and thus held at
arm's length from national narratives: it definitely explores feminine
agency, but not only in the way of second-wave feminism. It is markedly
postmodern in its stress on the performative, and its gender representations
are downbeat and wry rather than liberationist. It certainly prompts reflection about questions of postcolonial identity, among other themes, but
Enright avails of the distancing afforded by her historical data to do this in
subtle and non-parochial ways. Questions of national identity are fleeting-
ly invoked via Eliza Lynch's own Co. Cork origins – is she 'the right kind'
of Irish?[6] – and the Scottishness of Stewart the doctor and Whytehead the
engineer (from Edinburgh and Orkney respectively). But these topics take
their places within a larger project: to use the *décalage* between nineteenth-
century Europe and its present or former colonies to show the melting
away of apparently solid European systems of order and belief in the utter
difference of Latin America. Enright weaves all these themes together in an
exceptionally elegant and morally disturbing narrative.

Pleasure presents the teenage Eliza – beautiful and clever, and brought
up in North Co. Cork, of middle-class parents – as a *demi-mondaine* in
1854 Paris, giving English lessons and also working as a high-class pros-
titute. She encounters Francisco Solano López, the son and heir of the
dictator of Paraguay, on his tour of Europe, and goes back with him as
unofficial consort. Married off in obscure circumstances at 15 to a
French army veterinarian to discharge a parental debt,[7] she has hitherto
lived by her wits. In Paraguay she acquires empress-like wealth as
López's mistress and is drawn into his prosecution of the catastrophic
War of the Triple Alliance (1865–70). Denied official wife status, she
watches his growing paranoia and the brutality which eventually leads
him to destroy vast numbers of his countrymen. The moral flagrancy of
Lynch's evil-queen role affords Enright the opportunity to explore (having
borrowed her from history) a female character who is empowered by
wealth and luxury but exists outside the bounds of the bourgeois world.[8]

In choosing this material Enright was entering a field of
contestation, broadly between negative views of both López and Lynch

in Anglo-American historiography, and a different, especially Paraguayan, version of the two as inspiring nationalist leaders (despite the eventual insanity of López, his cruelties and military rashness, and Eliza's life of luxury). López certainly became reckless and over-reaching, but the war's cause was Brazil's expansionism, to which Paraguay had to respond to avoid being dominated in the region, and to attempt to preserve the advanced programme of modernization initiated by Carlos Antonio López, Francisco's father.[9] Enright takes care to provide a counterpoint to Anglo-American interpretations of the facts, partly by means of the diary-like narrative she creates in Eliza's own voice. But in the other, alternating sections, mainly told from the viewpoint of Dr Stewart, the reader gets a vivid account of the horrors inflicted during the last phases of López's failed campaigns and of his murderous instability. There is an implied sympathy with the felt need of Paraguayan nationalists to redeem their history. But Enright's representation of Eliza, adroit as she becomes in performing her role as feminine nation-avatar while retaining all her carnal humanity, also amounts to a pointedly interrogative while oblique comment on the Mother-Ireland stereotype.

Pleasure focuses on the profound shock of characters born and bred in Europe at encountering the quintessentially different landscape, physical and political, of Latin America. Enright shows this primarily through Stewart, who finds his whole world-view shattered. Her story-material has, then, a distinctly 'masculine' character: the figure of Joseph Conrad looms behind the book. Indeed, its intertextuality with *Nostromo* deserves further analysis in its own right. In constructing by *bricolage* his imaginary Republic of Costaguana, Conrad drew heavily on G.F. Masterman's account of his imprisonment and torture by the López régime, *Seven Eventful Years in Paraguay* (1869).[10] Enright's narrative is both a kind of pre-quel to *Nostromo* and a comment, a century later, on Conrad's great 1904 fiction of failure and disillusionment amid cruelty and chaos, and of the hardened heart. A study of the two together would find particular interest in the contrasting representations of femininity: a major theme of *Pleasure* is the gender system and what might happen to it in a decolonizing country thousands of miles from the Europe that sustained it. It is the defect of Conrad's sweeping anatomy of civilization in *Nostromo* that he left this system largely untouched. His Emilia Gould, angel of her cool white mansion, remains a pool of quietness and loving calm amid the disintegration of Sulaco, and Conrad sees to it that the domesticity she elaborates in her 'old Spanish house' retains its mystique unparodied and undisturbed.[11] The constructed and performative mode of Eliza's simulacrum of housekeeping is all the more marked by contrast. Lynch differs from Mrs Gould above all in being placed – jointly with Stewart – at the centre of the plot, and being conceived as a reflective agent. Another significant disparity of perspective is evident between that tendency to approve Britishness which, at least ostensibly, characterizes Conrad's thinking, and Enright's counterweighing of Stewart's taciturn probity with Eliza's flamboyant Irish quickness of feeling. Stewart's interior reflections on the men who have served López's régime unmistakably invoke the language of Conrad's own dodgy Englishmen, the clipped inarticulateness studiously ignoring the realities of class, greed and power:

> It was the money that maddened them now, the better sort of British man trapped in Asunción ... Still, they held on. If anyone were to funk, it would be late at night after too much to drink with something blurted and wrong – the chances a chap had of making it overland to Buenos Aires ... or whether López was 'sound' ... Stewart ... would sit ... silently answering each in disgust that, No, a chap had no chance ... López went to the wrong sort of *school*, don't you know.[12]

In her 'Acknowledgements' Enright, noting Anglophone prejudice in the historiography, says drily that Lynch 'seems to provoke in her English-speaking biographers all kinds of sneering excess'.[13] In tone, *Pleasure* itself flamboyantly outflanks the restraint and understatement typical of colonial and post-colonial adventure-stories (such as those by Greene and Farrell, which have their ancestry partly from E.M. Forster). Enright's style combines an intense, sensational eye with the dry detachment adopted in such writings; English-ironic is only one of the tones adopted in *Pleasure*, and that in sometimes parodic instances in the Stewart sections. The narration is conducted as a series of alternating scenes, moving forward, then back, so that story time and discourse time are at odds. Though there is a clear chronological frame – 1854 to 1873 – the effect is deliberately disorientating. So are the switches of viewpoint between Lynch and the outwardly phlegmatic Stewart (whose surface calm is broken only by rare bouts of drunkenness). He sails with her and López to Paraguay and remains throughout their history in that country, accompanying them on their final flight to López's death in the Northern mountains at the hands of Brazilian troops. A third-person narrator recounts the Stewart sections, whereas we are often drawn into Eliza's contrastingly volatile direct consciousness by her own narration, diary-like. A framing narrator flouts Victorian decorum with the intentionally blunt beginning: 'Francisco Solano López put his penis inside Eliza Lynch on a lovely spring day in Paris.'[14] But both strands of *Pleasure* exhibit an atmosphere of dreamlike, sometimes feverish, immediacy. Enright represents extreme otherness without assuaging the anxiety it produces by subordinating it to a master-narrative.

Hermione Lee argues that Enright places at the centre of her narrative 'so-called women's subject matter … domestic details, clothes, female bodies, sexuality and pleasure, pregnancy and childbirth'.[15] The most salient such topic, however, is food: of the ten sections, seven are called after (mostly luxury) food or drink: 'Fish', 'Melon', 'Asparagus', 'Veal', 'Truffles', 'Champagne', 'Coffee', and three invoke gracious domesticity: 'Flowers', 'Clean Linen' and 'A Little Dog'. Eating is a primary narrative image, insisting on the irreducibility of the body: Enright's vision is Swiftian in linking both with death in general and killing in particular. A series of arresting motifs connects bodies with food and food with bodies, producing a disconcerting vision of life as a process of consuming and being consumed.[16] This emphatically displaces the larger, 'masculine' themes, those of Rankean historiography (government, the military, high politics), so that they jostle for attention with the more immediate life of the embodied self. But Enright does not relinquish them, only forces them to accommodate and contend with that embodied life. Though one of the two centres of consciousness in the book is a man's, and he does try to reflect on the conduct of the war, on the character of Dictator López, Eliza's moral nature, and the existence of God, he too finds himself obsessed with physicality and beset by a yearning above all for comfort both bodily and emotional, placed as he is amid the suffering of others and an overwhelming strangeness. The tormented and the gratified body both force themselves unavoidably on our attention.[17]

Enright renders the physical facts of existence so opaque as to disrupt the conventional arrangement of facts and values, that is, as a hierarchy where the former are transparent to the latter. The body-food images include people relishing meals and starving for the lack of them, but also bodies being themselves eaten. As the *Tacuarí* docks at Asunción, the 'scrabbling crowd' Eliza sees through her porthole reminds her of her first voyage on the Queenstown-Plymouth packet, as her family flees Famine Ireland: a woman among the desperate 'poor at the door' grazes the 10-year-old Eliza's cheek with a 'purple knuckle', 'saying, in a soft kind of way, that she would eat me, I was so lovely and fat'.[18] This sheer fleshliness of bodies is always in evidence. During their grand tour of Europe, López brings her to be spectator for a day at the Crimean War; they picnic on cold chicken in a honey glaze while hussars 'risk their body parts and lose them ... She would recall with perfect simplicity the dryness of the chicken ... its cold, dimpled skin; the crunch where the fat met the bone.'[19] Motifs of this constant two-way traffic are pervasive: meat being incorporated into human flesh and human flesh being turned, one way or another, into meat.

Enright anarchically links eating with love, beauty and the ideal, thus overriding the immanence-transcendence dualism which structures Western thought about both women and the body. When Stewart is woken from a drunken stupor by a dog licking vomit out of his hair; he mistakes it for his mother's hand caressing him.[20] When Eliza wears an especially beautiful sky-blue dress, which to her is 'armour ... and transcendence', he looks at her 'as a man looks at a good dinner before he eats it'.[21] This inextricable embroilment of beauty with disgust, appetite and need is never more brilliantly expressed than in an early scene.[22] During a stop on the river passage to bury a dead sailor Eliza sees fifty or more brilliant butterflies 'as though in colloquy' on the sand by the Paraná ('the most astonishing blue. I have not seen such a blue since leaving Paris'). They

> sat and stirred like ladies in a garden, their skirts parting to show underskirts of more beautiful blue ... They spread them to sit, and played with their fans, and flicked open their parasols in the sun.[23]

Asked why they gather on certain spots, Miltón says 'they go where an animal has pissed, or a man has pissed. Then he rolled out his tongue, as though to lick.'[24] Eliza remembers 'the salon of the Princess Mathilde' in Paris where women sat 'all clustered and fluttering, when a rich man speaks. And when he leaves the room, a general business with fans, as we settle on his words and eat.'[25] During this same pause while the sailor's grave is dug, Whytehead takes Eliza's French maid Francine out of sight to have sex. As she walks back barefoot on the riverside earth, she is bitten by a sandfly and infected with the flesh-eating disease called leishmaniasis, of which she eventually dies.[26] Summoned to tend to her, Stewart looks upon 'the open meat of her face', her mouth and nose obliterated.[27] The doctor's distancing professional language – 'it was a classic presentation' – cannot save him from horror.[28] Later, drunk at his own wedding, he tries to escape the memory of her frightful death, and his own painful empathy with such suffering, by assuming a brutalized attitude towards women ('I like them when they're sick').[29] He tells himself this is because 'they broke a man's heart',[30] but the reader sees how it comes from the cultural placing of women as native to flesh and earth: how the mortality of all bodies is indissolubly entailed by women's first making all men within their own. Yet despite the necessary repression, assisted by whisky, of these normally abjected truths, Stewart sometimes can glimpse how 'in the body, that was where the truth of it was'.[31] All is prey, even fruit is not safely Edenic: Eliza gives Stewart a basket of cherries with 'thick, dark skins' and 'red as an old wound'.[32]

Enright's representations are unflinching but not voyeuristic: such is the energy of her imagination, her exactness of words, and the pertinence of the fictional items she pinpoints, that everywhere the language of metonymic description (scene-setting, background) is infused with the force of metaphorical signification. Literal instances of hunger and feeding take their place in the food-flesh narrative which destroys conventional boundaries between fact and symbol, along with fundamental taboos. Thus the starving Stewart, doing surgery on the battlefield, involuntarily salivates at the sight of a wounded man's last meal in his open abdomen;[33] and the dogs found raiding 'his medical heap of discarded flesh' are cooked and eaten.[34] We become increasingly aware of the fundamentally paradoxical relation between the capacity for rational consciousness and the incontrovertible fact of bodiliness. A third term, compassionate inter-subjectivity, is largely unattended to in the world which the book constructs, though not in the book itself, which brings it forcefully before the reader's mind. This is what is daily betrayed in mutual consumption, in war, in the brutal exercise of power and the struggle between wealthy and wretched.

Narrative items are presented as dissociated and discrete, often in partial, glancing form, so that we must piece together an event from fragments and, as I have suggested, metonymy is always poised to become metaphor. This technique increases the excess of sense-experiences over explanations. Patricia Waugh has argued that dwelling on 'the luminous detail' is a characteristically postmodernist form of resistance to the discredited 'totality' of concepts.[35] Enright's narrative does this at the micro-level of each sentence, and also in her consistent privileging of scene over summary in narrative method. Waugh's view that 'Totalising systems create the "same", the universal, through exclusion of the "other"' and that 'Postmodernism has been referred to as a romance of the marginal or the other',[36] throws light on the nature of the radical critique underlying the apparent sensationalism of Pleasure. It presents experience as discontinuous, while inescapably concrete because based in the bodily.

At the level of thought, meanwhile, naming and rational reflection are always already the product of representation, and never give access to unshakable truth. Tending the wounded on successive battlefields, Stewart can gain an overarching vision of the war only by thinking of it as a painting on a giant commemorative canvas.[37] This both distances it and places it within a familiar ideological structure (the history painting) which makes it tolerable to think about. The resulting 'magnificent canvas' dwarfs both individual endeavour and suffering. One might read this conceit of Enright's as an instance of what Lyotard calls 'the unpresentable' or the postmodern sublime: a terror, something unspeakable except *as* a representation.[38]

Shuttled between the warp of Stewart's intensifying bewilderment and the weft of Eliza's slow river journey – along the thousand-mile navigable length of the river Paraná – towards the landlocked heart of Paraguay, we are drawn into the fabric of the book. The further one reads, the more Stewart reels away from the readable and the familiar. His own sense of shrinkage and fear of complete self-loss is an index of this process.[39] Enright's project depends on the fictional realization of extreme, out-of-proportion and – to realism – unconscionable circumstances.

Performing the prosperous expatriate, Stewart paces Whytehead's tobacco field, 'all alive with the wind and the shifting backs of peons labouring among the leaves', while the two discuss, not the war, but 'the weather, like gentlemen' and 'put their shoulders to the wheel, which was the wheel of History itself'.[40] Yet their social markers, including the sense of progress, coherence and moral solidity in a (white, professional) man's career, are obliterated by their radically unsettling awareness that they are part of a brutal system of exploitation.

Whytehead has set up a quintessentially English domestic life, sustained by his icon of Victoria, respectable Other of the outrageous Eliza. Whytehead, who has impaled his hand on a nail and needs the wound tended by Stewart, sits 'gazing into the middle distance from behind his florid, solid moustache'.[41] The two men's conversation has a wonderfully surreal moment:

> He would like to marry Whytehead, Stewart thought. There would be enormous comfort in it. No need for speech. Everything ordered and on time. A little woman who works a hole in her hand, when you are away.[42]

The weirdness of this passage is far from gratuitous: gender roles are being rearranged to a purpose. Stewart, carer for the sick and wounded, capable of compassionate scruple, is himself in a sense feminized, acquiescent to Eliza's dominant role (which possibly occasions his compensatory fantasies of a sexual conquest of her, edged with aggression).[43] Here, however, he switches back to play husband, comically, to Whytehead's preposterous 'wife', with the macabre alteration that in place of her needlework, this 'wife' inflicts a wound on her own body. This cries out to be read as a version of that alleged feminine lack prominent in psychoanalysis: the penetrable vagina as wound where the phallus is not. Overdetermined in significance, this 'hole' doubles as a stigmatic emblem of Whytehead's self-torment, his 'own little crucifixion' as Stewart thinks.[44] Another tormented body. Eventually Whytehead – Chief State Engineer and supplier of mined metal for the war – hangs himself after the string of defeats. Like Stewart he is a failure in his own eyes, overwhelmed by the incommensurable realities of Paraguay's terrain and its political tyranny, itself a consequence of previous colonization. There is also a homologous failure of the gender system, overtly challenged by the flair, creativity and determination of the Irish 'whore' Eliza.

Eliza herself, before ever seeing Paraguay, already exists in a semi-permanently marginal position. Her multilingualism gives her potential leverage, making her an interpreter between forms of difference normally irreconcilable and an expert at passing between systems:

> She romped in French, married in English, and she ate in the Irish of her childhood kitchen. She had school Latin and spa German, but her fate, now, was in Spanish, and she would die in Guaraní, which is to say, obscurely. The lover in her head spoke Russian, in whispers. The devil in her head spoke Portuguese.[45]

Lynch's outsider status is also partly the product of her hybrid Anglo-Irish origins. But what ensures her dislocation from the bourgeois social order is her louche past and downright scandalous present, which preclude the attainment of respectability. In making such a character the novel's principal centre of consciousness, Enright chooses to present Victorian and Second-Empire values from an extreme and unsympathetic distance. In her version the crucial determinants of Eliza's life are economic and patriarchal ones. She has never had a choice but to live by her wits. Enright vividly represents both these social constraints on the development of Eliza's moral life, and the impulses towards compensation driving her to seize and consolidate her opportunity for security and prominence. In alternating Stewart's tormented reflections with Eliza's own narrative, Enright shows the hypocrisy of the Victorian sexual double standard as indissolubly linked with the ideologies, themselves interconnected, of modernization and the exploitation of the less developed world.[46] Stewart, himself painfully aware of the moral strain between probity, as nurtured in him by his Edinburgh aunt, and his desire to get rich, is well placed to observe that Eliza has an inner life and experiences impulses of attachment and social communion, as well as emotional devastation (he alone observes her visiting the grave of her stillborn daughter).

Yet he still thinks about women in strikingly polarized categories such as 'Angel of Mercy' and 'Angel of Death'.[47] Stewart, tending to the wounded, experiences maleness as lack, recalling Freud's Oedipal myth of phallic-male and castrated-female modes of being. On these occasions Stewart faced the problem of the women whenever their anatomy ambushed him in the operating hut – every time he panicked that a man's member had been blown away and grubbed through blood and hair looking for the non-existent wound. Every time he unbuttoned a shirt and found a breast, or two, beneath, he would sigh at the problem of the women.[48]

Women's bodies are either too much ('a breast or two') or too little (the member which has been 'blown away'). The 'non-existent wound' both recalls and undermines the notorious account in classical psychoanalysis of how the infant boy discovers the alleged castratedness of women, including that of his hitherto all-powerful mother.

Thus, a respectable woman must suppress her desire – the natural consequence of her embodiment – and meekly subsist within the symbolic order which is founded upon her very subordination. If she seeks the fulfilment of her sexual will, or if, as in Eliza's case, her chastity (the object of social fetishization) has been compromised, she incurs exclusion from social acceptance and possibly even the means of subsistence. Asunción society replicates these Manichean qualities of the European gender system. The beauty and talent of 'La Lincha', in the absence of married status, inspire in men only the desire to possess her sexually, and in respectable women the averted gaze and snubbing rejection. Eliza's need for personal recognition is thus bluntly denied. Having achieved sexual happiness in her mating with López (and been so carried away that she fails to protect herself from pregnancy), she had begun to anticipate a more general self-fulfilment in the prospect of her new life in Paraguay. As the boat draws alongside the dock in Asunción, Eliza recalls the jealousy she saw in all the men she had to do with as a young girl, and hopes that 'here … I will be safe'; for 'they were all … jealous of me, as a man might be jealous of a painting that he may pay for, but will never properly have. As men are jealous of all beautiful things.'[49] This reflexive moment demonstrates both her ample awareness of her object-status to men, and her countervailing presence to herself as a thinking, self-aware subject. In the event, Asunción high society, adhering to Spanish-colonial mores, draws away its skirts in disgust from the spectacle of Eliza when she appears, flagrantly pregnant, on the ship's gangway: as this 'vision smiles her visionary smile', all the family carriages drawn up to greet the returning heir wheel away in the dust.[50] This initial ostracism is unremitting. Among the Spanish aristocrats 'with more surnames trotting after them than they had horses',[51] men may sow 'wild oats' but female sexual will is still kept in an iron cage of restraint.[52] Nevertheless, though the mere illicit appendage of a man, 'the tart from County Cork'[53] creates an exalted, queenly identity of her own, using an inherent aesthetic flair which informs her dress and her surroundings even in the glorified tent where she establishes herself during the protracted wars, and that capacity for 'pleasure' (sexual, culinary and visual) which gives the novel its title.

Enright's rendering of Eliza shows her as living her (female) body, but performing her femininity as a succession of social selves which she constructs with careful craft and full consciousness of their effect. A sub-theme of the book is the agonistic encounter between her burning, intelligent will and her own embodiment, entailing, as I have noted, ideological as well as physical constraints. Thus, late in her pregnancy, she feels with chagrin that she is now like a feeble daddy-long-legs, 'the beastie with my belly huge and my limbs all feeble and waving, and bits gone'.[54] At the end of the long voyage from Europe, she experiences a crisis at her dependency ('as [her] belly grows, [she] withers away').[55] She looks at López and sees 'what he is'; when she turns, distraught, to her maid Francine and asks what she must do, Francine replies simply '[y]ou must love him. There is no other way'.[56] This Eliza decides to do, and together the two women squeeze her great belly, already contracting, into her clothes so that she can make her opening appearance: 'I must love him, because through such narrow gaps in our lives we all must squeeze and crawl.'[57] The slow river journey, with its long final phase like a birth canal between the Paraná's walls of impenetrable vegetation, shows Eliza recomposing her life: as the metaphor suggests, at the end she is delivered not just of her first child but of her own new Paraguayan self.

It is not, then, that Eliza does not inhabit her changing roles, and indeed the book shows her as trapped within them, in contrast to the insouciance of some postmodernist notions of pure joy in the free play of performances. While in the war she becomes an icon of civility and culture to the troops and the whole country, Stewart sees below these glittering surfaces. Gleaning the rumours about her sumptuous but isolated life, he thinks: 'You could say she has everything, except the satisfaction of having it. Also perhaps, that she cannot relax, because she is not real.'[58] Yet Enright's vision seems utterly sceptical about anyone having a real essence beyond the performative.

There is a revealing tête-à-tête between the principals, in the longest Stewart section, sardonically entitled 'Truffles'. In a conversation between the pair, Eliza shows her piercingly clear understanding of the workings of the sex-gender system, within which she is contained and controlled:

> For every enemy that he [López] has, I have two, because for every man that hates him there is another who says that whatever he does it is at my urging; because a woman's ambition is a fathomless thing.[59]

She concludes: 'A woman has no limits, because she may not act. She is all reputation, because she may not act. So, even as we do nothing, our reputations grow more impossible, and fragile, and large.'[60] By contrast, a comment by Conrad's narrator in Nostromo about Mrs Gould, the ideal of feminine love and domesticity, is withering about women who would seek to 'act':

> It must not be supposed that Mrs Gould's mind was masculine. A woman with a masculine mind is not a being of superior efficiency; she is simply a phenomenon of imperfect differentiation – interestingly barren and without importance.[61]

This insists on the laws of sexual difference; Lynch, by contrast, evidently is gifted with a 'masculine mind', but also with a nuanced feminine awareness of the impression she is making. So she knows when and how to mask her intelligence with flirtation and signs of sympathy. She has to a degree thwarted the constraints of gender while staging superb performances from its repertoire of quintessentially feminine roles.

The classical novels of modernism often, implicitly or otherwise, substitute an aesthetic, virtual world, where order and beauty obtain, for the irredeemably failed and tainted one of actuality. In contradistinction from this, Pleasure shares with other postmodern texts a representation of the aesthetic realm as not exempt from implication in oppression, as itself capable of being made instrumental. The beauty of Eliza's mises-en-scène and of her person seem works of art which she has made, even Nietzschean constructs of her will, and while being intimations of transcendence so enchanting as to break men's hearts (as Stewart's is broken), are devastatingly instrumental, disposable and impermanent too. They are also obscene because of their conjunction with cruelty, death and the laying waste of the land and the people.

Near the beginning of the book as Eliza lies having sex with López, she thinks: 'She had tried to be good, had wanted to be good, but the curtains had cost her a month of fucking and they were far too blue.'[62] This interweaves the aesthetic – the curtains too blue to be tasteful – both with the work she has had to put in for their acquisition ('a month of fucking') and, in addition, with the nature of that work, which infringes the clear rubrics of 'goodness'. The formulation of the bourgeois-feminine moral imperative is tellingly naive, as if Eliza has carried the simple framework of childish prohibitions into her otherwise knowing adult life. Within this framework, for a girl, to be good is not to fuck, but that is an aspiration which is literally beyond Eliza's means. Fanning's and Lillis's research suggests that the real Lynch seems in fact to have been married off quasi-coercively to the shady Quatrefage by her mother. They also cast strong doubt on her engagement in prostitution prior to meeting López.[63] It is not, then, that Enright celebrates mindless physical excess and domination, but that she resists the dualistic subordination both of the body and the feminine which underpins Western thought. And in the public sphere she does not glide over cruelty, but refuses hypocrisy about allegedly advanced civilizations. The Eliza-Victoria analogue might be turned back upon Britain: is there much to choose between the hideous violence practised by López and witnessed by Eliza on the flight to Cerro Corá, and, for example, the lashing of sepoys to cannon in the reprisals – systematic, military, officially sanctioned – after the Indian Mutiny?[64] Stewart himself experiences how they are all brought face to face with the unconscionable, thus radically disturbing the civilized surface of the 'gentleman's' life: wealth *is* exploitation, states depend upon domination, no self exists which is distinct from its social acts and roles, and love is mixed up with power. The violent disorder of Paraguay is combined with the terrible vulnerability of all human embodiment to overthrow the self-assurance of nineteenth-century European ideology and to show everyone as equally engaged in improvisation. Eliza's resourceful challenge to that ideology in the practical conduct of her life does not keep her from its moral taint. Nobody in Pleasure is freed into moral security or emotional peace. By the end almost nothing is left standing in its ideological world: systems, states, gender roles and relations, the would-be moral innocence and practical value of work well done (medicine, mining) – which in Conrad might have withstood much – are all razed to the ground, just as uncounted thousands of Paraguay's people have been mown down. Yet from her own dark vision, within the dystopia it has shown, Enright salvages one site of consolation and of utopian hope: the Guaraní people's belief in the existence of a 'land without evil'.[65] This would be especially interesting for a full post-colonialist reading of Pleasure. Can it be seen as a false note? Enright is too sanguine to represent the Irish or Scottish as unequivocally subaltern, and she subtly registers their complex positioning and the shifts they must make in the world. Is her representation of the 'Indians', by contrast, an exoticizing one? There are layers of representation overlaid here: by 1857 the indígenas had already become the object of romantically originary Indianista romance in neighbouring Brazil.[66] It is true that we see them exclusively from either Eliza's or Stewart's viewpoint, though there is irony and nuance in these glimpses. Eliza is shown as quickly gaining an affinity with Miltón, whose naming may not be entirely sardonic and who becomes her personal servant, even accompanying her back to Europe when all is over. Enright works to distance this from sentimentality: offhandedly affectionate, Eliza is also amused in a rather Voltairian way: 'He has taken, my little savage, to telling me things. It is a flattery of sorts.'[67] Yet there are traces of stereotyping: herself expert in appearances, Eliza is intrigued by his poise and thinks 'he ignores me well', as he stands stock still in the bow of the Tacuarí.[68] Stewart finds that the Guaraní soldiers refuse to 'lend' him the names of places he points to,[69] and Eliza at first finds herself baffled, looking into the 'mineral eyes' of Miltón, to imagine 'what these people might believe; whether they even have souls like ours – lost or otherwise':[70] an inscrutability topos? However, this is explicable as Eliza's attempt to come to grips with her new milieu by applying prejudices from the old, and the joke is on her. In fact, indigenous Guaraní speakers in the 1850s shared a largely amalgamated culture with the ethnic Spanish, and extensive intermixing had taken place even before Francia's policies of ethnic hybridization.

121

Simple racist binaries are hard to sustain in Paraguay. López calls his father a 'nigger'; but when she asks him 'what they believe', he identifies himself too as a 'native' and says he believes in nothing.[71] Nevertheless, Enright does risk projecting a hierarchy of transcendence and immanence onto European-'Indian' differences, and perhaps implicitly treating such immanence as mute blamelessness. 'Indians' are repeatedly characterized as keeping silent, and also as particularly valuing silence. Stewart notices that 'they do not listen to words', but watch the body, and 'make you feel not so much wrong-footed but wrong-faced';[72] when a romance of inter-ethnic union is performed in Eliza's new theatre, crowds of 'Indians' at first stand 'enormously silent'.[73]

Enright makes the millenarian, mythic nature of the Guaraní thought-world play with a ghostly, fitful illumination upon the different European sensibilities of her two main characters, and about these beliefs – perhaps these alone in *Pleasure* – she suspends her otherwise unremitting irony. The recurring, poetic moment in her representation of the Guaraní focuses on their belief in a 'land without evil' somewhere to the north.[74] When, sailing upstream, the *Tacuarí* comes to the confluence of the Paraguay and the Paraná, the water is streaked with red. Down-to-earth Whytehead gives a geological explanation (no doubt empirically correct), Eliza a florid symbolic one in the European literary manner: 'It might be some battle ... or a wounded god, staining the far waters red',[75] and López a geographical location. He says it comes from the far north, from the Mato Grosso, the very region of which his rash invasion exacerbates the war, at this point still in the future. Last, Miltón 'sidles by' to say that 'the red earth comes from a place without evil', explaining that 'it is indeed blood' that comes down the Paraná,[76] a symbolic anticipation of the blood of the thousands yet to be shed. The scene has elegance and poignancy.

On the nightmare final trek into the northern Cordillera by the ragtail army weakened by hunger and disease, a small Guaraní girl attaches herself to Stewart, walking beside his stirrup. As they struggled on, 'the farther they went in the northern hills the smaller and more helpless' she seemed, until she was gone. He thinks: 'So perhaps it was true. They were going to a more innocent place, after all.'[77] Reality is intolerable and he is powerless to change it, so he tries to escape into *indígena* belief and rewrite mortal illness as a recovery of innocence and a shedding of suffering.

The effect resembles the consolatory moment which concludes Pat Barker's *The Ghost Road*.[78] Rivers, the English doctor, has done anthropological research on a Pacific island. Serving in a London military hospital in the 1914–18 war, he is cast into despair by the terrible death of a young soldier whose extruded brain has hung for days outside his dying body. As Rivers sits by the bed, he sees the shaman Nijru from the island come slowly down the hospital ward at dawn, chanting the song of exorcism which both acknowledges that all is always passing away and salves grief: '*There is an end of men, an end of chiefs ... then go down and depart. Do not yearn for us, the fingerless, the crippled, the broken. Go down and depart, oh, oh, oh.*'[79] But the scenes are also different. Barker makes a recuperative contrast between the poetic faith of the shaman and the felt powerlessness of Rivers, at the heart of positivist Western medicine. Enright does not so load Guaraní mythology with transformative feeling. In *Pleasure* the 'land without evil' is no more than the place of hopeless yearning: the doomed *indígenas* march in their thousands like automata 'in dull-eyed ranks and rows, ever advancing' towards a common destruction.[80] In the end it seems that only the powerless can sustain belief in another, better world, and only they are absolved from guilt and responsibility.

NOTES

1. This is a revised and shortened version of an article with the same title which first appeared in the *Irish University Review*, 35, 2 (2005), pp.349–73. I thank the editorial board for permission to reprint this.

2. A. Enright, *The Pleasure of Eliza Lynch* (London: Vintage, 2003).

3. But see S. Cahill, '"A Greedy Girl" and a "National Thing": Gender and History in Anne Enright's *The Pleasure of Eliza Lynch*', in *Irish Literature: Feminist Perspectives*, ed. P. Coughlan and T. O'Toole (Dublin: Carysfort Press, 2008), pp.203–22.

4. See P. Coughlan, 'Irish Literature and Feminism in Postmodernity', *Hungarian Journal of English and American Studies*, 10, 1–2 (2004), pp.175–202.

5. Enright, *The Pleasure of Eliza Lynch*, p.122.

6. Ibid., p.141.

7. Ibid., p.123.

8. Enright's version of Eliza parallels historical women such as Queen Matilda, Joséphine and Eva Perón, whose role as adored embodiment of Argentina echoes the real Eliza Lynch's self-exculpatory *Exposición y Protesta* (Asunción: Fundación Cultural Republicana, 1875). I thank Carla Lane for linguistic help with this text. I have drawn historical

information mainly from R.A. Nickson, *Historical Dictionary of Paraguay*, 2nd edn (Metuchen, NJ and London: Scarecrow Press, 1993); P.H. Box, *The Origins of the Paraguayan War* (New York: Russell and Russell, 1967); J.A. Fornos Peñalba, 'Draft Dodgers, War Resisters and Turbulent Gauchos: The War of the Triple Alliance against Paraguay', *The Americas*, 38, 4 (April 1982), pp.463–79; and J. Plá, *The British in Paraguay 1850–1870*, trans. B.C. McDermot (Richmond and Oxford: Richmond Publishing and St Antony's College, 1976). M. Lillis and R. Fanning's readable *The Lives of Eliza Lynch: Scandal and Courage* (Dublin: Gill and Macmillan, 2009) brings new facts to light about many biographical and historical matters but dismissively relegates *The Pleasure of Eliza Lynch* to 'the tradition of northern fantasies about the exotic possibilities of South America', p.27.

9. See Nickson, *Historical Dictionary of Paraguay*, p.353, and D.M. Hanratty and S.W. Meditz (eds), 'Library of Congress Country Study on Paraguay', *Library of Congress*, http://memory.loc.gov/frd/cs/pytoc.html, accessed 26 September 2005.

10. See N. Sherry, *Conrad's Western World* (Cambridge: Cambridge University Press, 1971), pp.147–99, 99–132.

11. J. Conrad, *Nostromo: A Tale of the Seaboard*, ed. J. Berthoud and M. Kalnins (Oxford: Oxford University Press, 2008), p.31.

12. Enright, *The Pleasure of Eliza Lynch*, pp.116–17.

13. She pointedly disclaims any historiographical intentions, explaining that, 'Some facts seem to remain constant and it is around these facts that this (scarcely less fictional) account has been built. This is a novel, however. It is Not True [sic]', (ibid., p.231). This did not prevent reviewers of two popular histories on Lynch – both, by a strange coincidence, appearing late in 2002, months after Enright's – from commenting on *Pleasure* rather as if it too laid claim to historical accuracy. Thus a curious remark by Jean McNeil, who seems to base her judgement on these works alone: 'Enright's fictional Eliza meditates on her pregnant state and understands she has become "evil". But *after reading the biographies* it's hard to believe Eliza was capable of lush subjectivity, that she was anything other than a utilitarian individual, inhabiting an interior desert of bare acts' ('The Shadows of Elisa Lynch', *Independent* (UK), 18 January 2003; emphasis mine). This itself reads quite like 'sneering excess' to me.

14. Enright, *The Pleasure of Eliza Lynch*, p.1.

15. Hermione Lee, 'All Reputation', *London Review of Books*, 17 October 2000, pp.19–20.

16. During the war a story circulates that Eliza sustains herself by eating the flesh of the dead, and that, 'She said it tasted like pork, but gamier – like the truffle-hunting boars you get in the Auvergne' (ibid., pp.134–5).

17. The book weaves an elegant web of narrative images which only becomes fully visible on a re-reading; right at the outset, for instance, Eliza's sparsely furnished room in the rue St Sulpice nevertheless contains 'a statue of the flagellated Christ', prefiguring of the fate of so many Paraguayans (ibid., p.1).

18 Ibid., p.207.

19. Ibid., p.13.

20. Ibid., p.69.

21. Ibid., p.103.

22. Recalling Swift's 'Celia, Celia, Celia shits' ('The Lady's Dressing-Room', 1.116), but pragmatically rendered, stripped of Swift's misogyny.
23. Enright, *The Pleasure of Eliza Lynch*, pp.26–7.
24. Ibid., p.27.
25. Ibid.
26. Enright first, however, sets the reader wondering if Whytehead has given Francine syphilis.
27. Enright, *The Pleasure of Eliza Lynch*, p.66.
28. Ibid.
29. Ibid., p.83.
30. Ibid.
31. Ibid.
32. Ibid., p.67.
33. Ibid., p.134.
34. Ibid., p.135.
35. P. Waugh, *Practising Postmodernism, Reading Modernism* (London: Edward Arnold, 1992), pp.32–6.
36. Ibid., p.34.
37. Enright, *The Pleasure of Eliza Lynch*, pp.125ff.
38. J.F. Lyotard, *The Postmodern Condition* (1984), quoted in Waugh, *Practicing Postmodernism*, p.30. The War of the Triple Alliance has been called the *original* 'war to end all wars', that is, the first modern Armageddon.
39. Enright, *The Pleasure of Eliza Lynch*, p.133.
40. Ibid., p.112.
41. Ibid., pp.110–11.
42. Ibid., p.111.
43. Ibid., p.150.
44. Ibid., p.111.
45. Ibid., p.3.
46. See ibid., pp.12, 14, 105, 128 for reminders of the aspirations towards modernity and 'opening the nation' which marked the régimes both of Francisco Solano López and of his father, the old Dictator.
47. Ibid., p.122.
48. Ibid., pp.131–2.
49. Ibid. p.209.
50. Ibid., p.50.
51. Ibid., p.51.
52. The cage around female choice is more than metaphorical: it is literally realized in the fate of a former object of López's desire, Carmencita Cordal, which is caught by the reader in glimpses, dispersed amid the principal narrative. In piecing together these fragments, it emerges that Cordal has refused the youthful López, upon which he and his brothers hideously murder her preferred suitor by dragging him after their horses through Asunción. When Cordal goes insane as a result, she is eventually kept in a cage

and – 'that witch Cordal'– later raped for a dare by the teenage Pancho, López and Eliza's eldest son – see pp.57, 197. As the old Dictator is dying, Carmencita Cordal, Ophelia-like, 'started to walk at night and was seen abroad, naked, or bloodstained or dressed in white. In the morning, people found flowers jammed between doors and their lintels, and wreaths floating downstream', p.61. Enright attends only tangentially to the specific motivation of López; significantly, however, he presents to Eliza his and his brothers' killing Carmencita's fiancé as, in a classic instance of *machismo*, 'a thing we had to do', p.101. The incident is factual. See Box, *The Origins of the Paraguayan War*, p.180.

53. Enright, *The Pleasure of Eliza Lynch*, p.2.
54. Ibid., p.102.
55. Ibid., p.209.
56. Ibid., pp.209–10.
57. Ibid., p.210.
58. Ibid., p.59.
59. Ibid., p.151.
60. Ibid.
61. Conrad, *Nostromo*, p.51.
62. Enright, *The Pleasure of Eliza Lynch*, p.8.
63. Lillis and Fanning, *The Lives of Eliza Lynch*.
64. 'The murder of women and children enraged the British, but in fact some British officers began to take severe measures before they knew that any such murders had occurred. In the end the reprisals far outweighed the original excesses. Hundreds of sepoys were shot from cannons in a frenzy of British vengeance (though some British officers did protest the bloodshed)'. 'Indian Mutiny', *Encyclopaedia Britannica*, 2000.
65. Enright, *The Pleasure of Eliza Lynch*, p.57.
66. José de Alencar's 1857 novel *O Guaraní*, a romanticizing tale of Amerindian life, was made into an opera and followed by other such fictions (*O Guaraní: Romance brasileiro*, ed. Darcy Damasceno [Rio de Janeiro: Instituto Nacional do Livro, 1958]).
67. Enright, *The Pleasure of Eliza Lynch*, p.159.
68. Ibid., p.20.
69. Ibid., pp.179–80.
70. Ibid., p.19.
71. Ibid., p.21.
72. Ibid., p.180.
73. Ibid., p.62.
74. Ibid., pp.157–8.
75. Ibid., p.158.
76. Ibid., pp.157–8.
77. Ibid., p.187.
78. P. Barker, *The Ghost Road* (Harmondsworth: Penguin, 1996).
79. Ibid., p.276.
80. Enright, *The Pleasure of Eliza Lynch*, p.127.

CHAPTER EIGHT

'History is Only Biological': History, Bodies and National Identity in *The Gathering* and 'Switzerland'

KRISTIN EWINS

A nne Enright's second novel, *What Are You Like?*, published in 2000, opens with a father cradling his baby daughter only days after his wife has died. His thoughts take him back to the moment of conception: 'He thought, once, about how he had made her – the map on the sheet when he was done. She was another country, that was all.'[1] The strangeness of the child to the father is conceptualized in terms of foreignness: she is a different country from his own, configured by the biological stuff that made her. From the beginning, Enright connects nationhood, biology, sex and family history. Conception becomes a mapping out of the child's development away from her originator. In the novel, the alienating psychological urge that divides children from their parents becomes subtly interwoven with the idea of the Irish diaspora. The large-scale dispersal of Irish citizens across the globe, and especially across North America, is conceptualized microcosmically through one family. The Irish diaspora, as it is pictured here, is as much about a bodily and psychological severance – a loss of identity – as it is a physical journey. Berts, the father, brings up his daughter Maria in Dublin. Disaffected and frustrated, as a young woman Maria leaves Ireland for New York. Her restlessness is as much a part of her body as of her mind. Its source is, we discover, biological: unknown to herself, she has been yearning for her lost twin sister, Rose. Another example of diasporic Irishness, Rose was adopted by an English middle-class couple at birth and has grown up in London with the same indefinable restlessness as her sister. By accident, the twins find the complementing part of their selves, and the novel concludes with this biological-psychological connection. The journeys that separate the sisters and then bring them together again model the loss and rediscovery of Irish identity – via New York, London and Dublin – ending with redemption and self-discovery. The healing of the self also becomes the piecing together of a fragmented national identity.

What Are You Like? was published in the same year that Enright gave birth to her first child. Writing about nursing her baby in an essay for the *London Review of Books*, Enright elaborates her understanding of the intimate relationship between our biological embodiment, family relations and a sense of belonging: 'motherhood', she writes,

> happens in the body, as much as the mind. I thought childbirth was a sort of journey that you could send dispatches home from, but of course it is not – it *is* home. Everywhere else now, is 'abroad'.
>
> A child came out of me. I cannot understand this, or try to explain it. Except to say that my past life has become foreign to me.[2]

By emphasizing body and mind as equally central to her experience of childbirth, Enright connects psychology with physiology. The effect is to locate her experience in an actual place. Rather than being a 'journey', childbirth, to Enright, becomes 'home'. But, at the same time, the experience has upset a carefully mapped out order, from which she had assumed she could travel away. By making childbirth the place in which her body and mind feel at home, any other place 'is "abroad"'. 'Everywhere' indicates actual physical locations, but the quotation marks around 'abroad' also suggest that these places may not be quite foreign after all. The relationship to these other places is uneasy and tentative, and the locations 'everywhere' may refer to are diffuse. In the sentence that follows, however, physical space is exchanged for historical space. It is now 'my past life' that has become 'foreign'.

By juxtaposing these two senses of foreignness, Enright manages to conflate historical time and physical place. Something similar goes on in the process of diaspora. The ambiguity of 'abroad' sums up some of the contradictions of the Irish diaspora that involve both a change of physical space and a sense of historical distance. The attempt to understand what makes up history, both personal and political, has continued to be the driving force of Enright's fiction since the publication of *What Are You Like?* In this essay, I will examine how history and national identity invest the physical and psychological journeys that Enright's characters take in *The Gathering* and a recent short story, 'Switzerland', from *Taking Pictures*.[3] I will show how Enright exploits the links between the Irish diaspora, the body, sex and family history to engage with questions of nationhood, sexuality and religion. I will go on to explore the ways in which she tackles the chaos and pain of the Irish diaspora and contemporary history most forcefully through her dark comedy, thus unearthing a bleak-hopeful impetus for healing and redemption from a tattered and fragmented past for the individual as well as the community.

The Gathering is told by the thirty-something, middle-class, stay-at-home-mum Veronica Hegarty. The eighth out of twelve children, she returns to the family home to tell her mother of the suicide of Liam, the most wayward of the siblings and her favourite brother. Veronica looks to the past to gain a better understanding of what went wrong in Liam's life and why he killed himself. By searching for answers to her questions about Liam and herself in her family history – especially what she imagines as the youth and courtship of her grandparents, Ada and Charlie – Veronica demonstrates the interconnectedness between members of a community: how one life crucially affects another. Typically for Enright, this type of history has a sticking-power which is felt in the bones and in the flesh. The opening of the novel is a good example of this:

> I would like to write down what happened in my grandmother's house the summer I was eight or nine, but I am not sure if it really did happen. I need to bear witness to an uncertain event. I feel it roaring inside me – this thing that may not have taken place. I don't even know what name to put on it. I think you might call it

129

a crime of the flesh, but the flesh is long fallen away and I am not sure what hurt may linger in the bones.[4]

It is typical of Enright to maintain an aura of uncertainty around the historical events themselves: in this case, as we later discover, instances of abuse that may or may not have taken place, and that Veronica may or may not have observed. Despite the uncertainty about the status of these events, they take on a metaphorical significance. Whether or not Veronica's memories capture what really happened in her grandmother's house there is a sense of guilt that is almost tangible. It is by looking back into family history, and by imagining a series of scenes from her grandparents' youth, that Veronica attempts to figure out the origins of this guilt; or, more precisely, the first seeds of Liam's suicide. As well as a family history, invested as it is with references to the Catholic Mass, this becomes a story of original sin; which is at the same time a sin of origins, of the flesh, of family, of biology: the paedophilic assault of Liam by his grandmother's late landlord, Lambert Nugent.

As she recalls the decaying face of an anonymous man suffering from tertiary syphilis – his sexual history literally written on his body – Veronica sums up the physical nature of history:

> History is only biological – that's what I think. We pick and choose the facts about ourselves – where we came from and what it means ... What is written for the future is written in the body, the rest is only spoor.
>
> I don't know when Liam's fate was written in his bones. And although Nugent was the first man to put his name there, for some reason, I don't think he was the last. Not because I saw anything else going on, but because this is the way these things work. Of course, no one knew how these things worked at the time. We looked at the likes of Liam and had a whole other story for it, a different set of words.
>
> Pup, gurrier, monkey, thug, hopeless, useless, mad, messer.[5]

The passage explains some of the novel's meandering search for origins. It may seem a little controversial that personal identity should be so determined. Veronica more or less accepts that, at some point, 'Liam's fate was written in his bones'; and the novel itself comes back to this point again and again. Past experience can help explain what someone becomes, 'thug, hopeless, useless' and so on, and release him or her from sole responsibility for his or her actions. When, more comically, one of the Hegarty sisters annihilates her distinctive family nose with plastic surgery, there is a suggestion that this historical determinism – history written on the body – could be broken. At the same time, the extreme measure of surgical intervention only helps to reinforce the claustrophobia of the family, or closed community, from which so many of Enright's characters want to sever themselves.

The preoccupation with the biological nature of history and identity – not least national identity – has been a trademark of Enright's fiction: in her magic realist first novel, The Wig My Father Wore, family guilt is embodied in the wig that everyone sees but no one mentions; The Pleasure of Eliza Lynch opens with a measured description of the sexual penetration of the body of that spectacular Irish Parisian courtesan, and follows Eliza's pragmatic use of it to become, for fifteen years, Paraguay's most powerful woman; and, as we have seen, in What Are You Like? twins separated at birth are attracted to one another across the Atlantic by a biological force. The concentration on the physical recurs in another essay Enright wrote for the London Review of Books, in which she marvelled at the universal reproduction and spread of the human cancer cells from an ordinary American woman, Henrietta Lacks. The cells had been stolen by two scientists before Lacks died in the early 1950s and were reproduced prolifically, to the point of infiltrating a vast number of cell samples across the world. The possibility of the posthumous reproduction of Lacks's cells moved Enright to reflect in her essay on the relationship between human biology and a person's self:

> The question is moot: the closer you get to the body, the harder it is to see. On a cellular level, we are each a community, or several communities, and the relationships are not always clear: some cells 'commit suicide', for example, but the question of intention must be a false one. Under the microscope, the question of 'self' is so diffuse and so complicated that it might as well not arise.[6]

What is most puzzling to Enright is the way in which selfhood is rooted in physical being – there is something to be grasped about the self from looking at the body – while escaping close-up analysis, evading the very question of where selfhood resides. The ubiquity and multiplication of cells generate a strikingly physiological image of human beings as cellular 'communities', which somehow connect with one another: in this case, the fact that Lacks's cells could multiply to such an extent that they not only outlived their original carrier, but nowadays have infiltrated a vast number of test cells in laboratories worldwide. The question of selfhood remains located in the physical stuff that makes us. However, when we look too closely – again, at a cellular level – we cannot grasp selfhood at all.

In *The Gathering*, though, Enright locates selfhood precisely in bodily sensations. Veronica remembers Liam, sunk into alcoholism, visiting her in hospital after the birth of her first daughter: 'He was reduced, by the sight of her, to someone I knew in my bones.'[7] Then in Brighton,

> He is back in my head like an expanding smell – a space that clears to allow him look out of my eyes and be disgusted by arse or tit, or 'cold tit', even, by flesh that is never the right temperature or the right humidity, being too *sweaty*, or flesh that is *saggy*, or *hairy*, and the women, especially, who inhabit this sad human sack too craven or too beautiful (except, of course, for their holes), and in the end, who do you sleep with, who do you kiss?[8]

Bodies, death, sex, desire: this is a recurrent pattern in the novel and, it may be argued, in all of Enright's work; the influence, perhaps, of Angela Carter who taught Enright as an MA student in creative writing at the University of East Anglia. In a recent interview, Enright listed Carter's collection of feminist rewrites of traditional fairy tales, *The Bloody Chamber*, alongside Shakespeare's *King Lear* as significant influences.[9] And the family dynamics and sexual envy of Lear loom large here as elsewhere in Enright's fiction. The body, of course, is the central location of power battles in these works: the politicizing of sexualized bodies in Carter's radical fairy tales, and the fetish of dismemberment and suicide in *Lear*.

So it is physically – on her skin, in her bones, as a smell – that Veronica remembers her brother. For all its secular, even blasphemous, demonstrations, the novel is shot through with resounding religious metaphors. Veronica's urge to reveal Liam's true history is the desire for her own *vera icon*, recalling the occasion when her namesake saint received the imprint of the face of Christ on a towel on the way to Calvary. All the talk about the sharing of blood and flesh within a family conjures up the image of the Eucharist, exploring the, specifically Irish, Catholic version of a communion: an act which works against the Irish diaspora and pulls together family and national culture with extraordinary strength. As Veronica says: 'I do not think we remember our family in any real sense. We live in them, instead.'[10] Or in the terms of Enright's brutal humour: 'Bad news for [my sister] Bea and my mother and all the vultures who will flock to 4 Griffith Way for the wake … is that there will be another ten days at least to wait before they can feast on Liam's poor corpse.'[11]

The most striking emblem of this peculiarly Irish communion is the gathering around Liam's body in the family home for his wake; the occasion that gives the novel its title. Here, the disparate members of the Hegarty family manage to reconcile some of their differences in the serenity that follows their brother's death. Significantly, the twelve Hegarty children have spread across the world, settling in Canada, South America, England as well as Ireland. Hence they function as a microcosm of the Irish diaspora. Such uncontrolled dispersion is symbolically reflected in the family home, a sprawling architectural nightmare of endless extensions. The house grew up with the family, as Veronica reflects:

> This is my house too. I was inside it, as it grew; as the dining room was knocked into the kitchen, as the kitchen swallowed the back garden … The place is all extension and no house. Even the cubby-hole beside the kitchen door has another door at the back of it, so you have to battle your way through coats and hoovers to get into the downstairs loo. You could not sell the place, I sometimes think, except as a site. Level it and start again.[12]

There is a sense of unsustainability in the situation: the house could not be sold on as it is, it is too much of a patchwork for that. The idea of adding bits onto the house over time ties in with Enright's preoccupation with the Irish diaspora. When the Hegarty siblings come back to the house from all over the world for Liam's wake, they fill the different extensions with their diverse personalities, and the house comes to embody the fragmentariness of national and familial identity.

In her well-known public address of February 1995, 'Cherishing the Irish Diaspora', the then President of Ireland, Mary Robinson, set out to make the 'term the people of Ireland ... as broad and inclusive as possible' and concluded that the seventy or so million people worldwide of Irish descent proved that 'Irishness is not simply territorial'.[13] Robinson points out the significance of the title of her address:

> I chose the title of this speech – cherishing the Irish diaspora – with care. Diaspora, in its meaning of dispersal or scattering, includes the many ways, not always chosen, that people have left this island. To cherish is to value and to nurture and support ... The men and women of our diaspora represent not simply a series of departures and losses. They remain, even while absent, a precious reflection of our own growth and change, a precious reminder of the many strands of identity which compose our story.[14]

Despite the pragmatic enthusiasm of Robinson's talk, absent from Enright's writing, Robinson's emphasis on the double nature of the Irish diaspora suggests a way of appreciating Enright's deep engagement with psychological as well as physical diaspora. In Enright's terms the loss of a sense of home, self, nationhood – almost always, and certainly in The Gathering, a journey away from Ireland – is necessary for healing and redemption to take place. This fixation with journeys and an expansive notion of Irishness had begun much earlier. In an interview with Caitriona Moloney, and about to set off for New York, Enright speaks of the road to the airport as 'the most important road in the country'.[15] The interview was published in the collection Irish Women Writers Speak Out, which had emerged out of Robinson's call for a broader conception of Irishness.[16]

The redemptive associations of the Eucharist reverberate throughout The Gathering. In an essay published only a week after The Gathering came out, Enright notes her own ambivalence about Catholicism:

I still believe in God, in some reluctant, furtive part of me. I'm not proud of it. I understand atheists, who are averse to religious people as they might be averse to fat people, as being actually quite dangerous in their weakness. So I am weak (and slightly fat, indeed) and a bit too ethnic, if it comes down to it. I just won't shape up and become a proper person who believes in nothing at all.[17]

At times, though, Enright uses humour to puncture the religious overtones:

If you ask me what my brother looked like after he was dead, I can tell you that he looked like Mantegna's foreshortened Christ, in paisley pyjamas. And this may be a general truth about the dead, or it may just be what happens when someone is lying on a high, mortuary table, with their feet towards the door.[18]

Bodies in the novel are never so expressive as in death, and The Gathering is scattered with corpses: Liam's drowned in the sea, severed body parts carted back and forth between hospital wards, dead bodies in morgues or laid out for wakes, touched and observed, or pictured, as Liam's is here, as 'Mantegna's foreshortened Christ, in paisley pyjamas'. The image takes the serious Christian topic of Christ in death and plays with it by putting on some paisley pyjamas. It is the very bodiliness of the corpse – being only body – that brings it in line with such blasphemy. In a review of Enright's recent collection of short stories, Taking Pictures, Hermione Lee observed that,

Like Eliza Lynch, a million miles away from County Cork, or the disappearing Hegarty brother, the people in these stories are never at home, or happy with the idea of home. The self-exiled, self-mocking Irish are always on the look-out for a false story, a sentimental cliché about Irishness.[19]

There seems to be something of this going on in Veronica's attempt to recreate the personal history of her grandmother from memory and imagination. Some of these stories assembled from the past turn into a parodic version of 1920s courtship:

135

Lambert Nugent first saw my grandmother Ada Merriman in a hotel foyer in 1925 ...

She walked into the foyer and did not look about her and sat in an oval-backed chair near the door. Lamb Nugent watched her through a rush of arrivals and instructions as she removed her left-hand glove and then picked off the right. She pulled a little bracelet out from under her sleeve, and the hand that held the gloves settled in her lap.

She was beautiful, of course.[20]

Enright plays with the idea of history as cliché. A few lines before this passage, Veronica observes that 'history is such a romantic place, with its jarveys and urchins and side-buttoned boots'. Although in this novel Veronica attempts to work out her family history and find the roots to Liam's suicide by assembling and imagining her grandmother's life, patched up from clues, memories, physical evidence and a lot of filling in the gaps, history only ever becomes a partial redeemer. Uncertainty remains with us at the end, and the fluidity of history, that is so powerfully presented through Enright's style, leaves us with the protagonist looking forward instead of backwards.

Enright's preoccupation with history continues in the short stories collected in *Taking Pictures*. In one of the finest of these stories, 'Switzerland', Irish Elaine travels with her American lover Tim from Dublin to Venice, then from Dublin to Mexico. Just like in *The Gathering*, the reliability of history in these short stories, and in 'Switzerland' in particular, is questioned by the potential of story to invade its sphere. On Elaine's request – 'Tell me about potatoes'[21] – Tim tells her about his great-aunt going mad on arriving at Connecticut from Connemara:

Rubbed the eyes off potatoes because she thought they were looking at her.

You just made that up.

No, it is true, he said. She went dotty. Quite literally. Ants, flies, mildew, mould – it was the spots that drove her crazy. She thought they were eyes. She thought the world was boiling with eyes. Gravel, for instance. Think about it.

Eyes or eyeballs? she said.

Actually, I made it up.

He wore a little fake history on his back; a white shirt, very thick cotton.[22]

Enright's removal of quotation marks around spoken phrases and sentences loosens the style to accommodate the fluidity of history making. It is unclear which parts of the story are made up. The lover claims that it is true, then admits that he made it up. Enright's description of the 'fake history on his back' is a puzzling image. The characters' own stories help make up their history, even when they are fake. Enright evokes both the physicality of history and the uncertainty of it, similar to representations configured in *The Gathering*.

Again, history is written on the body: from a restaurant table on the Zipolite beach in southern Mexico the couple spots

hippies and junkies who were madder than his great-aunt Louise.

One of them sat on the sand nearby as they were having dinner. He looked about seventy years old. A beach-bum, afflicted by sores – they were infected mosquito bites, or needle marks, perhaps. He stretched out his legs and looked in horror at the scabs, his face puzzling and straining, as though he expected maggots to crawl out of them. Then he attacked one with his nails, tearing at the skin . . .

They looked at him. History, there on the beach.[23]

History in the story is depicted as something concrete: the man embodies history itself. The body is again at the centre of Enright's engagement with history. Rather like the case of tertiary syphilis in *The Gathering*, this is an infected body, 'afflicted by sores', worn, full of scabs. There is even a suggestion of the man as a corpse, with the attributed expectation that maggots should be crawling out of his scabs. In this case, however, it becomes less clear whose history we are observing: is it the man's poverty-ridden past, or Mexico's itself? Or, does he reflect their own tattered histories, national and personal, in a more problematic way?

Removed from Ireland by two generations, Tim is fascinated by the Irish: 'You know what I like about Irish women?' he asks Elaine,

I like the way they still call themselves 'girls'. And I like the weather in their hair. Which is romantic of me, but I am Irish too, you know. So I like your big family; all those brothers and sisters bubbling up, like the froth on milk. And, I hate to say this, but I love your accent. Also your dark lipstick, and all the history flowering up your back.[24]

History flowers up Elaine's back very much like the suggestion in the earlier quote that Tim is wearing 'a little fake history on his back': hers may be more genuine, bubbling up as those very physical siblings around her, whereas his is made-up stories. However, the two kinds of history they present, both pictured in terms of something physical carried on one's back — one actual, the other anecdotal and fabricated — remain equally significant. There is no sense in Enright's fiction of privileging one type of history over another, even when uncertain or largely made up. History is always also a form of story telling. Even though Elaine, rather like the Hegartys, has sought to escape the sprawling family and the claustrophobia of Ireland itself, the warmth and congeniality of an Irish welcome balance the picture. When she tries to wean Tim off his enchantment with Ireland by taking him to see her family in Cork — 'This fucking country, she said. You have no idea. Come down to Cork with me. That'll change your mind' — instead,

He loved them all, and they loved him. Her brothers bringing him down to the local for a pint and her father talking about tornadoes in America, and was he ever in one, at all? And it was all the Big Yank in the front parlour, and no one asked them once about Italy, or Mexico, or the North Circular Road for that matter. No one asked anything, except would he like a cup of tea, because in this house, it became clear, questions were out of the question.[25]

Here, in the family home, they make love 'under the table where, looking up, Elaine saw a crayoned boat she had drawn, one endlessly idle afternoon, when she was nine or ten. A green boat with a blue sail. Her own secret sign.'[26] Here we have that longing for escape that seems to be at the heart of Enright's characters, and that, after all, has been one of the reasons for the Irish diaspora. The story ends with her lover asking her: 'Where do you want to go? he said. Where to you want to go, now?'[27] A little earlier he had suggested 'We could live in France'.[28] As Bernard O'Donoghue has noted in his review of the collection, France is invoked as a place of impossible escape in the next story in the collection, 'Green', in which 'the narrator – a well-educated grower of organic vegetables – reports that she had told her mother that she "wanted to start over somewhere else. France – why not?"'[29] There are curious links with James Joyce's *Dubliners* (1914) here, as O'Donoghue notes, 'the repeated invocation of France as an escape establishes it as a symbol of the unrealistic, as Buenos Aires was for Eveline':[30]

> That was a long time ago; she and her brothers and sisters were all grown up her mother was dead. Tizzie Dunn was dead, too, and the Waters had gone back to England. Everything changes. Now she was going to go away like the others, to leave her home.
>
> Home! She looked round the room, reviewing all its familiar objects which she had dusted once a week for so many years, wondering where on earth all the dust came from. Perhaps she would never see again those familiar objects from which she had never dreamed of being divided.[31]

The green boat with a blue sail recalls the ship that could take Eveline away from her troubled home to a new life with Frank in Buenos Aires. This, of course, is a step away from home too daring to take:

> Through the wide doors of the sheds she caught a glimpse of the black mass of the boat, lying in beside the quay wall, with illumined portholes. She answered nothing. She felt her cheek pale and cold and, out of a maze of distress, she prayed to God to direct her, to show her what was her duty. The boat blew a long mournful whistle into the mist. If she went, tomorrow she would be on the sea with Frank, steaming towards Buenos Ayres.[32]

Enright's portrait is much more hopeful, but it captures the same tension between the desire to leave and start afresh, away from Ireland, and the compulsive yearning to come back, as in Tim's case, or to stay.

A specifically Irish home is something Enright's characters keep returning to, even when ostensibly wanting to leave it behind. The tension between the desire for home and the wish to abandon it is concentrated in the alienation from Irishness within Ireland itself. In *The Gathering*, Enright turns this self-alienation into a joke in a letter Veronica recalls from Liam on a school trip to an Irish-speaking region:

> 'Meanwhile', he writes from Gweedore, the year he was fourteen, 'we get numb bums from sitting on the beach and not drinking vodka, or "bhodhca" as it is called here. Billy Tobin got sent back up for speaking English so Michael and me have developed a way of speaking English <u>as if it is actually Irish</u> which is great fun and not very comprehensible. Iubhsaid try it iurseldh some time.'[33]

Moving to England for Liam and Veronica in their youth is moving to the squalor of a three-story squat in North London's Stoke Newington. On the whole, Veronica's experience of England is one of unreality:

> The funny thing ... about that first journey through the British night for us – fresh off the boat, fifty paces across our first foreign soil and then stepping up again on to the iron floor of the train – was that we always thought that we were nearly there. We looked out the window and, after a period of darkness, there were so many lights we assumed they were the coming lights of London town. Except that we never arrived. And it seemed to us that England was a single city from one side to the other, without pause.[34]

Ultimately, it is Ireland itself that offers redemption, receiving Veronica at the end of a symbolic journey of self-discovery – a journey to England and back.

In a confrontation with her husband, Veronica says: 'Your daughters will sleep with men like you. Men who will hate them, just because they want them.'[35] In her first interview after winning the Booker Prize, Enright noted her fascination with the links between hatred and desire:

> One of the things I wanted to do in the book was explore how desire and hatred are closely bound up ... that sense that someone – usually a man – is enraged by the fact that he desires someone – usually a woman ... You hate what you desire because you desire it. That's why we speak about something that sounds so violent, namely fucking. I wanted to write about sex in a different way

from that bad-boy stuff that men write so often, to think about the violence in desire.[36]

And about her husband Tom, Veronica notes: 'his desire runs ... close to hatred. It is sometimes the same thing.'[37] Desire, sex, death and separation are what fragments and drives Liam away from Ireland, and Veronica away from her husband. In *What Are You Like?*, along the same lines, Maria compares desire to grief.[38] The communion – redemption – that heals the cracks in the familial relationships is ultimately driven by love and coincides with the return to Ireland. The hatred and pain felt by his family when Liam emigrated to England can now, after his death, be overcome by the shared joy at discovering that Liam had produced a son that they can all love unproblematically. It is love, too, that pieces together Veronica and her marriage, again using images of foreignness and other countries:

> I do not want a different life. I just want to be able to live it, that's all. I want to wake up in the morning and fall asleep at night. I want to make love to my husband again. Because, for every time he wanted to undo me, there was love that put me back together again – put us both back together. If I could just remember them too. If I could remember each time, as you remember different places you have seen – some of them so amazing; exotic, or confusing, or still.[39]

This is a forward-looking ending, hopeful of a future, perhaps another child. History as a physical presence speaks about what we are, but however essential, it is inadequate to describe everything about who we are precisely because it cannot, and perhaps should not, ever be fully grasped. There is something impossible about history. Even when it is pinned down to the most physical, bodily sensation, Enright tends to allow for yet another story to take precedence. As I have shown, this vague sense of history lends itself to an exploration of the body and national identity, and a specifically Irish diasporic condition. The simultaneous urge to escape and return home is crucial to all of Enright's writing. For Veronica in *The Gathering* – and for all of Enright's characters – journeys are of two kinds only: looking at the people queuing at Gatwick airport, she wonders are they going home, or are they going far away from the people they love. There are no other journeys. And I think we make for peculiar refugees, running from our own blood, or towards our own blood; pulsing back and forth along ghostly veins that warp the world in a skein of blood.[40]

In this concluding passage, the diasporic urge becomes as much a human condition as an Irish obsession. The reference to blood and its pulsations through the body underlines the physical nature of our actions: what drives us to leave or come back is beyond free will; it is there already, in our blood. Again, this is sheer psychologico-historical determinism, however attractive the thought of a globe wrapped in veins connecting us all may be. Nonetheless, the passage also illustrates the key points I have made in this essay: that history, in Enright's fiction, is rooted in the body; that national identity develops through personal as well as community history; and that love, conceptualized here as blood ties, offers redemption in a semi-secularized Irish context which is, nonetheless, deeply invested with the ritual of Catholicism – the blood of Christ, for instance, forging a communion between people. The Irish diaspora becomes both a metaphor and an actuality, and its physical presence in the history, bodies and relationships of her characters forms a core narrative strand in Enright's fiction.

NOTES

1. A. Enright, *What Are You Like?* (London: Jonathan Cape, 2000), p.4.

2. Enright, 'My Milk', *London Review of Books*, 22, 19 (2000), pp.34–5.

3. Enright, *The Gathering* (London: Jonathan Cape, 2007); *Taking Pictures* (London: Jonathan Cape, 2008).

4. Enright, *The Gathering*, p.1.

5. Ibid., pp.162–3.

6. Enright, 'What's Left of Henrietta Lacks?' *London Review of Books*, 22, 8 (2000), pp.8–10.

7. Enright, *The Gathering*, p.53.

8. Ibid., p.76.

9. S. Rustin, 'What Women Want', *Guardian*, 15 March 2008.

10. Enright, *The Gathering*, p.66.

11. Ibid., p.74.

12. Ibid., pp.4–5.

13. M. Robinson, 'Cherishing the Irish Diaspora', Address to the Houses of Oireachtas on a Matter of Public Importance, 2 February 1995, http://www.oireachtas.ie/viewdoc.asp?fn=/documents/addresses/2Feb1995.htm.

14. Ibid.

15. Enright, 'Anne Enright interview by Caitriona Moloney', in *Irish Women Speak Out: Voices from the Field*, ed. C. Moloney and H. Thompson (Syracuse, NY: Syracuse University Press, 2003), p.53.

16. Mary Robinson is mentioned positively five times in the book. See Moloney and Thompson, *Irish Women Speak Out*, pp.6, 28, 80, 83, 192.

17. Enright, 'Diary: Listen to Heloïse', *London Review of Books*, 29, 9 (2007), p.43.

18. Enright, *The Gathering*, p.64.

19. H. Lee, 'Pawed, Used, Loved and Lonely', review of *Taking Pictures*, by Anne Enright, *Guardian*, 1 March 2008.

20. Enright, *The Gathering*, p.13.

21. Enright, 'Switzerland', in *Taking Pictures*, p.103.

22. Ibid., p.103.

23. Ibid., p.109.

24. Ibid., p.106.

25. Ibid., p.113.

26. Ibid.

27. Ibid.

28. Ibid.

29. B. O'Donoghue, 'Anne Enright's Tales of the Ordinary', review of *Taking Pictures*, by A. Enright, *Times Literary Supplement*, 5 March 2008.

30. Ibid.

31. J. Joyce, 'Eveline', *Dubliners* (London: Penguin, 1992 [1914]), pp.29–30.

32. Ibid., p.33.

33. Enright, *The Gathering*, p.118.

34. Ibid., pp.77–8.

35. Ibid., p.219.

36. Enright quoted in S. Jeffries, 'I Wanted to Explore Desire and Hatred', *The Guardian*, 18 October 2007.

37. Enright, *The Gathering*, p.145.

38. Enright, *What Are You Like?*, p.132.

39. Enright, *The Gathering*, p.260.

40. Ibid., p.258.

CHAPTER NINE

Waking the Dead: Antigone, Ismene and Anne Enright's Narrators in Mourning

GERARDINE MEANEY

And yet how otherwise had I achieved
A name so glorious as by burying
A brother?[1]

Reflecting in 2008 on the link between her groundbreaking work on gender and her more recent work on war, Judith Butler proposed a relationship between liveable and grievable lives: 'it is very often a struggle to make certain kinds of lost life publicly grievable'.[2] This essay takes Butler's exploration of the 'politics of mourning' as its starting place for a reading of The Gathering and of the short story, 'My Little Sister' from Taking Pictures.[3] While The Gathering concerns a sister's mourning for her brother, 'My Little Sister' chronicles a woman's bewilderment and grief at her sister's death. Both explore 'what it means to understand certain lives as more precarious than others', and both are narrated from the position of 'those excluded from official public discourse' who 'somehow are still talking'.[4] This essay asks if the mournful narrators of these fictions can be understood in terms of the myth of Antigone and 'to what extent ... can Antigone figure for us [in] the position of the speaker who is outside of the accepted discourse, who nevertheless speaks, some-times intelligently, sometimes critically, within and against that

145

discourse?'[5] What does it mean to narrate from this edge where discourse meets death and difference? These fictions of mourning and survival are written in that aesthetic territory on the borderlines of what Julia Kristeva describes as the 'true-real' where the outside of language manifests itself in language,[6] a territory which Jean-François Lyotard made paradigmatically postmodern, where that which cannot be represented is present in representation.[7] They also challenge the terms of the theoretical definitions of this territory. For if Enright's fiction inhabits these spaces, where madness, psychosis and death are predicted, it also postulates the possibility of exceeding that paradigm, reconfiguring it with the force of the desire to 'be able to live'.[8]

This essay proposes a reappraisal of Antigone's relationship with her sister, Ismene, so often dismissed as a cypher for conventional femininity, and reads Enright's mournful narrators in terms of that relationship. Ismene is a more complex figure than she initially appears. She fears to act with her sister and counsels her to act more in accordance with the social expectation of femininity: 'My poor, fond sister, how I fear for thee!' She does not sacrifice herself for her brother or what is due to her mother, as Antigone does. She is, at least initially, a conventional rather than a heroic, singular woman. 'We must remember, first', says Ismene:

> that we were born women, as who should not strive with men; next, that we are ruled of the stronger, so that we must obey in these things, and in things yet sorer. I, therefore, asking the Spirits Infernal to pardon, seeing that force is put on me herein, will hearken to our rulers. For 'tis witless to be over busy.

There is a hint in that reference to using one's wits, that Ismene is a pragmatic woman rather than a willingly submissive one: 'A hopeless quest should not be made at all', she argues. She has no appetite for self-destruction and she identifies herself as weak: 'to defy the State, – I have no strength for that'. Antigone considers her sister 'guilty of dishonouring laws which the gods have established in honour' and aligns her own honour with death: 'I owe a longer allegiance to the dead than to the living.' Ismene's response to her sister's declared hatred of her for her weakness is surprising: 'though thine errand is foolish, to thy dear ones thou art truly dear'. Ismene's loyalties are with her living sister rather than dead brother. When Antigone is condemned by Creon, it transpires that self-preservation is not Ismene's overwhelming principle, for she tells her sister, 'now that ills beset thee, I am not ashamed to sail the sea of trouble at thy side', and there are circumstances in which she is prepared to give up her life for another: 'Sister, reject me not, but let me die with thee', she pleads with Antigone. When the latter scorns her belated desire to die, Ismene exhibits loyalties and strengths which have been obscured by her earlier common sense. This has been dismissed as cowardice by commentators who have tended to follow Antigone's judgement of contempt on her sister.

When Antigone speaks, in perverse obedience to Creon's law 'she defies that law', and, like Veronica in *The Gathering*, her speech exceeds 'the law that governs acceptable speech'. Veronica observes: 'I feel it roaring inside me – this thing that may not have taken place. I don't even know what name to put on it.'[9] Inhabited by the Real which has so uncertain a hold upon reality, unable to put a name on it, but talking all the same, Veronica rehearses the theoretical impasse characteristic of current theoretical debates which argue Antigone's significance as both the limit of symbolic power and the excess which can challenge it, the possibility and the impossibility of change. This essay will argue that Enright's narrators in both *The Gathering* and 'My Little Sister' exceed that impasse and that they do so because, like Ismene, they retain their attachment to life.

While 'My Little Sister' and *The Gathering* are stories about the dead, they are primarily concerned with how to live, though they are not staged as a triumphant reassertion of the narrators' egos over the drives towards death that destroy their siblings. Enright's narrative mode is characteristically an uncanny doubling of the first person:

> As I write, I look out of the window and check with the corpse I have sitting in the Saab at the front gate. He is always there (it is always a he), a slumped figure in the front seat who turns out, on examination, to be the tilting headrest. But even though I know this, I am drawn to his stuffed, blank face, and wonder why he should be so patient. He lets his gaze rest endlessly on the dash, like a man who is listening to the radio and will not come into the house.[10]

This is the ultimate first-person, plausible narrator of realist fiction and its opposite, for nothing could be further from the unified and unifying ego. The phrase, 'As I write, I look out of the window', effects the conventional occlusion of authorial voice and novelistic artifice by the first-person narrator who speaks, acts and even writes within the fiction. The second part of the sentence completely undoes this convention: 'and check with the corpse I have sitting in the Saab at the front gate'. This is not simply an untrustworthy narrator or a perfectly realized impersonation of insanity, however. The next sentence reverses the movement from the sane and familiar to the psychotic. 'He is always there (it is always a he), a slumped figure in the front seat', it begins madly: 'who turns out, on examination, to be the tilting headrest', it ends sanely.

In this one narrative persona there is a consciousness whose reality is a psychotic symptom and a clear-headed and critical narrator who 'on examination' knows and names her distorted view of reality. They are neither polarized nor even in conflict: 'even though I know this [that 'he' is a headrest], I am drawn to his stuffed, blank face, and wonder why he should be so patient'. The corpse symptom is domesticated, a man waiting outside his comfortable suburban home listening to the radio, but not entirely so for this activity implies that he neither wants to go in nor is wanted there. The narrative voice is not, in the end, at home with its own madness: 'I do not actually want him in the house', but she does not wish to banish it entirely as yet, and indeed derives some comfort from it: 'that does not mean I am happy to see him always in my car, this man who talks to me quite bluntly of patience and ability to endure'.[11] The symptom is personified as the locus of the narrator's sanity, outside waiting, not yet home, quintessentially unheimlich (uncanny). This disorientating and compelling narrative voice, with neither the subjectivity of the first person nor the objectivity of the third, is crucial in Enright's fictions' oscillation between the mundane and the menacing, as when Veronica in The Gathering describes her sister 'Kitty – a woman weirdly like my little sister, though much too old'.[12] This dynamic of unease gives even the most quotidian scene the atmosphere of a good ghost story, the sense that something is going to be revealed but that it will not, in any conventional way, make sense. The drive towards psychosis and death is countered by the desire to live again, but living requires an accommodation with the truth that madness reveals.

In *The Gathering*, the narrator describes her style of interior decoration in her 'Tudor-red-brick-with-Queen-Anne-Overtones' house:

> I started with all sorts of pelmets when we moved in, even swags. I wanted the biggest floral I could find for the bay window at the front – can you imagine it? By the time I had the stuff sourced, I had already moved on to plain Roman blinds and now the garden is properly grown in I want … nothing. I spend my time looking at things and wishing them gone, clearing objects away.
> This is how I live my life.[13]

Enright's descriptions of objects and places evoke those of another occasionally surreal minimalist, Muriel Spark, a key conduit of the influence of the 'new novel' on English language fiction. Spark was a dazzling exponent of the technique of dislocating externalization, where objects and the external world are described in almost psychedelic detail and clarity and the internal world of her characters not described at all. The effect of this is very similar to the paradox at the heart of Enright's descriptive style, where 'things' are looked at in detail and at length as a way of 'clearing objects away'. The heroine of Spark's 1973 novel, *The Hothouse by the East River*, defines the technique, in describing the bafflement of her therapist: 'He's looking for causes and all I'm giving him are effects'.[14] Spark's acrobatics over the abyss are nonetheless sustained by an architecture of omniscience. Author-ity (however parodic or fictional) persists in the implied third-person omniscient narrator, tantalizingly and powerfully present precisely because we cannot help looking for causes and all she is giving us are effects. While Enright's novels often evoke the depths of their narrators' subjectivity, which Spark eschews, there is no sense in *The Gathering* or 'My Little Sister' that this internal space can be fully mapped, or that it enjoys a stable boundary from the external world. In Enright's fictions its symptoms occasionally become objects, like the headrest man, and objects exhibit an intentionality often missing from subjects, like the headrest ghost, 'still game … like a thousand mechanical friends in a thousand cartoons'.[15] Observing the landscape through the train window as she goes to fetch her brother's body, Veronica tries 'to find the line along which the landscape holds still and changes its mind, thinking that travel is a contrary kind of thing, because moving towards a dead man is not moving at all'.[16] In the contrary relationship here between subject and object, stillness and movement, mind and matter, the causes implied are quite as opaque as the effects.

This withholding of causes is the central narrative device of 'My Little Sister'. The mystery of why Serena contracts anorexia haunts her older sister, who is left without an explanatory narrative and leaves the reader similarly stranded:

> I went through her life in my head. Every Tuesday night before the goddam therapy, I sifted the moments: a cat that died, my grandmother's health, Santa Claus. I went through the caravan holidays and the time she cried halfway up Carantoohill and sat down and had to be carried to the top. I went through her first period and the time I bawled at her for stealing my mohair jumper. The time she used up a can of fly-spray in an afternoon slaughter and the way she placed horsey on my father's bocketty leg. It was all just bits. I really wanted it to add up to something but it didn't.[17]

There is an easy way to read this story in contrast to The Gathering. The loss of the sister cannot be ritualized, translated into the public world in even the limited way that the loss of the brother is in the novel when his sister bears witness, offering us the kind of explanation that remains tantalizingly out of reach in 'My Little Sister'. This is to miss the point, for in both cases the truthful telling of the stories by the narrator demands the same ambiguity, an acknowledgement that the lost siblings remain an enigma. The implied depth of the subjective experience of the dead is terrifying, threatening to return to engulf the survivors, who bear witness but are incapable of an authoritative narrative which would close the border between the living and the dead, the present and the past. The Gathering opens with the impulse to tell and the impossibility of being sure of what story to tell: 'I would like to write down what happened in my grandmother's house the summer I was eight or nine, but I am not sure if it really did happen. I need to bear witness to an uncertain event.'[18] In this regard, Enright's work challenges the distinction between postmodernism and realism in fiction: the narrative's realism resides in its self-reflexive uncertainty. This is not the residual modernism which remains integral to much Irish writing and Irish writers' self presentation. Enright's humorous dismissal of Nabokov as an immature taste is typical: 'I used to think Nabokov was brilliant when I was in my early 20s, I thought he was the business – all those beautiful sentences, all this very refined yearning – and now I just think he's a boring old narcissist. He speaks not at all to my life now.'[19] Her appropriation of Joyce as an honorary woman writer, who 'writes domestic and introspective books, not the slightest bit socially aware',[20] is equally humorous. On the one hand, humour is Enright's device for the undermining of cultural authorities; on the other, her insouciance in the face of the canon is a deadly serious act. According to Lyotard, modernism puts forward the unpresentable 'only as the missing contents'.[21] The psychic and stylistic economies implied by Enright's narratives are not organized around any such fetish. In 'My Little Sister', the refusal of an originary trauma which the narrator can even partially recover makes the author a powerful, resistant presence in the story, a withholder of comprehension analogous to the lost sister who never does explain herself: 'with Serena you are always asking yourself what went wrong, or even, Where [sic] did I go wrong? But believe me, I am just about done with all that – with shuffling through her life in my mind.'[22] Bearing witness may be a burden in The Gathering; in 'My Little Sister' the inability to finish Serena's story means her loss is never over: 'I am trying to stop this story, but it just won't end.'[23] This narrative without an ending oscillates between self-defence and guilt. Recalling bringing her little sister to the bus stop on her own school lunch break, the narrator is obliged to clarify that this 'is not me complaining, it is me saying that she was cared for endlessly, by all of us'.[24] On one level the story accepts the fact that some acts are definitive, some losses absolute. The death of the sister marks the point at which reality is marked by the absence of the Real, where life is marked by death and the socio-symbolic order cannot obscure the limits of comprehension, nor the power of what cannot be said, nor human mortality: 'So, she died. There is no getting away from something like that. You can't recover. I didn't even try. The first year was a mess and after that our lives were just punctured, not even sad – just less, just never the same again.'[25]

The older sister's mourning process is characterized by intermittent attempts at self-vindication: 'there are just some things you can not do for a child. There are some things you can not help.'[26] The narrator searches in vain for a cause, a reason for her sister's insanity. First she remembers a brush with mortality, when the two little girls witnessed a car accident as children, then an encounter with a flasher. Neither incident nor the encounters with death and sexuality they initiate have seemed serious enough to act as originary traumas for the extremity of the little sister's symptoms, not least because they were also experienced by the older, surviving sister. The narrator acknowledges: 'I'm scraping the barrel here. We had a great childhood. And I'm fine, that's the bottom line. I'm fine and Serena is dead.'[27] Survival is as incomprehensible as death and is equated with guilt, 'nothing was enough, and everything was too late'.[28] Unlike the protagonist of The Gathering, this narrator cannot manage to be properly haunted, possibly because the little sister is so overwhelmingly present in her absence. She has never really left the land of the living so she can hardly come back from the dead. In a sense the anorexic is a ubiquitous shadow of femininity, a modern icon of feminine self-hatred, of alienation, 'weighed down' by the western tradition of denigration of the material and the body.

Yet, this particular sister is resolutely not a textbook anorexic:

> They say anorexics are bright girls who try too hard and get tipped over the brink, but Serena sauntered up to the brink. She looked over her shoulder at the rest of us, as we stood and called to her, and then she turned and jumped. It is not too much to say that she enjoyed her death. I don't think it is too much to say that.[29]

The narrative does not fit. The story rehearses a variety of narratives which would translate the unbearable reality to a story with cause and effect; the psychological one tried out with the trauma stories, the gothic one of the murderous boyfriend occurring to the narrator long afterwards when she reads of a murderer with the same name as her sister's boyfriend. Neither of them are remotely adequate to what has happened. What is left is a gap in reason, a fracture in reality, in time and in generation, like the encounter with the dying Serena after one of her disappearances:

Then one day I saw a woman in the street who looked like my gran, just before she died. I thought it was my gran for a minute: out of the hospice somehow ten years later and walking towards St Stephen's Green. Actually I thought she was dead and I was terrified − literally petrified − of what she had come back to say to me. Our eyes met, and hers were wicked with some joke or other. It was Serena, of course. And now her teeth were yellow as butter.[30]

The relationship between the sisters here can be read as analogous to that of Antigone and Ismene, but the mourning is that of sister for sister. The little sister plays the role of resistance, precisely mapping out the path of self-assertion as living death. Her surviving sibling is an agonized and haunted Ismene: 'Thou canst not say that I did not protest.' In 'My Little Sister', this protesting narrator seeks to shelter her sister from the real, but in the ninety-one days after she first left home she somehow became part of it, a harbinger not just of death but unreality: 'She was mysteriously gone from the bed across the room, she was absolutely gone from the downstairs sofa, and the bathroom was free for hours at a time. Gone. Not there. Vamoosed.'[31]

Serena's refusal of food is initially a refusal of the mother's nurture, of the mother as origin of life, and so the maternal becomes conflated with death:

My mother, especially, was infatuated by her absence. It is not enough to say she fought Serena's death, even then − she was intimate with it. To my mother, my sister's death was an enemy's embrace. They were locked together in the sitting room, in the kitchen, the hall. They met and talked, and bargained and wept. She might have been saying, 'Take me. Take me, instead.' But I think − you get that close to it, you bring it in to your home, everybody's going to lose.[32]

Again the logic of the unheimlich takes over, with Death taking up residence in suburban sitting rooms. There is a kind of reversal of the psychoanalytic identification of the maternal and death drives here. In Freud's Das Unheimlich, he identifies the uncanny as 'that species of the frightening that goes back to what was once well known and had long been familiar',[33] explicitly identifying the fear of being buried alive as the source of the most powerful affects of the uncanny because it inverts the desire to return to the womb. In an association which is relevant to a reading of the myth of Antigone, condemned to be buried alive, Freud identifies the mother's body with the place of death and the force of attraction of the maternal with the death drives. In this framework, both Veronica's and Antigone's affiliation to their mothers' 'ancient impulse',[34] to enact the rituals which will return their dead brother to the family, is identified with the desire to dissolve back into the maternal, the desire not to be. This framework is invoked in 'My Little Sister', where the mother is locked in an 'enemy's embrace' with death.[35] The location of this embrace within her suburban sitting room and the mother's attempt to bargain with her enemy, to effect substitutions, challenges the paradigm, however. The scene is doubly uncanny. It affects 'the alteration of a small detail in a well-known picture that all of a sudden renders the whole picture strange and uncanny'[36] which Žižek identifies as the characteristic source of the uncanny. It dislocates 'what was once well known', the psychoanalytic paradigm for understanding the repression of the maternal within an Oedipal framework, and makes it strange in the figure of the mother raging at the mortality of her daughter. This maternal subject very far from that which has been mythologized in Jocasta, the mother of Antigone and Ismene as well as Oedipus.

Perhaps it is this multiplication of feminine subjects raging at the limits of the symbolic and the inexorability of the Real as death that forces the story towards its un-ending. The final paragraph encapsulates and exceeds the rage of the living against the dead who have abandoned them, the guilt of survival and the bitter acknowledgment that the anorexic is a scapegoat, like Oedipus, for a sin of unknowing:

> even now, I find myself holding my breath in empty rooms. Yesterday I set a bottle of Chanel No.5 on the dressing table and took the lid off for a while, I kept thinking ... about those ninety-one days, my mother half crazed, my father feigning boredom, and me, with my own bedroom for the first time in years. I think of Serena's absence, how astonishing it was, and all of us sitting looking at each other, until the door opened and she walked in, half-dead, with an ordinary, living man in tow. And I think that we made her up somehow, that we imagined her. And him too, maybe

> – that he made her up, too. And I think that if we made her up
> now, if she walked into the room, we would kill her, somehow, all
> over again.[37]

In this narrative, grief and incomprehension are inconsolable. The older
sister cannot move on from the fact of her sister's absence, which she
finds embodied even in her daughter's eyes. In the absence of a compelling narrative to make the 'bits ... add up to something',[38] Serena
continues to have effects precisely because she has no cause.

In contrast to the bewilderment of the narrator in 'My Little Sister',
in The Gathering, the central protagonist's tragedy is that she knows why
her brother could not live, though she did not know she knew: 'It went
on slap-bang in front of me and still I did not realize it. And for this, I
am very sorry too.'[39] Her 'innocence' of the reality of what she saw has
made her guilty. In reparation she takes on the role of Antigone, tending
to her dead brother: 'This is how I live my life since Liam died. I stay up
all night. I write, or I don't write. I walk the house.'[40] Like Antigone, she
observes rituals at her mother's behest, resenting her sister Bea's preoccupation with what 'Daddy would have wanted'.[41] Veronica organizes
the return of Liam's body, though the bureaucracy she has to contend
with to arrange his burial according to maternal tradition are rather
more benign than Creon:

> The British, I decide, only bury people when they are so dead, you
> need another word for it. The British wait so long for a funeral that
> people gather not so much to mourn as to complain that
> the corpse is still hanging around ... They do not gather until the
> emotion is gone.[42]

Enright has herself stated that she has 'been fairly radical in wondering
what those definitions are, what the constructions are of gender, of
nationality and of identity in general. I haven't come to any answers.'[43]
The Gathering challenges the fundamental building block of these
constructions:

> All big families are the same. I meet them sometimes at parties or
> in pubs, we announce ourselves and then we grieve – Billy in
> Boston, and Jimmy-Joe in Jo'berg, doing well – the dead first, then

the lost and then the mad. There is always a drunk. There is always someone who had been interfered with, as a child. There is always a colossal success, with several houses in various countries, to which no one is ever invited. There is a mysterious sister. These are just trends, of course, and, like trends, they shift. Because our families contain everything and, late at night, everything makes sense.[44]

Veronica reconfigures this story: 'I have disturbed the ghosts. They are outside the door of my room, now, as the ghosts of my childhood were; they are behind the same door. Their story is there ... These are my nightmares. This is what I have to walk through to get downstairs.'[45] She endures 'Christmas in Hades', but, unlike Antigone, she returns from the underworld and re-makes her family to accept the truth of her brother's loss to gain his son, 'Oh there's no doubting the child ... It's Liam. To the life.'[46] This is not an easy substitution of the innocent boy with the Hegarty eyes for the ruined man: 'it is too uncanny'.[47]

In re-writing the Antigone story, among others, The Gathering addresses the central paradox of that story, much rehearsed in philosophical, psychoanalytical and literary discourse.[48] Antigone is a mythic figure of feminine resistance, iconic of the defiance of totalitarianism throughout most of the twentieth century and, for post-Lacanian psychoanalysis, representative of the refusal of symbolic order. However, recent critiques of this understanding of the myth have argued that her 'initial "No!" to Creon is entirely consistent with, and binds her to, her family destiny and paternal law'.[49] Veronica's role in The Gathering problematizes this polarized understanding of Antigone as either political or familial, and of the polarization of feminine identity into either submissive immanence figured in Ismene or radical transcendence. Veronica carries out the ancient duty of the women in the family to take care of the dead: 'Some ancient impulse of my mother's means she wants Liam's body brought back to the house before the removal, so Liam can lie in state in our ghastly front room. Though come to think of it, I can't think of a better carpet for a corpse.'[50] The incongruity of the front room and Veronica's consumerist disdain for its carpet are integral to the temporal games the novel plays. This, like all good ghost stories, is about the refusal of the past to be past. In this respect, it is also like the story of

Antigone, who, while she has been appropriated to signify the possibility of a different future, was originally destroyed for honouring an archaic attachment to the old rules of kinship over the new rule of the state. The Gathering exceeds these formulations, as any attempt to 'bear witness' must, by making Veronica both Antigone and Ismene. Veronica's declaration that, 'I do not want a different destiny from the one that has brought me here. I do not want a different life. I just want to be able to live it, that's all',[51] is very much the perspective of Ismene. Her dedication to truth and the dead is pure Antigone: 'The truth. The dead want nothing else. It is the only thing that they require.'[52]

Antigone tells Ismene, 'thou chosed'st life, and I to die'. The positions represented by the sisters in Sophocles' characterization are quite simply affiliation to life, defeat and deceit, or death, fidelity and truth. Enright's narrator combines both positions and outlives them. Perhaps this is the root of the power of the novel's ending, itself another beginning in life's cycle of beginnings: 'then again, I have been falling for months. I have been falling into my own life, for months. And I am about to hit it now.'[53] Antigone never gets her own life, nor can Ismene live without her. Paradoxically it is the fact that Veronica encompasses the ordinary weakness of an Ismene, who does not 'want a different destiny',[54] as well as the strength of Antigone that facilitates telling the untellable truth. Veronica's ability to go mad is essential to her ability to bear witness and to recover a sane life. For Veronica not only exceeds the familial, she exceeds the singularity of a lone female voice against the law of silence. Her dead brother's injunction to give truth to the dead conjures up Uncle Brendan, 'lost to Largacytl and squalor. How many years of it? He probably died wondering who he actually was.'[55] She interrupts her journey home with her brother's body, diverting from the familial narrative, and gets off the plane to drive to find St Ita's, the psychiatric hospital where Brendan was an inmate, and finds the stories of her brother and her uncle are part of a larger story when she encounters the grave of the inmates: 'There are no markers, no separate graves. I wonder how many people were slung into the dirt of this field and realize, too late, that the place is boiling with corpses, the ground is knit out of their tangled bones.'[56] This encounter with the ghosts of the mad paradoxically marks the beginning of Veronica's sanity. The headrest ghost has been banished by Kitty: 'I look back, helpless, at Kitty in the front seat of the car.'[57] At this moment of helplessness and strange sisterhood, Veronica is at one with the dead: 'They have me by the thighs. I am gripped at the thighs by whatever feeling this is. A vague wind. It clutches at me, skitters between my clothes and my skin. It lifts every hair. It grazes my lip. And is gone.'[58]

This sense of being ambushed by the dead reprises a recurrent element in the story which initially inspired Enright when she began writing The Gathering: Joyce's 'The Dead'.[59] The novel is careful to establish the 1925 scene in a very Joycean geography. Great Denmark Street where the Belvedere Hotel is located, is two minutes' walk from Leopold and Molly Bloom's putative address in Eccles Street. Charley drives off to a pub called The Hut in Phibsboro, which parallels the route of the funeral procession to Glasnevin in Ulysses, but the reference to ghosts is a most explicit reference to 'The Dead':

> A spent coal slips in the grate with a whispering 'chink'.
> Here come the dead.
> They hunker round the walls and edge towards the last heat of the fire: Nugent's sister Lizzie; his mother, who does not like being dead at all. Nugent's ghosts twitter soft and unassuaged, while Ada's make no sound at all.
> Why is that?
> She is an orphan. Of course.[60]

In 'The Dead', the sweet sadness of ballads and songs evokes desolating memory and the loss of love in the past becomes inextricable from the destruction of love in the present. In that case, the moment of epiphany is a moment of communion with the dead, not recovery of life as in The Gathering. In the century between Joyce's and Enright's narratives of the burdens of memory and knowledge, the resurgence of traumatic memory has become a fetish of Irish cultural practice and commentary. The construction of familial relations as the capillary network of tragic consequence has become a defining feature of Irish drama and fiction. Very often the beautiful narrative edifices built on recovery of memory obscure the ongoing realities of those whose memory of the terrible past is recuperated into a cultural trope. This location of events in living memory in an incomprehensibly remote past is perhaps an understandable form of disavowal given the horrific nature of the abuse of children, but it is also a politically expedient one. The cultural agonizing around the Ryan Report[61] has not been translated in Ireland into, for example, the practical, necessary, expensive and urgent business of improving services and protection for children in the present (unaccompanied minors are routinely misplaced by the care system, their fate outside the narrative of an Ireland that has left the callous past behind). In effect, the symbolic confrontation of past abuse displaces the necessity of doing anything about it in the present. Butler's comments that it is 'a struggle to make certain kinds of lost life publicly grievable' resonant powerfully with the discovery in 2010 that the Irish Health Service Executive did not record the numbers of children who died in its 'care', even in the twenty-first century. In this context, the past really is in the present tense.

In Enright's work the relationship between the past and present is unstable, but it is not simply that the past trauma interrupts the present and must be put in its proper place, recuperated into a linear narrative of past and present, cause and effect. In The Gathering nothing is more suspect than closure. It is opening up new stories, not concluding them, that makes it possible to go on into the future. It is significant that, as in 'My Little Sister', temporal distortion is a key technique and experience in The Gathering. The distant past can be in the present tense: 'Here is my grandfather, Charley Spillane, driving up O'Connell St to his future wife in the Belvedere Hotel.'[62] The Gathering both uses and critiques the structure of psychological narrative and the technique of finding causes in memory and resolving the effects of past trauma. It also asks political questions about the way in which the recovery of memory substitutes for engagement with its consequences in the present. In contrast to the Irish narratives which keep abuse narratives resolutely in the past, The Gathering forces us to confront both the suffering boy and the bitter ruined addict, to complicate our identifications and challenge our sympathies, to make the process of acknowledgement of the past as difficult as it needs to be if it is to be more than a new form of denial. In Hegel's formulation, influential on Lacan and Irigaray, Antigone is the servant of history, who loyally fulfils the role of translating the dead into the national past. National identities are very much part of the fabric of 'The Dead', but the relationship between the living and the dead generation is not imagined as the terrible abstraction of the nation, but in the embodied intimacies of social relationships. Loyal to those the nation cannot abstract – its others, the forgotten dead in the unmarked graves, the drowned brother, the mad uncle – Veronica proposes a radical continuity. Seeing her brother in his son, she coalesces the narrative distortions of memory and time into nature's own temporal doubling, the continuity of eternal recurrence and eternal difference that begins again with the narrator's possible pregnancy at the novel's end. The Gathering's ending offers more than a moment of epiphany as the narrator falls back to an earth which cannot contain her.[63] 'In the 80s and 90s, people talking on the radio about abuse were not just breaking a silence, they were actually forming new words', Enright says. 'It's not just that they were articulating something that could not be said out loud, it was that they didn't even have the words in their minds.'[64] Veronica understands that without that public discourse, her private revelation could not have occurred:

> Over the next twenty years, the world around us changed and I remembered Mr Nugent. But I would never have made that shift on my own – if I hadn't been listening to the radio and reading the paper, and hearing about what went on in schools and churches and in people's homes. It went on slap-bang in front of me and still I did not realise it. And for this, I am very sorry too.[65]

Being sorry is, of course, not enough. The question posed by Enright's narrative is whether having found the words, the reality can be changed. The Gathering negotiates between the demands of the dead for truth and the desire of the living 'to be able to live', between the desires of Antigone and Ismene. It is an uncannily hopeful novel, which ends convincingly with a future.

Enright's mourning narrators engage in complex negotiations between memory, truths, and living which end inconclusively, as they should. If 'My Little Sister' rehearses the polarized relationship of Ismene and Antigone, giving voice to the bewildered ordinariness of the former, the uncertain narrator of The Gathering fuses the potentialities of the tragic daughters of Oedipus. Antigone rejects Creon and the state he rules. Ismene tries to negotiate between their rival absolutes. For all her declared weakness in Sophocles' original text, Ismene becomes not just a speaking subject, but also a political one. When Creon asks her, 'wilt thou also confess thy part in this burial, or wilt thou forswear all knowledge of it?', she replies, 'I have done the deed, – if she allows my claim, – and share the burden of the charge.' Antigone will not allow this false claim, despising her sister as 'a friend in words' not deeds. Ismene lies and it is not cynical to say that this is what makes this woman of words political. She pleads for clemency not for herself but for her sister, attempting to deploy an emotional register equally unacceptable to Antigone and Creon, whom she asks, 'wilt thou slay the betrothed of thine own son?' Creon's inability to respond in that register leads him to the fate to which he condemned Antigone: his 'life is but as death'. Her position – initially fearful but moved to defiance by cruelty, torn between loyalty and wit, attempting to appeal to the humanity of the powerful – is not heroic and it does not prevail against a dictator. It is nonetheless socially and psychologically viable, unlike that of Creon or Antigone, and it is capable of change. The mourning sister in 'My Little Sister' reaches the point where Ismene realizes that life 'bereft' of Antigone – and what she represents – is an unreasonable burden.[66] In *The Gathering*, she moves beyond it.

NOTES

1. All *Antigone* references are to the MIT Internet Classics Archive (http://classics. mit.edu/Sophocles/antigone.html) for ease of reference. Sophocles, *Antigone*, trans. R.C. Jebb, *MIT Internet Classics Archive*, MIT, accessed 1 July 2010.
2. J. Butler, 'Antigone's Claim: A Conversation with Judith Butler', an interview by P. Antonello and R. Farnetti, *Theory & Event* 12, 1 (2009), *Project Muse*, http://muse. jhu.edu.eproxy.ucd.ie/journals/theory_and_event/v012/12.1.antonello.html, accessed 1 July 2010. Butler discusses her books on Antigone in *Antigone's Claim: Kinship between Life and Death* (New York: Columbia University Press, 2000), and the aftermath of the September 11th attacks in *Precarious Lives: The Power of Mourning and*

Violence (London and New York: Verso, 2004).

3. A. Enright, *The Gathering* (London: Jonathan Cape, 2007) and *Taking Pictures* (London: Jonathan Cape, 2008). 'My Little Sister' was originally published as 'Little Sister' in *Granta 75: Brief Encounters* (2001).

4. Butler, 'Antigone's Claim: A Conversation'.

5. Ibid.

6. J. Kristeva, 'The True-Real', in *The Kristeva Reader*, ed. T. Moi (Oxford: Blackwell: 1986), pp.214–37.

7. J.F. Lyotard, *The Postmodern Condition: A Report on Knowledge*, trans. G. Bennington and B. Massumi (Manchester: Manchester University Press, 1984), p.81.

8. Enright, *The Gathering*, p.260.

9. Ibid., p.1.

10. Ibid., p.132.

11. Ibid.

12. Ibid., p.153.

13. Ibid., pp.36–7.

14. M. Spark, *The Hothouse by the East River* (London: Macmillan, 1973), p.48.

15. Enright, *The Gathering*, p.148.

16. Ibid., p.41.

17. Enright, 'My Little Sister', in *Taking Pictures*, p.61.

18. Enright, *The Gathering*, p.1.

19. Enright quoted in S. Rustin, 'What Women Want', *Guardian*, 15 March 2008.

20. Ibid.

21. Lyotard, *The Postmodern Condition*, p.81.

22. Enright, 'My Little Sister', in *Taking Pictures*, p.55.

23. Ibid., p.63.

24. Ibid., p.55.

25. Ibid., p.62.

26. Ibid., pp.55–6.

27. Ibid., p.57.

28. Ibid., p.60.

29. Ibid., p.59.

30. Ibid., p.62.

31. Ibid., p.63.

32. Ibid.

33. S. Freud, *The Uncanny*, trans. D. McLintock and H. Haughton (London: Penguin, 2003), p.124.

34. Enright, *The Gathering*, p.42.

35. Enright, 'My Little Sister', in *Taking Pictures*, p.63.

36. S. Žižek, *Looking Awry: An Introduction to Jacques Lacan Through Popular Culture* (Cambridge,

MA: MIT Press, 1992), p.53.

37. Enright, 'My Little Sister', in Taking Pictures, pp.64–5.

38. Ibid., p.61.

39. Enright, The Gathering, pp.172–3.

40. Ibid., p.36.

41. Ibid., p.42.

42. Ibid., p.182.

43. A. Enright, 'Anne Enright Reading from her Novel', Boston College Irish Seminar, Boston College Front Row, Boston College, 27 September 2007, http://frontrow. bc.edu/program/enright/, accessed 1 July 2010.

44. Enright, The Gathering, pp.184–5.

45. Ibid., p.215.

46. Ibid., p.245.

47. Ibid., p.246.

48. For commentary on this debate, see, for example, M. de Kesel, Eros and Ethics: Reading Jacques Lacan's Seminar VII, trans. Sigi Jottkandt (New York: State University of New York Press, 2009); I. Parker, Slavoj Zizek: A Critical Introduction (London: Pluto Press, 2004); Y. Stavrakakis, 'The Lure of Antigone: Aporias of an Ethics of the Political', Umbr(a), 1 (2003), pp.117–29.

49. R. Grigg, Lacan, Language, and Philosophy (New York: State University of New York Press, 2008), p.129.

50. Enright, The Gathering, p.42.

51. Ibid., p.260.

52. Ibid., p.56.

53. Ibid., p.261.

54. Ibid., p.260.

55. Ibid., p.156.

56. Ibid., p.160.

57. Ibid.

58. Ibid., p.161.

59. See J. Joyce, Dubliners (Oxford: Oxford University, 2008).

60. Enright, The Gathering, p.32.

61. The Ryan Report, published in 2009, is the findings of the Commission to Inquire into Child Abuse, which gives an account of the extensive and systematic abuse of children in Irish state institutions from 1936 onwards. The report can be accessed at http://www.childabusecommission.ie/.

62. Ibid., p.30.

63. In this regard the ending of Enright's novel has interesting parallels with E. Ní Dhuibhne's Fox, Swallow, Scarecrow (Belfast: Blackstaff Press, 2007), which also appropriates a tragic heroine and then reverses her tragic ending into a new

beginning.

64. Enright quoted in S. Rustin, 'What Women Want'.

65. Enright, *The Gathering*, pp.172–3.

66. When Creon admonishes her that she 'hath newly shown herself foolish' in her loyalty to her sister, Ismene replies, 'such reason as nature may have given abides not with the unfortunate, but goes astray ... What life could I endure, without her presence?'

CHAPTER TEN

What Am I Like?: Writing the Body and the Self

MATTHEW RYAN

A FLOATING ISLAND

Anne Enright has described early twenty-first-century Ireland as a floating island, like Jonathan Swift's Laputa.[1] Introducing a series of photographs of Irish life in the 2000s, Enright refers to the property-price boom and the wealth differential it has produced, making home-ownership increasingly inaccessible. This other, wealthy Ireland hovers as aspiration, prompting Irish parents to work and worry for their children in order to boost them onto this market-levitated land, while 'so many are left down below'.[2] It is an evocative image from the last days of the Celtic Tiger, a domestic market buoyed by transnational capital at its inflated extreme, before the same forces brought the economic crash.[3] The inhabitants of Laputa, it should be recalled, were preoccupied with a technological modernity and prone to a way of life abstracted from the immediate and material concerns of the surface world. In this, Swift's allegory fits the present. The globalization of finance markets brought wealth to some in Ireland, transforming them into 'a nation of small-time landlords', as Enright puts it, 'buying flats and houses in Budapest and Manchester, Orlando and Shanghai'.[4] This economic globalization is a particularly powerful instance of a form of life that abstracts the self from place, from immediate community and even from the individual body itself.

Traces of this social form appear in Enright's fiction and identifying them is the main task of this essay. Before proceeding to that analysis, however, I note not only the aptness of the Laputa analogy, but also Enright's ambivalence about this new form of life. She is alive to both the potential and pitfalls of global Ireland; home to 'tall young people with good skin' but also containing 'many who have been left behind'.[5] While Enright has misgivings about the exacerbation of social inequality in a globalized Ireland, certain designations of 'Irishness' might be abandoned gladly. Wry jibes at Irish stereotypes are common in her work, such as the Irish woman who castigates her Irish-American lover: 'can we, from now, for ever, forget the froth on the milk and the weather in my fucking hair?'[6] The Ireland of the 2000s, which Enright sketches, had taken flight not just from a depressed economy, but also from the hopes, assumptions and, indeed, stereotypes associated with Irish nationalism. As such, Colm Tóibín has celebrated Enright's rendering of a fictive Dublin that is finally 'post-national'.[7] While conceding this description of the way her fiction elaborates the liberation from received designations of gender and sexuality in particular, I want to also consider the obverse of that new freedom, the disorientation of the self and alienation from community. Boon and burden are twinned in Enright's fiction, often around sex and madness. So the trajectory away from an exhausted idea of the nation is not necessarily an escape into a generous global space. There is a tension in Enright's work: certain forces, which establish abstracted social relations that extend beyond the local community and which shift the configurations of self toward disembodiment, are set against an effort to emplace and embody those relations in localized contexts. In Enright's writing, the self is constituted in this tension. Specifically this manifests in the pull between the abstracting effect of writing itself and the representation of material experiences such as sex or death.

A consideration of a recent Enright short story, 'Green', will help to introduce this set of themes and formal concerns.[8] The story is brief, a snapshot of the life of an unnamed Irish woman who has returned to the rural village of her birth and set up an organic farm. The occasion of the story is the woman's resentful, but acquiescent, dealings with Gertie, a former school acquaintance who 'never did leave the town' and who now runs its only restaurant.[9] The farm has prospered without local support – 'they eat my *cime de rapa* ... in effing London town' – but a request from Gertie for a special order sends the woman into a rage against the smallness of the place.[10] As I suggested, this story carries an ambivalence about both the freedom offered in the escape from home and the apparent satisfying stability of return. Despite the mirror-imaging of the two women, a straightforward reading of cosmopolitanism over parochialism is not adequate. Indeed, Jeanette Shumaker has argued that Enright's use of 'uncanny doubles' is a refusal of any settled understanding of self. It, instead, points to the 'impossibility of stabilizing identity or answering ontological questions'.[11] This is true of this particular story also, with the first-person narrator unable to present a sufficiently-formed identity to counter the perceived challenge of Gertie's established position as the town's petit bourgeois.

The tension is, however, a subtle one. At first glance, the story offers an ideal image of life in the new Ireland, marked by only a small annoyance for the narrator. Rural life and agricultural production (tillage rather than pasture, so important to the nationalist pieties of the early twentieth century) is made over in the image of the 'glocal'.[12] The cosmopolitan techniques of organic farming are brought to the Irish countryside. There is a non-gender-specific division of labour between husband and wife in the farm work. Also, the narrator maintains a critically reflexive approach to the patterns of village life and her place within them. In all there seems a synthetic reworking of place and of home, made possible by the narrator's leaving and return and her continued preparedness to criticize the received conventions of that society. The re-working of home, however, is rendered most directly through images of soil. After recounting the way she 'shook the dust of that damn town off my feet' the narrator tells of making the soil productive and 'organic' by adding loads of especially brought-in manure, transforming the clay into a fine tilth: 'Muck into gold'.[13] In itself, soil imagery might not be sufficient to support a national-allegorical reading, even though it is, of course, a central trope in nationalist representations of place.[14] Yet, the polysemic title of the story, 'Green', licences investigation in this direction. Also, Enright's recent work has been shown to be structured, to a significant degree, by an allegorical mode.[15] So we might then proceed to a reading of the farm as an idyll of globalized Ireland – even a fantasy – prospering in specialized transnational trade; enmeshed with small-scale community; connected with the specificity of place while incorporating the new; balancing manual and intellectual labour. It is not, however, quite a fantasy of arrival at *being* or transcendence of *becoming*. The insufficient self, who cannot quite confront the town (in the figure of Gertie), finally enters into the area of lack that seems to power a motivating desire. The story concludes with the narrator between waking and sleep, in the early morning, her mind turning over a vision of the farm and herself, the light outside 'undecided'. She returns to a dream of hydroponics:

> A dream I have of water, an infinity of lettuce, row upon row of the stuff, coming out of a lake smooth as glass, so all you see is the lettuce and the reflection of the lettuce. And maybe, as I fall asleep, me also, floating in there, utterly still amidst the green.[16]

The transformed soil is, in the dream, done away with altogether and the self made into a floating island: frictionless, untethered and finally arrived at the still-point of a radically autonomous being. Rather than a vision of Ireland as an achieved *glocality*, this is a fantastic anticipation of transcendence of locality, a dream of placelessness. It is the unrealized life of the unmoored self; the Laputa-like self as fancy, lifted out from the designations of place. The abstraction from soil here is fantastically figured in the technology of hydroponics.

'Green' presents, in a remarkably condensed and subtle rendering, the ontological problem of constituting the self within social formations that tend to be dominated by techno-mediation and which pull the self toward forms of disembodiment. These are the social conditions of globalization. Under these conditions, the self of proximate or face-to-face relations remains, but it is increasingly channelled towards deterritorialized and disembodied modes of composition. These modes are usually recognized in the technologies of communications, information or transport, but in Enright's story they are brought to the soil or territory itself and, of course, to the body. Here, I am referring to globalization as a set of processes that exceeds the neoliberal extension of finance capital or commodity markets. This is globalization as a social or cultural phenomenon which conditions 'the practices and experience in which people symbolically construct meaning'.[17]

The particular form, which I am drawing out from Enright's work, is the dominance of the intellectual form of life as a mode though which the self integrates into 'world-space'.[18] By this I do not mean globalization transforms everyone into a traditional intellectual of the kind that might be found in the university. Rather, that the characteristic patterns of the intellectual form of life are generalized as modes of social integration. Typically, entering into the intellectual form of life has been achieved via abstracting modes, of which the key example is writing. Through writing, the intellectual is put into relation with absent others across time and space. With the proliferation of print cultures (from the book to the Internet), this abstracted social domain of the intellectual has become a dominant form for social relations. Intellectual-type social integration has then extended beyond that particular group and been generalized across the social whole. Its characteristics can be summarized as: technological mediation of social relations; the process of 'lifting out' or defamiliarization of received social context; and an associated ideology of autonomy in the formation of the self. Regarding the first of these, the key form of tech-nological mediation of the intellectual form is writing and print.[19] 'Lifting out' is then the process by which an individual assumes a reflexive posi-tion that enables a conceptually-distanced consideration of self and society. More concrete experience of social interaction is, in this process, set within a wider frame so that it comes to be seen as just one form among many. Mobility and fluidity are traits that emerge from such a formation of the self and they are a ready fit with the requirements of a globalized labour or property market. Enright's work, I argue, dramatizes the tension between this fluid formation and a more material social experience of the body and place. And in her own reflexive turn, Enright sets this tension in relation to the abstracting or 'lifting' effects of writing itself.

Within Ireland, the shift toward such a globally conditioned culture and reconfigured self has been articulated in terms of a nationalist/post-nation-alist division. For reasons of space, it is not possible to set out here a full account of post-nationalism. However an outline of the idea and its 'blurred provenance'[20] can be seen variously in revision of national historiography; Southern reactions against violence in the North; revelations of Fianna Fáil's fall from grace into corruption; and the dissipation of the moral authority of the Catholic church through child abuse and sexual scandals.[21] These relatively recent crises in the authority of nationalist social formations have, in turn, followed from a fundamental criticism that the national project of decolonization and independence had been unable to achieve its own sovereignty goals. The 'great nationalist push', as Conor McCarthy describes it, had in the course of the economic liberalization programme of Sean Lemass and T.K. Whitaker, been 'exposed as a failure, as destructive and even a sham'.[22] By the time of the Good Friday Agreement in Northern Ireland in 1998,[23] Fintan O'Toole was able to claim that the transnational political structures set in place by the Agreement were merely a case of the polity catching up with the social. Across the island, according to O'Toole, people were already constructing their identities in a fluid and postnational manner, replacing 'fixed visions of the future with the pleasures of contingency'.[24]

In fiction, however, it would seem that the trace of the nation is incorporated – rather than merely transcended – even where an evident criticism of nationalism is in play. Irish writers such as Desmond Hogan, Mary Morrissy, Colm Tóibín and, indeed, Anne Enright have been able to overturn many of those restrictive images of Irishness which have been associated with nationalist imaginings. Yet, at the same time, these writers mark out the absence left when the national frame is withdrawn from the formation of identity. It is not a nostalgic longing for the nation itself, but an indication of the not-yet-replaced formal capacity to combine abstract and material sociality; to place the self in a matrix of social integration that extends from the 'imagined community' of strangers to the sense of belonging in locality and small-scale community. In spite of the many criticisms that can be made of nationalist ideology, the nation as a form has been extraordinarily successful in drawing together differing levels of social experience, from embodied identification of the self to connection with unseen others in the territory. It is with this integrative capacity of the nation, or its absence, that post-nationalism must contend. The nation, as it has been understood, may be losing its capacity to make identity and community cohere, but the intellectual form of life, in its current nexus with the global economy, appears to be an insufficient replacement. Tóibín notes the persistence of violence and darkness in recent Irish writing, despite it having been produced in a context of relative economic 'brightness'. He alludes to a 'strange and confused ideology' lying behind phenomena like property-price booms and increases in luxury car sales.[25] Now that the promise of globalization has turned to peril for Ireland, it appears the economy has caught up with those persistent misgivings coded in Irish culture. The dream of transcendence, of a self constituted through disembodiment or placeless-ness, is haunted by the absence of those other, emplaced and embodied, levels of social experience.

Questions of embodiment appear as the key way in which Enright's fiction manifests this problem of social integration and the constitution of the self. For example, in her examination of The Pleasure of Eliza Lynch, Enright's third novel, Patricia Coughlan notes the centrality of food as a primary narrative image.[26] Coughlan goes on to relate this set of images to a broader vision in Enright's work which 'insists on the irreducibility of the body'.[27] For Coughlan the historical and political concerns of the novel, regarding the tumult of mid-nineteenth-century Paraguay at war, 'jostle for attention with the more immediate life of the embodied self'.[28] Enright does not relinquish the larger 'historiographic' themes, Coughlan observes, rather she 'forces them to accommodate and contend with that embodied life'.[29] In this Enright is also bringing manifestations of power and politics to the particularity of women's embodiment which, for Eliza Lynch, means the use of her sexuality by herself and others.[30] Eliza's embodiment of her historical circumstance is the familiar bind for women under patriarchy, to enter the discourse of gendered power through the particular 'powerless power' of her sexuality.[31] For Enright, writing about sex is also a reappropriation of the image of the female sexualized body from the dominant depictions in masculine writing. In an interview she complains that men have often written of sex 'as if it's the worst thing that could ever happen to anyone', imbuing their work with 'puritanical disgust and misogyny'.[32] Writing sex, then, is itself a process of bringing the body to a 'new space', quite apart from the depiction of the 'experience' of particular characters.[33]

In The Pleasure of Eliza Lynch, the forced encounter between history and the body is enacted through various metaphorical implications of food with sensuous pleasure, or with sustenance, or with death, or with the body itself as meat. The overarching historical circumstances of war and the exercise of power are brought to the immediacy of the body through the allusive fecundity of food imagery and its ready association with sexuality. So, if I can expand on Coughlan's reading, not only does Enright put the historical and the particular in tension, she also holds the material and the abstract in union by drawing the substantial experiences of the body into the abstracted world of writing. As Penelope Fitzgerald captured it, in Enright's writing, 'metaphors often become the things they stand for'.[34] This capacity to run across the abstract and material divide is a general trait of Enright's work, even where she is not dealing with historical figures or events. It means that Enright's writing, its content and its structure, is especially illustrative of the precarious position of the self that is constituted in the tension between abstract and material sociality, the generalized intellectual form of life which is characteristic of the present global moment.

This mode of writing-in-tension was established by Enright in her first novel, The Wig My Father Wore. There, the body is rendered primarily through images of sex and reproduction, which are placed in relation with the technologies of television production and reception. The novel is set in Dublin in the early 1990s. Grace (or Grainne), the first-person narrator, works as a producer on a dating game-show, LoveQuiz. The narrative is structured around Grace's relationship with Stephen, an angel who arrives at her door 'with an ordinary face on him' who, 'with broad comments' about her 'fertility', moves into Grace's house.[35] The question of rendering the materiality of the body is then complicated by the presence of the semi-embodied Stephen and the disembodied interaction enabled by television. In the novel, this is played out through various inversions and mergers of body and image, as we see in an early description of the television production office:

> People run around like it was a labour ward for the blind. They shout to make themselves clear, they whisper that the baby has no eyes. The phones are ringing, the vases stand empty, a male pin-up is stuck to the filing cabinet, ripped at the waist. In the corner is the hiss of an empty television, switched on, with nothing coming through. It is not simple.[36]

Television production is paralleled with human reproduction but the imperfect fit of the simile is also emphasized. The dating programme, in particular, draws out the contradictions. The face-to-face concerns of LoveQuiz – love and sex – are actually enacted at a distance and experienced through image. Despite the effort to 'keep it wet', television is essentially a mode of disembodied social interaction.[37] Television – like the telephone, or more like the computer and Internet in its entrenchment in the realm of simulacra – draws its affective power from the simulation of face-to-face interaction even as it enacts an altogether more abstracted social exchange.

Suspending the contradiction between these modes of interaction is a general requirement of living in a mediatized society, yet in The Wig their routine conflation is defamiliarized through dementia, ethereal transcendence and formal devices. In madness, escape and art, the contradictions become apparent. The novel offers three key examples: the manner in which Grace's father watches television; Stephen's disappearance in broadcast; and the novel's narrative structure. Regarding the first of these, the stroke-affected mind of Grace's father – his life on the 'wrong side of the mirror'[38] – licenses a number of conflations that bear out hidden incongruities. He sees the telephone and the television as the same and maintains a direct social engagement with television programmes. He sings along, converses and plays word games with the television as though it were a person. In effect, he steps over the contradiction of the distanced interaction which, for others, must be continuously suspended. This delusion of full presence is the final phase of a process of folding the body into the image of the body, which started with the simultaneous arrival of the eponymous wig and the family's first television set. The father's collapse of these levels into each other is a kind of negative example of living with the tensions of abstract and material sociality. In his condition, the complexity of the social situation is lost along with the distinction between types of social relations. He believes them all of a kind, making the relation with television images qualitatively the same as those with his family. This general reduction of the social to the level of material, proximate and local forms is homologous with a reactionary nationalism that draws everything into a parochial enclosure. The father's example provides one pole in the array of possible responses to the increased abstraction of social relations, here manifest in the disembodied social forms offered in television.

Stephen's disappearance, on the other hand, marks the opposite extreme. He materializes in the course of his relationship with Grace. He is fleshed out at her expense. Grace's body becomes radically amorphous: she loses a nipple, she guards her belly button, her flesh is made so soft she is 'afraid it might tear'.[39] Their sexual exchange takes the form of a contrary motion in embodiment. Yet, Stephen's somatic stabilization is finally dissipated in television. It is as though he acquires only enough body to allow him to become image. Appearing as a contestant on *LoveQuiz*, Stephen disappears during a live transmission. He 'hits the heart of the nation',[40] his signal-self spread across the island:

> It dropped without a sigh into a sitting room in Granard, where a woman was bathing a baby, into a parlour in Carrigaholt where a man left his dishes out in the rain, into a lounge in Abbeyleix where it was still too early for a drink. And everywhere was the slight, heavy smell of lilies.[41]

Stephen's televised signal is resonant with the role of the newspaper as described in Benedict Anderson's famous account of the 'imagined community' of the nation; they are both experienced simultaneously across the territory.[42] The linking of unseen others in a sense of simultaneous movement is the characteristic capacity of the newspaper which, Anderson points out, is essential for a conceptualization of the nation. In this way, print media have provided a key form of abstract social integration for the nation. Yet this is also a form of integration that has been augmented by communication technologies, which now extend its scope beyond the national territory. So a key social form that allowed the nation to be thought and lived is also a means for transcending the nation's integrative limits. Stephen's example, it would seem, belongs to this latter phase. His material being, gained through the face-to-face relation of love, is lost in this furthest extension of social relations. He is not bound to the territory or to local embodied relations. Rather his final and complete disembodiment makes him fully 'angelic', matching the sense of the term as used by Frantz Fanon when he described the dangers for post-colonial intellectuals in reconstituting identity through a 'universal perspective'.[43] There is a tendency, according to Fanon, for them to become, 'individuals without an anchorage, without borders, colorless, stateless, rootless, a body of angels'.[44] Here Fanon describes not only a post-colonial condition, but a characteristic of the intellectual form of life more generally; to shift from individuality toward a belief in the radical autonomy of the self and solipsistic self-authorship.

Enright has described *The Wig My Father Wore* as a 'bildungsroman, in reverse', meaning, 'the main character becomes more innocent as the book progresses'.[45] In the course of the narrative Grace negotiates the poles of response, as represented by her father and Stephen, synthesizing a position which avoids the contradictions inherent in each. She does not reduce abstracted social relations to material, nor does she surrender the body to its image. Rather she holds these levels of social interchange in tension. This is evident in the arrival at 'innocence' which concludes the novel. As in the short story 'Green', *The Wig My Father Wore* concludes with a dream. Grace dreams of cycling towards Stephen, who stands 'at the top of the hill with clouds behind him'. She rides along a bog road, 'between the sky and the bog' leaving a trail of milk spilling from a pierced bottle onto 'the road between Furnace and Lettermaghera'.[46] It is tempting to read certainty and simplification in this conclusion; that Grace is return-ing to the stability of place, calling out the 'Irishness' of the bog, the specificity of home in Furnace and Lettermaghera. She is, however, suspended in this dream-moment 'between' all these elements.[47] If the *Bildungsroman* is, among other things, a story of self-authorship in which the individual constitutes a self through experience of the world, then *The Wig*, to a large degree, remains true to the form. In the course of the novel, Grace enters into possible figurations of the self, yet the narrative trajectory is thwarted or denied its formal completion by not settling the question of the self at its conclusion. The 'innocence' of the narrative lies in its open-ended character, in its projection of the work of the *Bildungsroman* into a future beyond the confines of the narrative.

Indeed, the story of the self appears to be taken up in another form, ready to be written past the conclusion. Grace is pregnant. So a particular future is forming in bodily terms that have not, to this point, been artic-ulated in the novel. This pregnancy not only anticipates an as yet untried figure of the self for Grace, but also sets a pattern for her sister-characters in Enright's three subsequent novels. Pregnancy, as a beginning/end-point or as a state of being, plays a central part in all four novels. We get some insight into this centrality from Enright herself in a short non-fiction article, 'My Milk', published five years after The Wig.[48] She sets out her view of pregnancy, birth and lactation as extra-linguistic bodily experiences that in fact provide the ground for narrative:

> I have found a place before stories start. Or the precise place where stories start. How else can I explain the shift from language that has happened in my brain? This is why mothers do not write, because motherhood happens in the body, as much as the mind.[49]

The effort to write the self from the body, to grapple with the inherent tendency of writing to abstract away from the body, to traverse this gap while not doing away with it in some transcendental manoeuvre or mistaking it for pure material experience; this network of tensions can be said to be a general characteristic of Enright's work. It is also a description of Grace's state at the end of the novel. To move across these modes of experience, it seems, she has taken a cue from Hélène Cixous and is to start this other narrative of the self by writing it in milk.[50] Rather than a Bildungsroman in reverse, The Wig might then be understood as a form of Künstlerroman in which Grace arrives at the place where she can start her story; the body of work which is her self.

While the image of Grace writing herself out of the novel in milk – finding a path between hyper-abstraction and reductive materialism – is one of hope, the effort to reconcile the body with its image, and indeed with writing, is fraught with potential alienation. The resonance of two moments, from The Wig and What are You Like?, illustrates Enright's on going concern with this other side of embodied self-authorship. The first is a recollection from Grace's adolescence: shutting herself in the bathroom after a family argument, Grace cuts herself:

> I looked at my eyes in the mirror and had the feeling, those eyes could see. I looked at the blood in the mirror and was afraid the glass itself might bleed. So I put some blood on the mirror, a smear of solid red. It separated us out. I thought, Now the blood is in the room.[51]

In What Are You Like?, the scene of self-harm is prompted by Maria finding, in her lover's bag, a photograph of a girl who appears to be her 15-year-old self. Maria does not know of her twin sister, Rose, from whom she was separated at birth. She considers the photograph in a state of existential confusion: 'Maria looked at her and wanted to laugh. She had always felt like someone else. She had always felt like the wrong girl.'[52] Later that evening, 'She tested the knife above her ankle and after the cut, … she could feel everything, even the pain'.[53] Then, more than one hundred pages later, in the midst of Rose's extended fantasy of her neighbour's suicide, Maria's own suicide-attempt is inserted:

> The mirror is flat and cool against her skin. Maria can see the sheet of glass between the real blood and the reflected blood. It is very thick. It is very clean and calm. She is trying to open the bottle with her teeth. She looks into her own eyes. 'Hello.'[54]

These echoed scenes, across the novel and between the novels, have the characters writing in blood to reconcile or differentiate the 'uncanny double', the unknown twin, the disturbingly autonomous mirror-self. They resonate with each other in their portrayal of the failure to bring body and self together within the full range of social integration. Rather than providing a meaning-giving frame, the impermeable mirror stands between the numbed body and the image of suffering. Here self-harm becomes a type of solipsistic aesthetics in which writing on the body/writing on the mirror amounts to communication with only the bifurcated self. Indeed, this hermetic aesthetic is emphasized in the way Rose's part of the narrative takes the form of a thwarted *Künstlerroman*. She gives up her plan to be a concert pianist, finding herself unable to bring emotion to her over-technical playing, unable to let herself 'fall' into the 'bliss' of inhabiting a complicated piece of music. Instead she abandons the piano after a final mistake-strewn Mozart Sonata: 'One mistake after the other, until she felt like she was beating herself up.'[55] A pitfall of self-authorship that emerges from these repeated images of self-harm is the danger of the enclosed, wholly self-referential formation. These characters back themselves into a flattened or one-dimensional constitution of the self when confronted with an inadequate social circumstance, one which cannot provide the range of means for social integration. When restricted to a single level of articulation – an aesthetic sensibility, a disembodying technology, the body as pure material – the process of self-formation becomes corrosive. With this warning coded into the bodily/aesthetic imagery, the ethical drive in *What Are You Like?* is oriented toward a constitution of the self in relation to others. The movement of the narrative is then toward this relational self, formed across a number of levels of social integration, that incorporates proximate and distant, material and abstract, social relations.

I want to, finally, draw together two other significant portrayals of writing the self, in the figures of Anna and Veronica, from *What Are You Like?* and *The Gathering* respectively. Anna is the mother of the separated twins. After giving birth in a comatose state she dies from a tumour on the brain. Her death leads the father, Berts, to separate the sisters. Anna's first-person account (from the grave) is contained within a single chapter. The other figure, Veronica, is the first-person narrator of *The Gathering*. She is the grieving sister of Liam, whose suicide initiates the narrative. In differing ways these characters call up the limits of writing the self, even as they insist on the attempt. They are making themselves, we might say, but not under the conditions of their choosing. Anna's posthumous account sets out a waning faith in the capacity of writing to give shape to the alienation within her family, or to articulate her isolation from her husband, or to re-order her increasingly inchoate sense of the world:

> When I was dying, I thought I should write things down, but the words made no sense. I thought that if I could write I would not die, but that made no sense either. There is no story to living and then dying. There is no story to living and having a child, and dying. Not for me. No matter what order I put them in ... I am terrified, here in my grave, by words and what they might want.[56]

Anna's enclosed story of loss and isolation is told through an account of the reification of language – 'words and what they might want' – and the impotency that follows from it: the words 'were just themselves and did not join with anything else'.[57] Here the gothic device of the speaking/ writing dead draws out, in a reflexive manner, the '"unreal" or "antirational" nature of literature itself'.[58] In particular, the project of writing the self is set at odds with itself, recognizing at once its inability to fully articulate the body and the redundancy of it standing as an autonomous, closed sphere. Radical instability of the self and the social world – a characteristic gothic effect – is brought out as a condition for, and effect of, writing itself.

Likewise, Veronica is to write through the 'unreality' of writing. She is troubled throughout the novel by the failure to render the true fibre of the world. As Hedwig Schwall observes, not only is the protagonist of *The Gathering* a writer, she is also called Veronica, 'like the woman who caught the *"vera icon"*, the true image of God's incarnation. Can any other name set a writer a more demanding task?'[59] The documentary task for Enright's Veronica is, indeed, a daunting one: 'to bear witness to an uncertain event'.[60] The novel opens with her statement of intent:

> I would like to write down what happened in my grandmother's house the summer I was eight or nine, but I am not sure if it really did happen ... I think you might call it a crime of the flesh, but the flesh is long fallen away and I am not sure what hurt may linger in the bones.[61]

While the intention is clear, it is enacted with an awareness of the inherent limitations of rendering 'a crime of the flesh' in writing. Even the achievement of the Gospel-Veronica is qualified in the novel: 'He left His face on her tea towel. Or the picture of His face',[62] and Enright's Veronica plainly states her own limitations: 'I am not Veronica'.[63] In the novel it is exactly a *fleshless* reality which is equated with writing: 'I write it down, I lay them out in nice sentences, all my clean, white bones'.[64] So the potential failure to render this 'incarnation' haunts the narrative until an account of 'the crime' itself is attempted, mid-way through the novel. In the midst of intertwined plots, Veronica announces, 'an end to the shifting stories and the waking dreams. It is time to call an end to romance and just say what happened in Ada's house, the year I was eight and Liam was barely nine.'[65] What happened was the sexual abuse of Liam by their grandmother's friend and landlord, Lamb Nugent.[66] This, of course, does not mark 'an end to romance'. The fantastical history of Ada and Nugent, which has run through the first part of the narrative, does break off here, but it is replaced by other speculative gestures, such as Veronica's visualization of her own abuse at the hands of Nugent.[67] She quickly dismisses this scenario as unlikely.[68] 'Romance', then, does not quite write itself into verisimilitude. Instead, the narrative moves more directly toward the contemporary gathering of Veronica's siblings for Liam's funeral and wake. This temporal shift also marks a final modification in Veronica's avowed task: 'I know what I have to do – even though it is too late for the truth, I will tell the truth. I will get hold of Ernest [another brother] and tell him what happened to Liam at Broadstone.'[69] Significantly, this is to be a *spoken* truth rather than a *written* one. The misgivings about constituting a personal narrative through writing finally coalesce into the necessity of a face-to-face resolution. And this is projected into a space beyond the scope of the novel. This insistence on material presence is the final refrain of the novel, as Veronica prepares to return to her estranged husband and daughters: 'I have been falling into my own life, for months. And I am about to hit it now.'[70]

In her introduction to Kate O'Brien's novel *As Music and Splendour*, Enright describes the present difficulty for a contemporary writer 'discussing human intimacy': 'Anything buried or half hidden or forbidden can be found, explicit and open and wrapped in carry-out latex, on the Internet. This blight of the obvious infects, not just the secrets in a novel, but the way in which those secrets are revealed.'[71] One solution to the 'blight of the obvious', or perhaps a reconfiguration of the problem of revelation, can be seen in the way *The Gathering* approaches its hidden, bodily crime. To this end, the romance of an imagined sexual history between Ada and Nugent, frustrated by Catholic propriety, is one narrative device. The use of Biblical allegory is another. Yet another, which I have outlined here, is the examination of the three-way relation between writing, the body and the reconfiguration of the self in relation to others. This takes Enright's work of revelation beyond the narrative itself and even beyond the contemporary Irish context of re-examining the real history of child abuse. It, however, does not mean Enright's novel slips into a self-referential formal enclosure, of the writing-on-writing-on-the-body kind. *The Gathering*, like Enright's previous novels, is a depiction, and at another level an enactment, of the process of reconstituting the self in embodied relations through an abstracting mode of integration. In this, it reveals the current predicament of self-constitution that is immediately relevant to a globalizing, and would-be post-national, Ireland.

It is evident that Enright's writing works from the 'irreducibility of the body'. Here I have attempted to bring this somatic insistence into relation with the current tendency for social relations and the self to be constituted in the dominance of disembodiment. Not the least of the means of disembodiment is writing itself. To write the body is an action fraught with contradiction. Enright, however, utilizes this abstracting medium against its own tendencies, drawing attention to both its limits and its potential for re-framing bodily experience. As such, Enright enacts the precarious condition that is common to the intellectual form of life. She depicts the effort to make writing a technology that mediates across levels of social experience, rather than merely allowing writing to enclose the social within a highly abstracted frame. In this writing practice, she provides an analogue of how the intellectual form might properly over-take the nation as a socially integrative frame, if its inherent abstracting tendencies can be counter-balanced with embodied and emplaced social forms. The narrator of 'Green', we recall, dreams of a floating life. As she dreams, outside in the farmyard, a sycamore sucker oozes in a pulpy green mess. She had hacked it down in her sublimated rage against the limits of the town. The tree remains as a spectral presence in her mind; its sucker-ing, subterranean nature also ensuring its actual return. Enright shows how absence continues as a constitutive element of the present.

NOTES

1. A. Enright, 'The 00s: Anne Enright', in *Magnum Ireland*, ed. B. Lardinois and V. Williams (London: Thames & Hudson, 2005), p.226. See J. Swift, *Gulliver's Travels* (New York: Dell Publishing, 1974), pp.185–213. In Part Three of *Gulliver's Travels*, Swift describes the floating island of Laputa and its inhabitants. Laputa is the domain of a ruling class whose life and language is dominated by the abstract forms of mathematics and music: 'the whole compass of their thoughts and mind, being shut up within the two foremen-tioned sciences', p.197.
2. Enright, 'The 00s: Anne Enright', p.226.
3. See A. Enright, 'Sinking by Inches: Anne Enright on Ireland's Recession', *London Review of Books*, 32, 1 (2010), pp.21–2. See also F. O'Toole, *After the Ball* (Dublin: New Island, 2003) and *Ship of Fools* (London: Faber and Faber, 2009).
4. Enright, 'The 00s: Anne Enright', p.226.
5. Ibid., p.227.
6. A. Enright, 'Switzerland', in *Taking Pictures* (London: Jonathan Cape, 2008), p.110.
7. C. Tóibín, 'Introduction', in *The Penguin Book of Irish Fiction*, ed. C. Tóibín (London: Penguin, 1999), p.xxxiii.
8. A. Enright, 'Green', in *Taking Pictures*, pp.115–23.

9. Ibid., p.118.
10. Ibid., p.120.
11. J. Shumaker, 'Uncanny Doubles: The Fiction of Anne Enright', *New Hibernia Review/Iris Éire-annach Nua*, 9, 3 (2005), p.107.
12. See R. Robertson, 'Glocalization: Time-Space and Homogeneity-Heterogeneity', in *Global Modernities*, ed. M. Featherstone, R. Robertson and S. Lash (London and Thousand Oaks, CA: Sage Publications, 1995), pp.25–44.
13. Enright, 'Green', in *Taking Pictures*, pp.118, 121.
14. The work of Colm Tóibín displays a similar re-working of nationalist soil imagery. See M. Ryan, 'Abstract Homes: Deterritorialisation and Reterritorialisation in the Work of Colm Tóibín', *Irish Studies Review*, 16, 1 (2008), pp.19–32. See, also, Seamus Deane, 'National Character and the Character of Nations', in *Strange Country: Modernity and Nationhood in Irish Writing Since 1790* (Oxford: Oxford University Press, 1997), pp.49–99.
15. See H. Schwall, 'Anne Enright, *The Gathering*', *Irish University Review*, 37, 2 (2007), pp.594–5.
16. Enright, 'Green', in *Taking Pictures*, p.123.
17. J. Tomlinson, 'Cultural Globalisation: Placing and Displacing the West', in *Cultural Perspectives on Development*, ed. V. Tucker (London and Portland, OR: Frank Cass, 1997), p.23.
18. See P. James, 'Globalisation and Empires of Mutual Accord', *Arena Magazine*, 85 (2006), p.42. James writes that, 'globalisation is the extension of social practices across world-space where the notion of "world-space" is itself defined in the historically variable terms in which it has been practiced and understood. Globalisation is thus a layered and uneven matrix of processes, changing in its dominant form across history.'
19. See G. Sharp, 'Intellectuals in Transition', *Arena Journal*, 65 (1983), p.86. Sharp outlines the social constitution of the intellectual through print in this way: 'this form of social interchange constitutes the intellectual person in a way which "lifts" that person out of the constraints of more parochial contexts and extends the range of interchange across the boundaries of those contexts. Individuality as set within more parochial contexts is lifted too; qua intellectual, the person experiences himself or herself as a creator of meaning, as having passed on from individuality to autonomy.'
20. C. Graham, *Deconstructing Ireland: Identity Theory Culture* (Edinburgh: Edinburgh University Press, 2001), p.94.
21. See F. O'Toole, *Black Hole Green Card: The Disappearance of Ireland* (Dublin: New Island Books, 1994); and *The Lie of the Land: Irish Identities* (London and New York: Verso, 1997).
22. C. McCarthy, *Modernisation: Crisis and Culture in Ireland 1969–1992* (Dublin: Four Courts Press, 2000), p.33.
23. *Agreement Reached in the Multi-Party Negotiations, Belfast, 10 April 1998* (Dublin: Government Information Services, 1998), otherwise known as the 'Good Friday Agreement'.
24. F. O'Toole, 'Fear of the Future Set Aside as Ireland Embraces its Present', *Irish Times*, 23 May 1998. Terry Eagleton has argued that, as a branch of postmodernism, post-nationalism is prey to occlusions of its own assumptions, such as the essentialist assertion of anti-essentialism. Colin Graham provides an example in Richard

Kearney's post-nationalism. Kearney's position is characterized as unable to disentangle itself from the national form. Criticizing Kearney's teleological nostalgia, which preserves the nation by transcending it – making it a source for 'pluralist identity politics' – Graham asserts, 'Post-nationalism evolves from rather than rejects the nation; but its dependency on the maintenance of the conceptual value of the nation goes unrecognised.' This is a criticism which might be tested against many post-nationalist analyses and theorizations of politics and culture. See T. Eagleton, *Crazy John and the Bishop and Other Essays on Irish Culture* (Cork: Cork University Press and Field Day, 1998), p.324. See, also, Graham, *Deconstructing Ireland*, p.98; R. Kearney, *Postnationalist Ireland: Politics, Culture, Philosophy* (London and New York: Routledge, 1997).

25. C. Tóibín, 'Selling Tara, Buying Florida', *Éire-Ireland*, 43, 1 and 2 (2008), p.25.

26. P. Coughlan, '"Without a blink of her lovely eye": *The Pleasure of Eliza Lynch* and Visionary Scepticism', *Irish University Review: A Journal of Irish Studies*, 35, 2 (2005), p.354.

27. Ibid.

28. Ibid.

29. Ibid.

30. See S. Cahill, '"A Greedy Girl" and a "National Thing": Gender and History in Anne Enright's *The Pleasure of Eliza Lynch*', in *Irish Literature: Feminist Perspectives*, ed. P. Coughlan and T. O'Toole (Dublin: Carysfort Press, 2008), pp.203–22.

31. C. Moloney, 'Re-Imagining Women's History in the Fiction of Éilís Ní Dhuibhne, Anne Enright and Kate O'Riordan', *Postcolonial Text*, 3, 3 (2007), p.10.

32. A. Enright, 'Anne Enright in conversation at the Sydney Writers' Festival', ABC Radio Transcript, 8 June 2008.

33. See A. Enright, 'Anne Enright Interview by Caitriona Moloney', in *Irish Women Speak Out: Voices from the Field*, ed. C. Moloney and H. Thompson (Syracuse, NY: Syracuse University Press, 2003), p.59. Enright does note gendered differences in the experience of sex. She says of *The Wig My Father Wore*: 'Throughout, the book [Wig] contrasts a spiritual/ascetic male idea of love, Catholic in origin, with female sexual love that has not been widely explored in fiction, and which includes pregnancy and children as well as sex.'

34. P. Fitzgerald, 'Bringers of Ill Luck and Bad Weather', *London Review of Books*, 22, 5 (2000), p.8.

35. A. Enright, *The Wig My Father Wore* (London: Jonathan Cape, 1995), p.1.

36. Ibid., p.10.

37. Ibid., p.9.

38. Ibid., p.51.

39. Ibid., p.136.

40. Ibid., p.140.

41. Ibid., p.209.

42. B. Anderson, *Imagined Communities: Reflections on the Origin and Spread of Nationalism* (London: Verso, 1991), pp.35–6.

43. F. Fanon, *The Wretched of the Earth*, trans. R. Philcox (New York: Grove Press, 2004), p.156.

44. Ibid., p.155.

45. Enright, 'Interview by Caitriona Moloney', p.59.
46. Enright, The Wig My Father Wore, p.215.
47. For feminist interpretations of the novel's conclusion, see Elke D'hoker 'Reclaiming Feminine Identities: Anne Enright's The Wig My Father Wore', in Irish Literature: Feminist Perspectives, ed. P. Coughlan and T. O'Toole (Dublin: Carysfort Press, 2008), pp.185–201 and P. Coughlan, 'Irish Literature and Feminism in Postmodernity', Hungarian Journal of English and American Studies, 10, 1–2 (2004), pp.175–202. D'hoker notes Enright's use of magical realist techniques to convey a sense of 'in-between-ness' in The Wig My Father Wore. Of the images of 'return', in the final section of the novel, D'hoker concludes: 'Far from being post-feminist ... The Wig My Father Wore achieves an important form of feminist writing back, which does not shy away from traditional metaphors of femininity but reclaims them from a feminist perspective and translates them into contemporary Irish reality', p.196.
48. A. Enright, 'My Milk', London Review of Books, 22, 19 (2000), pp.34–5.
49. Ibid., p.35.
50. H. Cixous, 'The Laugh of the Medusa', trans. K. Cohen and P. Cohen, in New French Feminisms: An Anthology, ed. E. Marks and I. de Courtivron (Brighton: Harvester, 1981), p.251.
51. Enright, The Wig My Father Wore, p.111.
52. A. Enright, What Are You Like? (London: Jonathan Cape, 2000), p.37.
53. Ibid., p.40.
54. Ibid., p.158.
55. Ibid., p.128.
56. Ibid., p.235.
57. Ibid., pp.244, 246.
58. G. Smyth, The Novel and the Nation: Studies in the New Irish Fiction (London and Chicago, IL: Pluto Press, 1997), p.48.
59. H. Schwall, 'Anne Enright, The Gathering', Irish University Review: A Journal of Irish Studies, 37, 2 (2007), p.594.
60. A. Enright, The Gathering (London: Jonathan Cape, 2007), p.1.
61. Ibid., p.1.
62. Ibid., p.128.
63. Ibid., p.129.
64. Ibid., p.2.
65. Ibid., p.142.
66. Ibid., p.143.
67. Ibid., p.122.
68. Ibid., p.124.
69. Ibid., p.259.
70. Ibid., p.261.
71. A. Enright, 'Introduction', in K. O'Brien, As Music and Splendour (London: Penguin, 2005), p.v.

CHAPTER ELEVEN

Anne Enright's Machines: Modernity, Technology and Irish Culture

CLAIRE BRACKEN

Anne Enright's work is produced in an Ireland of late postmodernity, the term ascribed to the most recent manifestation of the modern. However, the technological and machinic configurations in her writing are more invested in twentieth-century versions of modernity than the digital and cyber technologies of the new millennium. Planes, trains and automobiles figure heavily in Enright's work, in addition to cameras, boats and televisions.[1] The nature of these machines signals an interest in the issue of modernity; machinic constructions are staple signifying emblems of the modern, given their historical links to the Industrial Revolution and technological advancement.[2] The term operates, primarily, as a signifier of change, as it is always placed in necessary opposition to the traditional/pre-modern space.[3] However, a rather different reading can be ascertained through an analysis of Enright's writing, whereby what constitutes the modern is revealed to be an established tradition itself. Modernity in her work spans a long time, ranging from late-nineteenth-century Paraguay and Francisco López's railway development project, through early and mid twentieth-century Ireland right up to the 'postmodern' present day. I will argue in this essay that the condition of modernity is set up in Enright's narratives in such a way that allows for re-thinking of the subject in relation to cultural change.

In an article on *The Wig My Father Wore*, Patricia Coughlan makes the point that protagonist Grace 'passes beyond the ideal of an atomised or autonomous self, associated with rationality, masculinity and modernity'.[4] Through an analysis of the machines in Enright's writing, this alteration in the subject can be further explored, revealing a reconfiguration of a masculine model of distanced rationality into a connective feminine self enmeshed in (rather than separated from) the structures of modernity itself.[5] Enright has stated in interview that 'a lot of the women, especially in my early stories, are women who have a relationship to a machine'.[6] In what follows, I explore the nature of that relationship, a body-machine compound in which the organic and inorganic are entwined. Reading the machine as a symbol of the modern, the body-machine will be considered as the self's negotiation of the conditions of modernity in the specific context of time and space. In both, the embodied female self is enmeshed in the machine, existing in both restrictive and creative relation to the conditions of modernity of which it is a part. The gendering of this is crucial, in that it allows a critical interrogation of the dominant structure of masculine, distanced subjectivity in the Irish post-colonial imaginary, an imaginary that, since its inception, has been marked by conditions of modernity via anxieties about national self-definition and cultural change. Irish feminist work has noted the ways in which such anxieties are played on and over the bodies of women, the materiality of the female body becoming fused with the materiality of the modern land: the mother-land.[7] On one level, Enright's female body-machines refer to these material conditions of modernity upon which the distanced masculine subject exerts authority. However, the drawing of this compound as enmeshed self also works to destabilize the construction of separated phallogocentric subjectivity, by presenting a viable self in connection, a *feminine* subject of modern Irish life.

MODERNITY, MACHINES, MEANING

Stuart Hall notes that:

> What is quintessentially 'modern' is not so much any one period ... so much as the fact that a society becomes seized with and pervaded by this idea of ceaseless development, progress, and dynamic

change; by the restless forward movement of time and history; by what some theorists call the compression of time and space.[8]

In this respect, modernity refers to a period of change. Modernity equals difference. However, by the same token, the modern can also be said to refer to sameness, in that the 'compression of time and space' also creates homogenization, examples of which include practices of colonialism and globalization. In this essay, I term an understanding of modernity-as-sameness (the restrictive experience of the uniform) 'repetitive assembly'. 'Chaotic disassembly' refers to modernity-as-difference, that is, the sense of instability that comes with change and difference, as the self is unable to cohere from a disassembled state. Technological and machinic representations can work to underwrite both the difference of temporal flux, as well as the sameness of homogenous repetition, in that they can function as markers of technological advancement, capitalist development, economic growth and consumerist commodification: mass producers *and* innovators of change. Machines can function in terms of repetitive reproduction; many operate to produce, in bulk, homogenous products, while others disassemble and breakdown. The question then becomes whether it is possible to have a more enabling and creative representation of the subject's experience in modernity and whether the figure of the machine can aid in this regard. Deleuze and Guattari, in their co-authored text, *Anti-Oedipus*, consider the operations of society through the figure of machine, acknowledging the processes of repetitive assembly and chaotic disassembly. However, they also present another configuration: machines that 'continually break down as they run, and in fact run only when they are not functioning properly', thus offering a vision of a creative assembly-disassembly process that is generative, productive and interactive.[9]

Enright's constructions of the camera (video and photographic) and television are generative of subjective experiences of chaos and repetition in respect to meaning-making. In the novel *The Wig My Father Wore*, video cameras operate in a disruptive television show space where disorder reigns. Despite the fact that 'nothing untoward has ever happened on the LoveQuiz', central character Grace, producer of the dating-game series, finds it difficult to coherently assemble an episode of the show: 'Get back on 1. Cue applause. Get back. Get back. Take it. That's our edit. And

2. Suffer on.'[10] The multiple camera perspectives emphasize a sense of chaos and a disassembled space, as Grace recounts the complications of arranging the camera shots, which speaks to a larger difficulty in the making of meaning and narrative signalled by the text. This establishes a link between the modern machine and the failure of representation, furthered in the novel through the image of the 'empty television': 'The office is a mess, full of the clatter-bang and howl-around of airwaves in crisis ... In the corner is the hiss of an empty television, switched on, with nothing coming through.'[11] Again a sense of chaos pervades; the office is a disassembled 'mess' and the 'airwaves in crisis',[12] which, aligned with the sounds of non-sense ('clatter-bang and howl-around'), contribute to the more general sense of meaninglessness that culminate in the final non-signifying image, the 'hissing' television with no message coming through.[13]

If the television and camera machines in The Wig are an expression of modern urban Ireland and the correlative disorientation that cultural change can bring, they also articulate the restrictively repetitious nature of modernity. Moving back to another time-space of Irish modern life, the 1960s, Grace remembers her family's yearly photograph: 'There is something embarrassing about our endless black and white family Christmas, the children lurching older, one year at a time, the turkey stay- ing the same'.[14] Louis Armand's point, that 'While machines accelerated the capacity for movement and locomotion, photography provided the analytical means of seeming to capture movement itself in stasis', is relevant here.[15] The 'stasis' indicative of the annual production, the 'end- less' reproduction of the same 'Christmas' pervades: the turkey stays the same, as does the black and white formatting. There is only moderate change with the contents (family members) 'lurching older', the 'lurch- ing' pointing towards the restrictive terms under which the subject is placed in a system of repetitive reproduction, the directionless nature of the movement emphasizing the absence of self-assembly. Returning to the more recent modern space of the narrative's present, repetition is also shown to form the basis of the LoveQuiz. The girls chosen to be contestants on the show are all the same: 'She looks like the girl-next-door because she is supposed to look like the girl-next-door. She looks like everyone else we've ever had on the show.'[16] Repeating the phrase 'looks like' three times figures the televisual image in a very specific way: the reproductive nature of television broadcasting, as mass media, comes to the fore here, evidenced in the expectation of sameness ('she is supposed to look like') embedded in the concept of the repeat.

The machines of modernity here are displayed as affecting the subject in two ways. In the first chaotic instance, there is disassembly – an inability to cohere and produce. In the second, there is a continuous practice of repeated assembly – an assembly of rather than by the subject. In both, the self is passive. One response to such passivity, presented in Enright's work, is detachment from the perceived-controlling-machine, a separation facilitating mastery and reverse control. In the main, this mastering of the machines is performed by male characters, for example, Grace's father who, when Grace was young, 'worked for the electricity supply board. He put on his hat and walked out the door and switched the nation on.'[17] In *What Are You Like?*, Berts's tinkerings with the machine are marked by an exertion of gendered power: 'A vindictive Lancia, as bad as his wife. The electrics were not the best ... He knew, as he stood at the side of the road with his head under the bonnet, that he would have to marry again',[18] while Veronica's husband Tom in *The Gathering* 'moves money around, electronically'.[19] Two male characters in the short story 'Taking Pictures' discuss cameras, simultaneously deriding newer models with 'auto-focus' as only for 'eejits'.[20] The implication here is that these 'eejits' do not have proper knowledge (control and mastery) over the machine, and that they become passively integrated into a machine-self assemblage.[21]

DRIVING IN TIME: FLYING THROUGH SPACE

An analysis of Enright's camera and television machines brings to bear two subjective experiences of modern life: chaotic disassembly and repetitive assembly. Her work presents the freezing of movement in space, as well as the inability to capture such movement: the stasis of fixed reproduction and the uncertainty of failed representation. One response to this is a process of separating out from the machine in an attempt to make active the perceived passivity of the self. However, Enright's work also charts another way, whereby the experience of stasis and chaos are not masterfully overcome, but rather inhabited and lived with. In the main, this is gendered feminine, since it is a response engaged with primarily by female characters. For example, in *The Gathering* there is an interaction of feminine body with the car-machine, which reflects on an experience of time. Veronica's Saab car and her night-driving facilitate a journeying into memory, as she moves through the grief of her brother Liam's suicide and links it with her family's troubled past: 'One night I give up steering the car one way or the other and let it go where it wants, which is north, as always ... all the way to Portrane', to the 'asylum' where her uncle was a patient.[22] Functioning as a time machine, the car enables fluid temporal movement, which resists the frantic time of the present, bringing Veronica back in time, into the past and memory.[23] Veronica's attempted rememberings, which are unstable and shifting throughout, are driven by a 'roaming'[24] nomadic consciousness of what Rosi Braidotti terms 'shifting locations',[25] which unsettles past/present divisions in a rhizomatic text of multiple temporal orders – Veronica's present and young adult and childhood pasts, in addition to the constructed pasts of her parents, grandparents and family.

John Urry makes the point that one of the features of the car is to free up time, to make an experience of temporality more fluid:

> Automobility ... develops 'instantaneous' time to be managed in highly complex, heterogeneous and uncertain ways. Automobility involves an individualistic timetabling of many instants or fragments of time. The car-driver thus operates in instantaneous time that contrasts with the official timetabling of mobility that accompanied the railways in the mid-nineteenth century.[26]

Veronica's rememberings are structured according to a machinic wandering. An embodied machine assemblage, she nomadically 'drives' her way through different versions of her present and past. As she tries to make sense of her brother's suicide, the car becomes a linking motif that directs her towards Nugent (as far back as 1925), Liam's abuse and the garage (where the car is housed and Veronica conjectures that the abuse took place). Veronica's sense of self is shown to merge with the car-machine early on in the novel, as she drives to the airport on the day that she finds out about her brother's death. In her grief, she drives 'the wrong way from home' and arrives at the airport, the last place she was with Liam: 'I don't think about where I am going, I think about the rain, the indicator, the drag of the rubber wiper against the glass. I think about nothing – there is nothing to think about.'[27] The repetition of the words 'think', 'nothing' and 'about' are used to emphasize Veronica's mind in a figurative state of automatic driving. In her grief, she unconsciously moves towards the memory of her brother, the machine functioning as an emblem of unprocessed thought. Just like the 'auto-focus' camera, Veronica is not presented as master of the machine. However, neither is she constructed as being managed by the technological; rather there is a blending of the two, a conjoining of the organic and inorganic: 'I should probably pull over but I do not pull over: I cry-drive all the way'.[28] The materiality of crying is integrated here with the driving process, with the organic making its mark on the representation of the machine. Parked in the airport, Veronica's memory of her brother is interwoven with the horror of the present situation: 'A plane roars low overhead and, when it is gone, I am hanging on to the steering wheel, with my mouth wide open. We stay locked like this for a while, me and the car, then I sit back and open the door.'[29] Her reaction is a physical scream while 'locked' with the machine, which functions to support her in her anguish, illustrated in the word 'hanging'. The intersections of self and machine, which produce Veronica as embodied machine assemblage, are made all the more insistent through the parallel imaging of the circle represented in her body's 'wide open' mouth and the 'steering wheel' of the inorganic machine.

The car is also a feature in Enright's 2000 novel, *What Are You Like?*, and can also be read in the context of time and remembering. In a chapter entitled 'Berts' Heart' set in 1976, an 11-year-old Maria is in the car with her father 'on the road to Dublin' after a visit with her deceased mother's family. As they drive, she thinks about her school homework:

> The Past Continuous – always, always, in the past. Or, at least, all the time.
>
> 'Mammy, didn't you always used to? …
>
> Because her mother was there once, but now she is gone. Her mother walked down the avenue once, in her summer dress, or

once with her coat, or once with her schoolbag ...

And each time she walked, she was already gone. There was no 'always' in it – just a kind of repetition. Nothing happened in that place that had not happened before, that would not happen again.[30]

Maria's thought processes, while journeying in the car, centre on the nature of time and the absence of her mother. In this instance, the past inheres, consistently repeating itself in the present and the future. What is particularly interesting is the way in which time is being configured as different temporal orders are crossed. Maria's absent mother represents a continuous past, a past that is 'all the time'. The use of the negatives 'nothing' and 'not' are important, as they imply, simultaneously, the complete stasis of the restrictive assembly of repetition (the mother that continues to repeat) and the complete disassembly of the negative (the mother that is 'gone' and absent). Furthermore, combined, both articulate the possibility of creative assembly and disassembly. Maria's memories of her mother cannot be fixed or curtailed, as they are opened up to possibility itself through the word 'nothing', which refuses the definition of what 'happened'. For this reason, remembering itself becomes a generative process in the present, leaving space open for different memories in the future, 'a kind of repetition' that is a repetition of difference. As Elizabeth Grosz notes, there is real potentiality in 'thinking the complexities of time ... in which the past, present and future are entwined'.[31]

Enright's car-machine does not cancel out the negative effects of the modern. However, articulating these effects at the same time, in the one representation, brings into relation the terms of assembly and disassembly, allowing for happenings of creative interaction between the two. For the feminine self, which can be likened to Deleuze's 'desiring machine' which both runs and breaks down, a more creative engagement with time becomes possible, one that allows fluidity to move, as well as opening up possibilities for the future. This potentiality runs alongside the more restrictive effects of modernity, which still remain, but now share space with moments a little more generative for the self. In this way, the car-machine of temporality articulates a virtual time in which restriction, disorientation and creative assembly are all possible and co-exist for the subject.[32] This necessarily affects conceptualizations of space, reconfiguring fixed spatial positioning in terms of nomadic movement. Veronica remarks in The Gathering that 'this is the way my mind runs' and we get the material and spatial sense of virtual time, as non-linear and rhizomatic.[33] Her mind 'runs' through space, rather than being fixed within it, thus highlighting a relationship with place that is in process rather than defined.

Such a relationship with space is perhaps most clearly articulated through the configuration of the plane in Enright's work, as the human-plane assemblage facilitates a configuration of the moving self. In The Gathering, Veronica looks down at the Dublin coastline as she flies home: 'I search the coastline for a beach, a bridge, an estuary ... I have just caught sight of it when I have lost it again, the plane banks and grabs a view of the sky'.[34] As Veronica moves through space in the plane, a body in the machine, she attempts to find a point of reference, a fixed place ('I search the coastline'). The effect here is of simultaneous connection and dislocation – she catches sight, only then to lose what she has seen. She assembles a relationship with place, only for that relationship to be disassembled. The fusion of machine and body is further emphasized here through the personification of the plane, which enacts a similar action to Veronica in that it 'grabs a view of the sky'.[35]

Throughout What Are You Like? links are made between journeying minds, dislocation and place.[36] Throughout the novel, Maria and her (separated-at-birth) twin sister, Rose, are both constructed as being lost.[37] The condition of being in-transit, of being in-between, functions to frame such feelings of isolation and uncertainty, something which is given shape by way of the figure of the machine. As Rose notes about homecomings: 'The first twenty minutes after she walked in the door her parents talked about how she had got there, the trains and buses, the minicabs and the weather ... There was never a clear way to get to the house she grew up in'.[38] What is being signalled here is the link between place ('house') and journeying, the way in which the concept of home is imbricated in the practice of travelling through space. As Veronica notes near the end of The Gathering: 'I look at the people queuing at the till, and I wonder are they going home, or are they going far away from the people they love. There are no other journeys.'[39] However, Enright's work problematizes any fixed arrival at home, as her characters are consistently configured as being on the move and making journeys. For example, at the end of *What Are You Like?*, the twin sisters, having found each other in Ireland (Maria's home), make another plane journey to another 'home' (Rose's England) and the reader is left with the sense of the impossibility of fixing home and, by extension, space. Rather, it is always in shift and in process.

In Enright's work, the machinic configurations of cars and planes, structured by complex inter-workings of chaos, reproduction and creative assembly, produce subjective experiences of space and time as nomadic movement and journeying. Both *The Gathering* and *What Are You Like?* present such journeyings in terms of the dislocated mind as it suffers a breakdown. Rose's experience of travelling through space, as she flies over the Atlantic Ocean, co-exists with the beginning of her breakdown: 'She thought that it would never end. That she would be on this flight for the rest of her life.'[40] Similarly, Veronica notes of her own psychic trauma and grief in *The Gathering*: 'I feel like I have spent the last five months up in the air.'[41] The plane-subject-machine functions here as an instantiation of the dislocated experience of moving through space, rather than being fixed and grounded within it. However, such experiences are also shown to generate the possibility of something more positive and productive, such as the meeting of the twins at the conclusion of *What Are You Like?*. While the experience of moving through space can produce feelings of unsettlement and dislocation, simultaneously it configures productive connections. Furthermore, landing is not always the utopia it promises to be: 'The airport terminal starts to slide past the window and it looks so much like a picture of a building, the whole ritual of landing feels so cinematic and fake, that I don't believe any of it for a while.'[42]

ENMESHED IN THE MACHINE: M-OTHER SUBJECT

Thus, Enright's machines present the reader with the subject of modernity's experience with meaning, time and space. Her work's machinic configurations suggest that the subject cannot *make* meaning, *direct* time, or *manage* space — the body is enmeshed in machinic structures rather than being located as separate or external to them. This expression of a feminine subject in modernity, a subject-with-machine, troubles the traditional construction of the masculine cyborg whereby there is a 'privileged bond between the male and the machine'.[43] However, while male cyborgs, as they are represented in popular culture, tend to be marked by metal, sealing them off from the world (as well as facilitating their power over that world), Enright's machine-bodies are notable for their connective qualities, an enmeshed feminine that is not and cannot be distanced. As detailed above, this subject experiences confusion, isolation and suffocation, *as well as* the possibility of creative play and difference.

In *The Pleasure of Eliza Lynch*, Enright's fictional account of the real life Irish woman who was the lover of the nineteenth-century Paraguayan dictator, Francisco López, the character Eliza becomes boat in the story, a floating machine: 'So I stand in the prow, very statuesque and still, while my belly boils.'[44] Eliza's boiling pregnant-belly is a representation of the boiler room in the Tacuarí boat on which she travels to Paraguay, a room in which a crew member was burned to death.[45] Enright perceptively illustrates here the way in which the mother's body is constructed as a tool (hence the machine image) in a patriarchal economy, an object that is perceived to be both life- and death-dealing, other to the 'proper' masculine subject. However, by writing the boat sections of the narrative in Eliza's first-person voice, giving subjective operations to the body-machine, the text opens up the possibility for a body enmeshed with the machine as a working viable configuration of the self.

The pregnant-machine also appears in *Making Babies* and the recent short story, 'Shaft'. In the former, for example, Enright comments on pregnancy: 'There was no technology for it: I was the technology – increasingly stupid, increasingly kind, a mystery to myself, to Martin, and to everyone who passed me by.'[46] What is striking in this description is the connective imagery. The emphasis placed on the word 'to', in addition to the punctuation of the colon, the hyphen, and multiple commas, highlights her sense of self as one in connection. But embedded within the 'to' is a restrictive functioning, signalled in the phrase 'everyone who passed me by', referencing a fixity in connection, an inability to move. The short story, 'Shaft', similarly constructs an embodied mother-machine, whereby the lift is an expression of the main character — a pregnant woman. As Enright herself notes: 'The thing about "Shaft", this is a woman in a machine. She is in a lift, and I really love the idea of this pregnant woman in this box, it's umbilical really — the rope.'[47] Considering her own pregnant embodied condition while in the lift, the woman thinks *We are all just stuck together*', a connection structured by suffocating confusion.[48] The lift is the space where she meets a man who stares at her stomach, but does not look at her. They are stuck together in this lift, hence they are connected, yet there is no meaningful interaction here. His desire to touch her belly positions her as an object of consumption, rather than a self in productive connection: 'So we were standing like that, him touching my belly, me looking at the ground, like some sort of slave woman.'[49]

In this way, Enright's enmeshed feminine selves are presented here in fixed connection as objects of consumption, demonstrating how an understanding of the feminine as enmeshed can produce a patriarchal construction of an undifferentiated m-other, antithetical to the distinct subject. However, Enright's fiction also works to negotiate this positioning of the enmeshed self, not by separating out the subject from connective processings, but rather by showing how the self can operate in this context. Such operations have been outlined above in respect to time and space. More generally, what we can identify in Enright's writing as a whole is the desire to write the enmeshed feminine body as self. Thus, she states of motherhood in Making Babies: 'My only excuse is that I think it is important. I wanted to say what it was like.'[50] Enright wants to speak the self from the space of the enmeshed. This project can be traced throughout all her fiction, as her female machinic characters (Grace-Television; Maria/Rose-Plane and Car; Eliza-Boat and Boiler; Veronica-Car and Plane) all negotiate a space for themselves within the context of their ongoing connectivities. The pregnant body exemplifies such selfhood, as it emphasizes connection in process and change: 'this peculiar, mutant, double self — motherandchild'.[51]

MODERNITY, POST-COLONIALISM AND THE IRISH SUBJECT

The emphasis that Enright's fiction places on the feminine body and its connectivity can be placed in productive dialogue with the ground-breaking work of Irish feminist critic Moynagh Sullivan. Sullivan critiques the field of Irish Studies for its masculinist paradigms, whereby the repeated questionings of Irishness and nationhood constitute an ongoing process of self-birthing. Her main argument is that subjectivity, as it is articulated in Irish Studies, is masculine-based, a subjectivity that requires the absence of the maternal body in order to sustain itself.[52] Self-birthing operates as a process of separating out, of distancing the subject from connections of materiality. In other work, Sullivan has made a connection between this process of subjective self-birthing and the Irish post-colonial imaginary more generally, whereby national selfhood is culturally inscribed as a masculine subject that distances itself from the 'motherland' through a dual process of rejection and incorporation.[53] If, as Joe Cleary notes, 'the inception of Irish modernity is invariably associated with British dominance on the island' in the sixteenth and seventeenth century, then it could also be argued that the inception of the subject of Irish modernity has the same beginnings.[54] Thus, the national subject (in the colonial and post-colonial periods) is a subject of modernity, whose masculine self-configuration is based on an objectified feminine space: Mother Ireland itself.

The subject of Irish modernity then, is a subject of separation, as it struggles to place order on processes of cultural change. Such struggles tend to be nation-based, deploying the feminine as a material other from which the masculine Irish subject is distanced. This has been consistently played out in the various historical, literary and cultural tropes of the woman-as-Ireland motif with its attendant masculine subjects of nation. The foundations of the modern Irish republic were based on a distinct gendered separation of public and private spaces, with the masculine occupying the active (and subjective role) of the public and the feminine relegated to a largely invisible and passive private sphere. This had the effect, throughout the twentieth century, of excluding women from being active subjects of the nation, as well as facilitating a construction of the national self that was self-sufficient, 'masculine' and in control. The citizenship referendum of 2004, a referendum which altered Irish law by taking away birth as a qualifier for legal Irish citizenship, deployed the body of an immigrant pregnant woman as a threat to the (white) body of Irish identity. The racial (m)other was configured in political discourse and popular media as parasitic body whose very condition was to enmesh itself in the structures of Irish society.[55] Hence the passing of legislation which attempted to keep such supposed connection at bay, the referendum itself acting as a separating mechanism designed to regulate the meaning of national identity. Integrating nationalist ideology, an ideology based on a masculine separated subject, with state policy is not new to the Celtic Tiger period, however. It can be symbolically traced both in de Valera's economic isolationist and protectionist policies, which used a model of distancing as the process through which national selfhood could be defined, and the Seán Lemass government of the 1960s which sought to redress the perceived passivity of the de Valera era with robust economic policies to place Ireland as an equal player in Europe and the western world.

In the specific context of Irish cultural criticism and modernity, the distanced subject is also a dominant structural frame. The primary question in this theoretical material is how to critique the condition of modernity while living within it. It seeks neither the utopic or the dystopic, but rather looks for a way to negotiate processes of modernity devoid of nostalgia for some type of 'before', as well as maintaining a scepticism for the present. Perhaps most prolific in this regard has been Seamus Deane, whose work examines the multiple meanings of modernity as articulated in Irish literature and culture in the nineteenth and twentieth centuries.[56] More recently, Joe Cleary's position in *Outrageous Fortunes* is that late-twentieth-century cultural production, both creative and critical, has been unable to provide a sustained critique of modernization processes, or present any viable alternatives to capitalist modernity in its current form.[57] Drawing on the work of Marshall Berman,[58] he makes the point that 'blind and uncritical enthusiasms or outright condemnations of modernity represent no substitute for an attempt to experience it whole, to see it dialectically as a world where "everything is pregnant with its contrary"'.[59] For Cleary, then, a proper and sustained critique of modernity and modernization processes comes from a critical distancing that enables the cultural critic to 'see' it 'whole'. The idea is to be a distanced subject who can clearly 'see'. Cleary's quotation choice (Berman quoting Marx) reveals a gendered dimension to the process, in that the 'world' looked at 'is pregnant with its contrary'. The object of study, modernity, constitutes an enmeshed form of the feminine, thus demonstrating the age-old and transferable nature of these discourses, passing from Marx to Berman to Cleary. In other work, Cleary specifically marks Irish feminism as an enmeshed subject unable to perform a proper critique of modernization discourse:

> Modernization theories and 'second wave' feminism are not only historically coincident with each other, both gaining momentum in the 1960s and 1970s, but they also share a structure of feeling in which contemporary Ireland is viewed as a 'traditional' society now undergoing an exhilarating liberation from the past.[60]

As a result, Irish feminism, according to Cleary, has 'a weak critique of modernization discourse', while post-colonial criticism, represented by Field Day, contains 'a stronger intellectual critique'.[61] Rehearsing problematic genderings of feminine weakness and masculine strength, there is a call here for a modern subject who can distance from the conditions of modernity and perhaps (actively) 'develop their own dreamworld' rather than (passively) 'accommodate themselves to the new order'.[62]

I am establishing a connection here between the way modern Irish subjectivity has been culturally inscribed and the specific critical ways modernity (as a condition) is discussed in Irish post-colonial criticism. What is general to both is a masculine subject predicated on some form of separation and distancing. Evidenced in the restrictive *and* creative self-machine assemblages in her work, Enright shares a resistance to 'blind and uncritical enthusiasms or outright condemnations of modernity'.[63] However, these same assemblages also point towards a major difference, which lies in the configuration of a connected rather than distanced subject. The fact that this subject is gendered feminine in her work suggests that the enmeshed female subject can be read as a refusal of a distancing process that ultimately requires the subsumption and rejection of the feminine.

Conjoining the material and the machine, Enright's work presents a different vision of modern selfhood modelled on the *presence* (rather than absence) of a feminine subject of on–going connectivity. The figure of the machine plays an important role in this regard. While Enright's works have been produced during moments of extreme social, cultural and economic change, the Celtic and post-Celtic Tiger periods respectively, her configurations of the machine are not so new. It is significant that the car in *The Gathering* makes an appearance in 1925, as this points to the founding years of the Irish post-colonial state, just as the said arrival of the television set in *The Wig My Father Wore* in 1967 corresponds with the year (10th May 1967) Ireland applied to join the then EEC. Thus modernity, represented by the machine in Enright's work, is an established condition in the Irish historical imaginary, stretching from the beginning of the twentieth century right up until the present day, and is intimately linked with post-colonial ways of thinking about nation and subjectivities of nation. Enright's representations of machinic bodies (in time and space) work to negotiate these established ways of thinking. In doing so, her work can be read as facilitating new modes of living in modernity that are neither dystopic nor utopic, but rather a realistic combination of restriction (repetitive assembly), disorientation (chaotic disassembly), and creative play. This has the important effect of reimagining both the gender and structure of subjectivity as it has been dominatingly configured in the Irish cultural imaginary.

ACKNOWLEDGEMENTS

Many thanks to Abby Bender, Susan Cahill and Mary McGlynn for their perceptive and illuminating comments on earlier drafts of this essay.

NOTES

1. Some notable exceptions include the Internet in *Making Babies* and mobile phones in *The Gathering*. Also, in her journalistic piece, 'What's Left of Henrietta Lacks?', Enright explores connections between cell proliferation, pregnancy and the structure of the Internet. See A. Enright, 'What's Left of Henrietta Lacks?', *London Review of Books*, 22, 8 (2000), pp.8–10; *Making Babies: Stumbling into Motherhood* (London: Jonathan Cape, 2004), pp.17, 52; *The Gathering* (London: Jonathan Cape, 2007), pp.23, 42.
2. Others argue that modernity has its origins in the early stages of the sixteenth century, when 'people are just beginning to experience modern life', due to colonialism and the globalization of European national spaces. See M. Berman, *All That is Solid Melts into Air: The Experience of Modernity* (London: Verso, 1983), pp.16–17.
3. For an exploration of this, see R. Kirkland, '"That Car": Modernity, Northern Ireland

and the DMC-12', Field Day Review, 3 (2007), pp.94–107, and 'Ballygawley, Ballylynn, Belfast: Writing about Modernity and Settlement in Northern Ireland', Irish Review, 40–41 (2009), pp.18–32.

4. P. Coughlan, 'Irish Literature and Feminism in Postmodernity', Hungarian Journal of English and American Studies, 10, 1–2 (2004), p.186.

5. Enright's work also establishes an interesting correlation between machines and writing which, because of space limitations, cannot be explored here. In The Gathering, as Veronica writes Nugent from the past she states: 'He must be reassembled; click, clack', thus positioning the writing process as a producing machine. See Enright, The Gathering, p.14. Enright specifically connects technology and writing in interviews. See A. Enright, 'Anne Enright Interview by Caitriona Moloney', in Irish Women Speak Out: Voices from the Field, ed. C. Moloney and H. Thompson (Syracuse, NY: Syracuse University Press, 2003), pp.63-4; 'Muscular Metaphors in Anne Enright: An Interview by Hedwig Schwall', The European English Messenger, 17, 1 (2008), p.22. See also the interview in this collection, where Enright states 'language is a machine. Quite a good one, actually', p.17.

6. A. Enright, Interview by Mark Lawson, Front Row, BBC Radio 4, 7 March 2008.

7. For example, see G. Meaney, 'Sex and Nation: Women in Irish Culture and Politics', in The Irish Women's Studies Reader, ed. A. Smyth (Dublin: Attic, 1993), pp.230-44 and M. Sullivan, 'Feminism, Postmodernism, and the Subjects of Irish and Women's Studies', in New Voices in Irish Criticism, ed. P.J. Mathews (Dublin: Four Courts Press, 2000), pp.243–51.

8. S. Hall, 'Introduction', in Modernity: An Introduction to Modern Societies, ed. S. Hall, D. Held, D. Hubert and K. Thompson (Malden, MA and Oxford: Open University Press, 1996), p.17.

9. G. Deleuze and F. Guattari, Anti-Oedipus: Capitalism and Schizophrenia, trans. R. Hurley, M. Seem and H. Lane (London and New York: Continuum, 1984), p.31.

10. A. Enright, The Wig My Father Wore (New York: Grove Press, 1995), p.16.

11. Ibid., p.10.

12. Ibid., pp.187–212.

13. See H. Hansson in this volume for a perceptive analysis of failed representation in the novel, with respect to the television, camera and mirror.

14. Enright, The Wig My Father Wore, p.109.

15. L. Armand, Technē: James Joyce, Hypertext and Technology (Prague: Karolinum Press, 2003), p.26.

16. Enright, The Wig My Father Wore, p.153.

17. Ibid., p.69.

18. A. Enright, What Are You Like? (London: Vintage, 2001), p.9.

19. Enright, The Gathering, p.39.

20. A. Enright, 'Taking Pictures', in Taking Pictures (London: Jonathan Cape, 2008), p.98.

21. See also A. Enright, 'Mr Snip Snip Snip', in The Portable Virgin (London: Vintage, 1991), pp.173–81. Stephen, the angel in The Wig, is the one male character who actively pursues emersion in the machine – he merges with the airwaves at the end of the

narrative. Grace's father, after his stroke, is said to be 'wired into the wrong channel', which seems to suggest that the masculine fear of connection is linked to a desire to retain a structure of subjectivity as rational and autonomous. See Enright, *The Wig My Father Wore*, p.74.

22. Enright, *The Gathering*, p.237.

23. Ibid., p.44.

24. Ibid., p.42.

25. R. Braidotti, *Nomadic Subjects: Embodiment and Sexual Difference in Contemporary Feminist Theory* (New York: Columbia University Press, 1994), p.172.

26. J. Urry, 'Inhabiting the Car', *The Sociological Review*, 54, s1, (2006), p.20.

27. Enright, *The Gathering*, pp.25–6.

28. Ibid., p.27.

29. Ibid., p.29.

30. Enright, *What Are You Like?*, p.53.

31. E. Grosz, 'Deleuze's Bergson: Duration, the Virtual and a Politics of the Future', in *Deleuze and Feminist Theory*, ed. I. Buchanan and C. Colebrook (Edinburgh: Edinburgh University Press, 2000), pp.230–1.

32. In Enright's personal memoir, *Making Babies*, she describes her thoughts as she drives with her child in the car seat: 'I am driving carefully ... she is trying to dress herself for school and wandering out of the house alone ... She is facing the wide world, and there is nothing I can do to help her ... I should write her a letter, but what could it say?' Written in the present continuous this piece, while tinged with maternal anxiety and fear, is also about imagining open-ended possibility. It is concerned with the present not limiting the future, ('I should write her a letter, but what could it say?') a limitlessness that is imagined from the space of driving itself, as the mother navigates the machine. See Enright, *Making Babies*, p.73. At another moment in the text, the car is conceptualized as a destructive machine of death for children: 'There is no worse trap than a car', p.140.

33. Enright, *The Gathering*, p.83.

34. Ibid., p.156.

35. Escalators also populate Enright's work, as symbols of the self moving through space. For example, see *The Wig*, p.11; *What Are You Like?*, p.214; *The Gathering*, p.189; 'In the Bed Department', in *Taking Pictures*, pp.31–7.

36. See M. Ryan in this collection for a detailed and comprehensive analysis of how Enright's work registers and negotiates processes of dislocation for contemporary selfhood.

37. 'Most of the time, Rose did not know who she was'; 'But Maria knows that she is lost': Enright, *What Are You Like?*, pp.136, 152.

38. Ibid., p.213.

39. Enright, *The Gathering*, p.258.

40. Enright, *What Are You Like?*, p.162.

41. Enright, *The Gathering*, p.259.

42. Ibid., p.158.
43. R. Braidotti, *Metamorphoses: Towards a Materialist Theory of Becoming* (Cambridge: Polity, 2002), p.234.
44. A. Enright, *The Pleasure of Eliza Lynch* (London: Vintage, 2003), p.206.
45. The ship-pregnancy analogy runs throughout the boat chapters, which suggest birthing imagery as a metaphor for water travel: 'after a hard morning pushing towards home', ibid., p.42.
46. Enright, *Making Babies*, p.25.
47. See A. Enright, 'Interview by Claire Bracken and Susan Cahill' in this collection, p.26.
48. Enright, 'Shaft', in *Taking Pictures*, p.131.
49. Ibid., p.132.
50. Enright, *Making Babies*, p.4.
51. Ibid., p.20.
52. Sullivan, 'Feminism, Postmodernism', p.250.
53. See M. Sullivan, 'Boyz to Menz(own): Irish Boy Bands and the Alternative Nation', *Irish Review*, 34 (2006), pp.58–78, and 'The Treachery of Wetness: Irish Studies, Seamus Heaney and the Politics of Parturition', *Irish Studies Review*, 13, 4 (2005), pp.451–68.
54. J. Cleary, 'Introduction: Ireland and Modernity', in *The Cambridge Companion to Modern Irish Culture*, ed. J. Cleary and C. Connolly (Cambridge: Cambridge University Press, 2005), p.3.
55. For an extended discussion, see G. Meaney, 'Race, Sex and Nation', *The Irish Review*, 35, 1 (2007), pp.46–63.
56. See S. Deane, *Celtic Revivals: Essays in Modern Irish Literature* (London and Boston, MA: Faber and Faber, 1985), and *Strange Country: Modernity and Nationhood in Irish Writing Since 1790* (New York: Oxford University Press, 1997).
57. J. Cleary, *Outrageous Fortunes: Capital and Culture in Modern Ireland* (Dublin: Field Day Publications, 2007). See in particular the chapter 'Modernization and Aesthetic Ideology'. Cleary also asks the question: 'Does contemporary Ireland still remain an appropriate site for tracking the ambiguities of the modern? Or have the successes of the move toward marginalization marginalized dissent?', Cleary, 'Introduction: Ireland and Modernity', p.14.
58. Berman, *All That is Solid Melts Into Air*.
59. Cleary, *Outrageous Fortunes*, p.212.
60. Cleary, 'Introduction: Ireland and Modernity', p.16.
61. Ibid., p.19.
62. Ibid., p.231. Post-colonial criticism on the specific subject of modernity and tradition also works to generate such distancing. Paying attention to what is constructed as 'past' or 'traditional' is interpreted as opening up space from the forward movement of modernity and allowing for the production of new meanings for past and present. See D. lloyd, *Irish Times: Temporalities of Modernity* (Dublin: Field Day, 2008); L. Gibbons, 'The Global Cure? History, Therapy and the Celtic Tiger', in *Reinventing Ireland: Culture,*

Society and the Global Economy, ed. P. Kirby, L. Gibbons and M. Cronin (London: Pluto, 2002), pp.89–106.

63. Cleary, *Outrageous Fortunes*, p.212.

CHAPTER TWELVE

Relationships with 'the Real' in the Work of Anne Enright

HEDWIG SCHWALL

Reviews of Anne Enright's work often describe it as iconoclastic.[1] This seems an apt qualification, as her representations of women are a perfect contemporary illustration of that most iconoclastic of pictorial motifs in the Flight to Egypt, where the mere passage of the Virgin Mary with her baby makes all the statues of the pre-Christian religions snap off their pedestal.[2] In her work, Enright overthrows the (Irish) Catholic paradigm, as her well-travelled, sexually active female protagonists debunk the image of the sorrowful, desexualized and idealized Irish mother. Anne Enright says of her own books that, 'They dealt with ideas of purity, because the chastity of Irish women was one of the founding myths of the Nation State'.[3]

This ethos seems entirely interiorized by the mother figures of Enright's novels. In the first novel, The Wig My Father Wore, this leads to the mother's absurd blaming of the daughter for her father's stroke;[4] in the second, What Are You Like?, Anna refuses an abortion, seeming to go along with the Catholic authority which stipulates that if a pregnant woman's medication would endanger the foetus, it is the mother who has to die.[5] However, in her case she is too far gone in her illness to realize what is going on: as a result, she leaves two motherless daughters.[6] In The Gathering, it is the daughter who blames both mother and grandmother, as Veronica accuses them of complying with Catholic mores: having too many children led to the neglect of her son Liam and his suicide.[7]

Fathers, on the other hand, are curiously 'irresponsible'. In *The Wig My Father Wore* the man's stroke disabled him in his communication, so that his reactions become odd and no one knows what or whom he 'responds' to. In *The Pleasure of Eliza Lynch* the father exploited his daughter's sexuality for financial gain and then disappeared, while in *What Are You Like?* Anna's husband, Berts, cannot cope with his bereavement and instead of mediating between the remaining members of his family he does the opposite, as he gives one daughter up for adoption, never mentioning the fact to anyone. Ignorance of their original family context and their parents' disastrous story causes both girls to be deeply disturbed. In *The Gathering*, the father gladly seems to obey the imperative of the Roman Catholic Church to see sexuality as the procreation of souls, but he does not seem to be able to respond to his children's challenges, especially not to Liam, who is reported to have been abused by his grandmother's landlord.

As Enright indicates, family matters are political matters, and they are directly linked to the dictates of a conservative Church which does not allow any questioning, dialogue or development. As we see from her political columns, Enright is clearly a political writer: 'The country was screaming at itself about contraception, abortion, and divorce. It was a hideously misogynistic time. Not the best environment for a young woman establishing a sexual identity.'[8] Writing offered a way out as it enabled her to create new worlds, inspired by philosophy and psychoanalysis. Talking of her philosophy courses she says: 'the really interesting people came ... [in] the psychoanalysis course ... The course I liked most was Freud. Especially *Das Unbehagen in der Kultur* .... I like all his death work ... I also had a Lacan phase'.[9]

Therefore, I want to look at three aspects of Enright's work: firstly, how she analyzes the Irish political situation; secondly, how she uses a deconstructionist twist to turn that reality into an alternative version which also seems inspired by Gilles Deleuze's reaction against phenomenology; and thirdly, I will turn to Lacanian psychoanalysis to see how Enright's revolutionary stylistics result in a specific representation of the body which allows the reader some insight into the complexities, the phases and layers of the subject's interactions between 'the self' and 'the world'.[10] Each of these aspects represents a step in Enright's 'feminine aesthetic':[11] first, she indicates the difference between her view and masculine Irish politics; second, she clarifies what the specificity of the feminine thing is; and finally, she shows how the feminine attention to the body brings about a new concept not only of woman but of the human being as a complex, multiple, divisible factor.

THE POLITICS OF VAGUENESS

In *The Gathering*, Liam is represented as the scapegoat of a culture that does not allow criticism or even an articulation of the components of its Catholic ethos, only complicity. As we have seen, it is mainly the mothers (grandmother and mother) who take the brunt for failing to thematize what was rotten in their culture:

> I am *saying that*, the year you sent us away, your dead son was inter-fered with, when you were not there to comfort or protect him, and that interference was enough to send him on a path that ends in the box downstairs. That is what I *am saying*.[12]

The repetition of the 'I am saying' indicates that the narrator's first and foremost aim is to articulate what has always been implicit: the fact that sexuality could not be discussed, as it was considered evil by the Catholic Church. Instead, Veronica's parents went along with this prohibition, which only deepened a vague sense of guilt, as we see in Veronica's mother whose *epitheton ornans* is 'vague': 'The *vague* daughter's endlessly *vague* pregnancies, the way each and every one of her grand-children went *vaguely* wrong'.[13] The mother's vagueness is further connected to the marital bed, 'where we were all conceived: I sense the chaos of our fate – or not so much a chaos as a *vagueness*'.[14] But not even the marital bed is the source of this chaos, it was passed on by Veronica's grandmother, Ada: 'This is the moment when we realise that it was Ada's fault all along. The mad son and the vague daughter ... This is the moment when we ask what Ada did – ... to bring so much death into the world'.[15]

Linking sexuality directly with 'fault' and death echoes the idea of original sin and the Fall, which, according to the Bible and its commen-tators, was also caused by a woman, mankind's 'arch-(grand)mother', Eve. The fact that the 'revolutionary' daughter, in her turn, blames the women, ironically indicates that even this narrator has internalized the misogynistic teachings of the Catholic Church which makes her focus on Ada's/Eve's 'first disobedience', that brought death into the world through 'original sin'.[16]

Yet the scene of 'original sin' in *The Gathering* is represented in a complex way. In the variations on the central scene that haunts Veronica, we find that Ada's landlord, Lamb Nugent, interferes now with young Liam, now with eight-year-old Veronica.[17] This scene seems to convey three things. Firstly, it seems a metonymy of a practice that was widespread in the country: not only does Veronica imagine that a pattern of sexual (child) abuse already ran in Nugent's family,[18] but also the fact that her school was named after St Dympna, who had to escape from her own father's sexual advances, suggests that it was a problem in (Catholic) institutions and families, as has been revealed over the past number of years. Secondly, Nugent's highly ambiguous position as both private and public figure (friend *and* landlord of the house) shows him to be a metaphor of the Catholic Church, which interfered with parents' sexuality.[19] And thirdly, the scene questions the silence surrounding child abuse, in which women are seen to be complicit. Veronica condemns Ada for not protesting against this child abuse: 'When I try to remember, or imagine that I remember, looking into Ada's face with Lamb Nugent's come spreading over my hand, I can only conjure a *blank*, or her face as a blank. At most, there is a word written on Ada's face, and that word is, "Nothing".'[20]

We could say that Irish society was ruled by dictates, based on metaphysics, which did not allow for any analysis of the ambiguities of sexuality. Sex was bad and that was that: it should not be talked about. Children were not allowed the 'right distance' from the power of their parents and the system that ruled them, to be able to find a (sexual) identity of their own. However, the narrator of *Making Babies* is determined not to undergo the effects of this oppressive culture where priests incite people to have children, but make the women culpable for the effects of sexuality. Instead, she wants to analyze the whole social context: 'The older I get the more political I am about depression … it is not because of who you are, but where you are placed'.[21] To Enright, depression is not a matter of an individual's shortcomings but of the position in which s/he is placed by society. In this stance, she sides with Deleuze: 'the anti-metaphysics of the subject proposed by Deleuze is inherently political: it is the kind of thought that aims at reconnecting theory with daily practices of change, transformation and resistance'.[22] This is the very thing Enright does in Making Babies: she reconstitutes an identity of her own in the rich bodily and verbal interaction with her babies. Freud will be a help, but the feminine experience will bring in entirely new experiences to model human interaction on: 'I don't think Freud ever discussed lactation, but the distinction between "good" and "bad" bodily products here is fine.'[23]

PHILOSOPHY: VENTURING INTO HYPERREALISM

In I love to You, Luce Irigaray engages in the very exercise Enright embarks on in Making Babies: both writers realize that the culture they live in is, in Irigaray's words, 'a civilization without any female philosophy or linguistics, any female religion or politics. All of these disciplines have been set up in accordance with a male subject.'[24] She argues that

> being born a woman requires a culture particular to this sex and this gender, which it is important for the woman to realize without renouncing her natural identity. She should not comply with a model of identity imposed upon her by anyone, neither her parents, her lover, her children, the state, religion or culture in general.[25]

In The Gathering, Veronica only half-heartedly dissents from the models imposed upon her by Irish society; however, it is Liam's final suicide which shocks the narrator out of her uncritical perception:

> I was living my life in inverted commas. I could pick up my keys and go 'home' where I could 'have sex' with my 'husband' just like lots of other people did. This is what I had been doing for years; and I didn't seem to mind the inverted commas, or even notice that I was living in them, until my brother died.[26]

This also goes for the narrator of Making Babies, but here it is a depression and two pregnancies which bring about a strong physical, mental and emotional overhaul in the body, enabling her to develop what Deleuze calls, according to Braidotti,

> a vision of ... a body freed from the codes of phallogocentric functions of identity. The un-organic 'body without organs' is supposed to create creative disjunctions in this system, freeing organs from their indexation to certain prerequisite functions ... In some ways, this calls for ... a way of scrambling the master-code of phallocentrism and loosening its power over the body.[27]

In giving accurate descriptions of the labour, parturition and intensive care that is part and parcel of 'making babies', this book's focus on exclusively feminine dealings with Others (babies) counteracts the phallogocentrism (Irish) women suffered so much from. In her precision, Enright gives us an excellent example of the Deleuzian re-modelling of perception. Unsurprisingly, one of the first 'organs' the author questions is the brain, which does not fulfil its 'prerequisite function' of giving the straight, clear, rational information that patriarchal tradition ascribes to it. Instead, Enright notices that the brain's 'indexes' are befuddled by associations which are entirely unpredictable:

> The milk surprises me ... The reflex is designed to work at the sight, sound, or thought of your baby ... but the brain doesn't seem to know what a baby is, exactly, and so tries to make you feed anything helpless, or wonderful, or small. So I have let down milk for Russian submariners and German tourists dying on Concorde. Loneliness and technology ... get my milk every time.[28]

As the brain fails to fulfil the expected principle of adaequatio, Enright further explores 'the joyful anarchy of the senses, a pan-erotic approach to the body' which Braidotti finds in Deleuze's theories.[29] However, what Deleuze calls anarchy, Enright calls hyperrealism:

> One of the pathways I have been negotiating as a writer has been my relationship with the real ... I like hyperrealism, as a description of what I do. Ideas of 'realism' are very culturally determined ... And I am very impatient with the real ... language strains towards

metaphor. And I follow on. And then sometimes I might make the metaphor radical, like I have an angel knock on the door instead of saying he looked like an angel. So it is linguistically determined, my relationship with the real ... My impulse is towards the real. That's where I am trying to get.[30]

This statement in itself may sound somewhat 'anarchic', as we hear a seeming contradiction between 'I am very impatient with the real' and 'My impulse is towards the real'. It seems that Enright wants to move from a reality that is informed by the patriarchal dictating paradigm to one that is inspired by a more feminine, interactional approach to things. In the former, as we have seen, some monolithic metaphysical authority overrules all articulation. In the latter, the focus is on the very physical kinds of dialogue between mother and child; as a result, the 'metaphysical' is found to be but a certain rhetoric of society. In order to force her way out of the paradigm of habit and to explore the paradigm of wonder, Enright practises a 'hyperrealism' which often harks back to the magic of childhood, as the interactional mode is still very strong there. Grace notices this, remembering her father's wig: 'I was very fond of it as a child. I thought that it liked me back.'[31]

That Enright's protagonists want to 'scramble the master-code' of tradition is a programmatic point that is stated in the very first sentence of her œuvre: 'Cathy was often wrong, she found it more interesting'.[32] Especially in her earlier work, experience is experiment, bewilderment is the norm. We find this throughout her first volume of short stories: 'So much sky makes ones [sic] bewildered – which is the only proper way to be',[33] and 'I was of course bewildered, because that is how I was brought up. I am supposed to be bewildered.'[34] Yet there is method in this bewilderment, this exploration of the 'hyperreal'. As Enright undoes 'male' hierarchies, systematically sabotaging the traditional value system, she seems to follow the (deconstructionist) tactics of systematically reversing a hierarchy of values which questions traditional categorization. The marginal is preferred to the central, the unstructured to the structured, energy over boundary, divided self over individual.[35] Likewise, actions which are traditionally regarded as intentional happen unintentionally and vice versa: 'She made extensive plans to ... start drinking again',[36] and 'her breasts ... have made the change from sexual to maternal, or tried to'.[37] In sexual matters, men are passive while women usually take the initiative (in most of the early short stories). The metaphysical and the physical change place when Grace has sex with her 'angel', Stephen. Not only does the spiritual aspect become palpable – 'the unutterable, the unspeakable and the inexpressible, lying by my side in hand's reach' – but as the relationship grows Grace loses substance to Stephen who becomes more physical.[38] Mental matters are treated as material ones while potential and real modes are mixed in Stephen when Grace notices how 'the blessings ever given or withheld seemed to sit in him'.[39] But the relations Enright focuses on most are those between the inside and outside world, and between body and mind.

Enright herself states she aims at 'a very feminine use of space',[40] which is linked to the fact that most protagonists, at some point, start 'housing' a baby. This often leads to a rather wild sense of space, again mostly in the early novels,[41] as we find when Anna, pregnant with Maria and Rose, 'put the cup into the milk, you could say ... she put the bag into the clothes ... [she would] bake a chicken in stuffing, wrap a sheet around the washing machine'.[42] In this 'inverting exercise', Enright once more echoes Irigaray: 'One method that I used to write Speculum and continue to use regularly – inversion.'[43] In 'The House of the Architect's Love Story', the simultaneous conception of a child and an idea of a house not only mix up the reader's ability to tell the difference between the inside and outside world, but also between literal and metaphorical images, which is one of the watermarks of Enright's prose.

The main 'deconstruction' of traditional hierarchies happens in Enright's privileging of body over mind. So a lover in her early work is intrigued by the opacity of his friend's body: 'Compared to her body, her mind was easy to understand'.[44] Thus 'scrambling the master-code of phallo(go)centrism',[45] Enright replaces a philosophy of nature with a 'perception of one's own' which focuses on nurture: 'I was reared with the idea that, for a woman, anatomy is destiny, so I have always paid close attention to what the body is and what it actually does'[46] – thus staying in line with de Beauvoir's famous observation that one is not born as a woman but becomes one.

Enright's protagonists completely correspond to Braidotti's presentation of Deleuze's nomadology which 'shifts the balance of power away from the mind and onto the body' and 'favours the unity of mind and body, not their binary opposition. The emphasis on affectivity here marks a pre-discursive moment.'[47] The pre-discursive is indeed the moment Enright and her protagonists like to concentrate on:

> I realize that I am actually moving towards being all interested in irresolute states; the emotions that happen before things become clear, so all these unsettled, unresolved things. I like the restlessness before it is arrested by words. I am interested in all the disturbance that goes before that, in that, sort of, agitation, of not knowing, or nearly knowing.[48]

It is the labyrinthine aspect of this body-laboratory that A.L. Kennedy appreciates in her review of Enright's The Gathering, as she notices: 'For Enright, the body, the mind, the will, the work, the heart — all work upon each other in a terrible, wonderful roar of life.'[49] My question is then: how does this jumble of 'mind, will, work, heart' work? Perhaps psychoanalysis can provide us with a red thread to enter this opaque maze of the body, that palace of mirrors 'full of lines going nowhere'.[50]

PSYCHOANALYSIS AS A WAY TO HELP ARTICULATING THE OTHER IN THE SELF

Based on Lacan's 'RIS system' of the Real (emotional and functional), Imaginary (imagined) and Symbolic (verbal) we could distinguish between four modes of perception/communication that are lodged in the body.[51] 'The real' is divided in two aspects: R1 which is the human being's prime condition, and R2 which comes into being after the Image function and the entrance in the Symbolic order of verbal interactions have been realized. So R1 is the state of being where the subject does not distinguish between subject and object, as in the baby who does not distinguish between himself and the caretaker, or in the person in a panic who 'loses his head' and his ability to articulate himself; I call this 'the arhetorical position'. Secondly, the imagined self appears when the child recognizes himself in the mirror. He starts to love his image because he can control it, which makes him believe he can convey an (illusory) image of himself to others. As the subject thinks it is master of its own discourse we call this 'the rhetorical position'. When children move to the Symbolic stage they learn to accept that one's body is moulded by a social aspect, which I call 'metarhetorical', as the inspiring discourse (grammatical rules, cultural structures) is beyond the personal rhetoric. So the Real, Imaginary and Symbolic aspect are developed. Yet most of the time all three are more or less in balance and unquestioned, which means that people act in a routine way, for which Lacan reserved the term R2. As this is a sheer functional, unquestioning mode, we call it the subject's 'unrhetorical' mode of communication. Now when Enright specifies that she is 'very impatient with the real', while stating that 'My impulse is towards the real' where 'emotions ... happen before things become clear'[52], this clearly shows that she wants to move from the routinely R2 back to the inarticulated R1.[53] In order to define the difference between these two kinds of 'Real', Lacan states that R1 is where the first emotional knots of fear and desire are tied. He sees it as a kind of umbilical knot, which disappears under later experiences and remains 'at the bottom' of the unconscious, *das Ding*. It is unprocessed and out of reach, but at times it is felt as a foreign Other in the self. Lacan calls it the fount of 'Pressure, urgency' of life itself, Freud's *Not des Lebens*.[54] This is precisely what sets Veronica writing in *The Gathering*; the whole novel is a laborious search for the traumatic roots of a childhood she shared with Liam.

So when we look at the modes of communication we find in Enright's bodies we see that her protagonists are always very impatient with routine 'reality': 'the eye we use, for example, to cross the road'.[55] In *The Gathering*, she is expelled from this routine by Liam's death which makes her see the 'inverted commas', the boundaries of her narrow kind of reality, and which makes her suddenly sense that other, arhetorical, traumatic reality. Veronica also clearly mentions the Imaginary communication of the 'rhetorical' body as she states: 'We know there is a difference between the brute body and *the imagined body*'.[56] A protagonist who excels in the rhetoric of her imagined body is Eliza Lynch, as it is her very profession to use her body language to convince people – and it works with her rich friend, Francisco López.[57] This imagined, rhetorical body is also what Grace finds in bed when Stephen mutely conveys the message that he is sulking when 'a line of piqued flesh lies exposed'.[58]

Thirdly, the body is affected and moulded by the Symbolic order. This goes from speaking/thinking along the grammatical rules to assuming an appeal, a task, or a role given by society. The 'metarhetorical' dimension is most explicit when one's perception is changed by a new function or status that is assigned by society, such as when one gets a new name or title. Or, as Elin Diamond puts it: when the Symbolic order affects the body it becomes an 'embodiment' or social incarnation: 'when the material body … enters discursive categories that make it mean when it becomes not the body but the visible form and social incarnation of the body: that is, an embodiment'.[59] In the passage where the pregnant narrator of Making Babies informs her mother that she will become a grandmother, this has a very positive effect:

> My mother said very little but, every time I looked at her, she looked five years younger, and then five years younger again. She was fundamentally, *metabolically* pleased. She was pleased all the way through, as I was pregnant all the way through.[60]

But as we can expect with an angry young woman who questions an unfortunate social code, the link between social and 'brute body' in Enright's work is usually problematic, such as when Veronica wonders how religious belief can be 'embodied': 'If I went looking for his personal belief I would not know where to begin, or in what part of his body it might inhere.'[61] Enright's figures want to look not so much at the ordering effect of the Symbolic order, but at the ways in which it clashes with the subject's own deepest secret, 'the Thing': 'What one finds in *das Ding* is the true secret'.[62] It is a kind of emotional navel, an opaque kernel which is 'fed' by deep-seated separation fears which remain unarticulated, due to an unsuccessful separation from the caretaker – in the Irish context, from the mother. Enright realizes that all human beings have to move away from this initial state of being: 'This peculiar, mutant, double self – motherandchild.'[63] However, this separation can be difficult, as many parents cannot let go, and instead smother the child with their worries: 'We slip like phantoms from our parents' heads, leaving them to clutch some Thing they call by our name, because a mother has no ability to let her child go.'[64] It is the struggle of the child to get away from parents that Enright concentrates on, a struggle which is mainly a matter of unconscious aggression and fear, or 'irresolute states ... unresolved things ... the restlessness before it is arrested by words'.[65] This conflict is symptomatic in Liam; his separation problem flashes up most clearly when he throws a knife at his mother. Veronica's brother is 'stuck' in the oral and anal stage: he drinks and his job is to dispose of organs in a hospital. His communication remains arhetorical: 'the place Liam worked best was under your skin'.[66] His remarks are never functional, but instead aim at trouble and vent frustrations without ever articulating them, so that Veronica's husband, after an angry bout from Liam, asks '"What was all that about?" ... he could smell what was going on in a room ... it was hard to say what exactly he had done to make you feel so off-key ... I don't think it was something he could control'.[67]

That Liam could not reach the Oedipal state is clear in that he could accept neither his father's authority nor his own responsibility as a father: each time he is called to commit himself, he leaves – until he leaves for his final destination, the sea (in French homophonous with the mother (la mer/la mère), and echo of his prenatal home.[68] Again none of these events are articulated, the knife-throwing is glossed over, canned by laughter, until Liam's fatal fusion with the waves of the sea[69] touches upon Veronica's 'urgency of life itself'[70] which hurtles her into her laborious translation into words of the vague anger her body houses: 'I need to bear witness to an uncertain event. I feel it roaring inside me – this thing that may not have taken place. I don't even know what name to put on it. I think you might call it a crime of the flesh.'[71]

Unlike her patron saint Veronica, this mother does not want to translate a divine body into an image, but an all too human body into words. In her endeavour to come to terms with the traumas she seems to share with Liam, the narrator comes across something which is neither bodily nor spiritual, neither an image nor a word, but something in-between: Lacan's 'object small o'. The most frequent kind of 'object o' is the gaze and the voice: they are observed in the phenomenal world, yet they do not belong to it. The eye is material and measurable but the gaze's emotional charge is not; the same goes for the voice. Especially when the gazer and the gaze are dissociated, the effect of the 'object o' becomes uncanny. This happens when Veronica meets Liam's son at Liam's funeral: 'He has the Hegarty eyes, we say ... and we look to see what human being looks out through them, this time. It is too uncanny.'[72] Uncanny, indeed, how the return of the familiar strikes one as being utterly unfamiliar, how identity proves to be non-identity. This and many other instances of this 'message of the Other' in Enright, perfectly fit Ned Lukacher's interpretation of the 'object o' as 'a kind of catharsis insofar as it clarifies the disorder, the illness that inheres within intellectual inaccuracy ... the untruth or perversity that is always constitutive of the truth'.[73] In her proclaimed aim to highlight the opacity of human truth, Enright often focuses on a catharsis which merely clarifies the disorder in her protagonists' psychological make-up. Though she can be very accurate in the rendering of her figures, it is the untruths they embody which are at the focus of her fiction, whether novels or short stories.

It is this mixture of truth and untruth which is at the heart of The Gathering, where the narrator is unreliable[74] because she cannot make a clear story out of the mess of images, words and objects o that tie her to Liam: 'I can feel his gaze on the skin of my cheek as he turns to look at me, uncanny and dead. I know what it is saying. The truth. The dead want nothing else. It is the only thing that they require. I look up too quickly, and he is gone.'[75] Though Enright's narrator is called Veronica, her protagonist can only find truth by 'looking awry'.[76] She is a far cry from the apocryphal heroine who could frame and fix God's own true face and gaze on the piece of textile, holding up a 'vera icon'. Instead, this exercise in 'remembering' Liam (again both metaphorically and literally) offers us a (post)modernist Veronica, one of Deleuze's 'nomadic bodies': 'open-ended, interrelational and trans-species'.[77]

Veronica, like Grace, the twins of What Are You Like?, and most protagonists of the short stories, all want to break open the mould of silent complicity which a male Catholic ethos imposed on Irish society. Some men and women stick to a 'metaphysically' ordained 'Symbolic order' to maintain their routine perception in 'vagueness'; Enright's protagonists, however, do not only notice the quotation marks of the 'absolute' imperatives of what male authority calls 'nature', but they also explore an alternative policy of their own, focusing on their bodies' reactions to the ways in which their culture tries to 'nurture' them. The result of that new focus is double: Enright's women figures explore the pre-discursive moment, 'the restlessness before it is arrested by words',[78] which can be scary; but acknowledging this arhetorical kind of perception allows for experiment from the bottom up. In their intense experiences, women monitor body rather than soul, and, in this Irigarayan inversion of the phallogocentric hierarchies, Enright seems to explore a kind of 'anti-metaphysics of the subject', which, like Deleuze's, is inherently political.[79] Enright's 'policy' is a literary one, allowing for 'creative disjunctions' in her figures' perceptions which question old hierarchies and lead to the development of 'a feminine use of space' – one which may affect the statuesquely suffering Catholic women Enright criticizes, making them fall off their pedestals, to hit real life.

NOTES

1. Kate Saunders observes how 'Enright begins with a slash right to the guts of this sprawling clan, exposing them with unswerving intimacy', K. Saunders, Review of The Gathering, The Times, 16 June 2007; Susanna Rustin talks about 'the subversive wit' with which she 'always wanted to grab the Irish audience', S. Rustin, 'What Women Want', Guardian, 15 March 2008; A.L. Kennedy finds Enright 'unflinching as she documents all the physical symptoms of emotion and memory', A.L. Kennedy, 'The Din Within', Guardian, 28 April 2007; Patricia Craig sees 'rage, violation, sadness and squalor as the narrator gets to grips with bitter truths, or possible truths', which are linked up with 'indigenous overbreeding', P. Craig, review of The Gathering, Independent (UK), 7 June 2007.
2. Examples can be found in, among others, Melchior Broederlam's depiction of the scene (1398), or Joachim Patinir's Flight to Egypt (ca 1520). They and many other 'Flemish Primitives' relish the legends surrounding this Bible passage (Mt.2, 13–15), in which Mary and Joseph flee for Herod's soldiers who are to kill all babies born in Bethlehem at that time. On the journey, the Virgin Mary is usually seated on a donkey, a mater/virgin dolorosa holding the newborn Jesus. As they pass 'pagan' statues on their way to Egypt, Jesus' mere presence makes them snap off their pedestals – a very 'plastic' way to show that the Christian paradigm is overcoming the pre-Christian one.
3. A. Enright, Making Babies: Stumbling into Motherhood (London: Vintage, 2005), p.194.
4. A. Enright, The Wig My Father Wore (London: Minerva, 1996).
5. A. Enright, What Are You Like? (London: Vintage, 2001).

6. What is stressed in this novel is the power of the Church's censorship over people's minds and domestic interaction. Berts, the father of the unborn twins, does not even dare to admit to himself he mentioned the word abortion. See Enright, *What Are You Like?* p.8.

7. A. Enright, *The Gathering* (London: Jonathan Cape, 2007).

8. Enright, *Making Babies*, p.187.

9. A. Enright, 'Muscular Metaphors in Anne Enright: An Interview with Hedwig Schwall', *The European English Messenger*, 17, 1 (2008), p.21.

10. I would like to point out here that Enright could certainly be considered a feminist, but she seems to aim at a more encompassing renewal in the representation of human interactions. Though most stories focus on women, her attention to the different ways in which the body registers and speaks is relevant to both women and men.

11. Enright, 'Muscular Metaphors', p.22.

12. Enright, *The Gathering*, p.213, my emphasis.

13. Ibid., p.223.

14. Ibid., p.187, my emphasis.

15. Ibid., p.223.

16. The Church has forever forbidden touch to women and not to men, as we see in the *Noli me tangere* passage of the Bible (John, 20:17) where Mary Magdalene is forbidden to touch the risen Christ, while Thomas is bidden to do it. For a more elaborate discussion of the *Noli me tangere* motif in *The Gathering* see H. Schwall, 'Distance and Desire: Civilisations and their Discontent', in *To Touch or Not to Touch? Interdisciplinary Perspectives on the Noli me tangere*, ed. R. Bieringer, B. Baert and K. Demasure (Annua Nuntia Lovaniensia, Leuven: Peeters, 2010).

17. In most reminiscences it is Liam who is abused by Nugent, but sometimes it is Veronica, and she often links this (phantasized) child abuse to her grandmother's knowing silence.

18. Enright, *The Gathering*, pp.35, 215.

19. 'Growing up in Ireland, we didn't need aliens – we already had a race of higher beings to gaze deep into our eyes and force us to have babies against our will: we called them priests.' Enright, *Making Babies*, p.5.

20. Enright, *The Gathering*, p.222, my emphasis.

21. Enright, *Making Babies*, p.186.

22. R. Braidotti, *Metamorphoses: Towards a Materialist Theory of Becoming* (Cambridge and Malden: Polity, 2002), p.124.

23. Enright, *Making Babies*, p.39.

24. L. Irigaray, *I Love To You: Sketch of a Possible Felicity in History*, trans. A. Martin (New York and London: Routledge, 1996), p.44.

25. Ibid., p.27.

26. Enright, *The Gathering*, p.181.

27. Braidotti, *Metamorphoses*, p.124.

28. Enright, *Making Babies*, p.45.
29. Braidotti, *Metamorphoses*, p.124.
30. Enright, 'Muscular Metaphors', pp.21–2.
31. Enright, *The Wig My Father Wore*, p.25.
32. A. Enright, '(She Owns) Every Thing', in *The Portable Virgin* (London: Vintage, 2007 [1991]), p.3.
33. Enright, 'Indifference', in *The Portable Virgin*, p.12.
34. Enright, 'Revenge', in *The Portable Virgin*, pp.38–9.
35. I have shown this in 'The Portable Virgin: Anne Enright's Translations of Philosophy into Literature', in *A New Ireland in Brazil: Festschrift in Honour of Munira Hamud Mutran*, ed. L.P.Z. Izarra and B. Kopschitz X. Bastos (Sao Paulo: Humanitas, 2008), pp.339–50.
36. Enright, 'Fruit Bait', in *The Portable Virgin*, p.115.
37. Enright, *The Wig My Father Wore*, pp.145–6.
38. Ibid., p.4.
39. Ibid.
40. Enright, 'Muscular Metaphors', p.22.
41. It seems that, as Enright is moving from the 'reality' she is impatient with to the one 'to which I am trying to get', the 'wildness' of the 'hyperreal' is toned down. In the volume *Yesterday's Weather*, most of the short stories which are steeped in a kind of 'magic realism' are left out of the collection, while *The Gathering* also moved to a more recognizable kind of reality. This 'maturing of tone' is also recognized by critics like Rustin, who quotes Enright's editor: 'I think she would probably agree that the writing now is more organic and fully formed.' S. Rustin, 'What Women Want', *Guardian*, 15 March 2008.
42. Enright, *What Are You Like*, p.5.
43. Irigaray, *I Love To You*, p.63.
44. Enright, 'Indifference', in *The Portable Virgin*, p.16.
45. Braidotti, *Metamorphoses*, p.124.
46. Enright, *Making Babies*, p.3. In her title, Enright refers explicitly to her function as a mother, but the whole purpose of the book is to pitch nurture versus 'nature', that is, not to give in to the female tradition of the suffering Irish mothers who think it is their destiny to suffer. Instead, her writing about motherhood must allow her to take a certain distance from it, so that she can assume motherhood in her own way.
47. Braidotti, *Metamorphoses*, p.125.
48. Enright, 'Muscular Metaphors', p.17.
49. Kennedy, 'The Din Within'.
50. Enright, '(She Owns) Every Thing', in *The Portable Virgin*, p.4.
51. H. Schwall, 'Lacan or an Introduction to the Realms of Unknowing', *Literature & Theology, An International Journal of Theory, Criticism and Culture*, 11, 2 (1997), pp.125–44.
52. Enright, 'Muscular Metaphors', p.17.
53. To give an example of the difference using the term water: if a person asks for a glass of water because she is thirsty, she is in the unrhetorical mode (R2); if a

confrontation with water would bring about a panic, or merely fascinate her, reminding of drowning or heroic fights against stormy seas, or vaguely recalling some incisive event in the past which marked the subject's unconscious in its core, the person would be in the arhetorical or R1 mode.

54. J. Lacan, *The Ethics of Psychoanalysis: The Seminar of Jacques Lacan Book VII; 1959–1960*, ed. J. Miller and trans. D. Porter (London: Routledge, 1999), p.46.

55. Enright, *Making Babies*, p.67.

56. Enright, *The Gathering*, p.223, my emphasis.

57. A. Enright, *The Pleasure of Eliza Lynch* (London: Vintage, 2003).

58. Enright, *The Wig My Father Wore*, p.151.

59. E. Diamond, 'The Shudder of Catharsis in Twentieth-Century Performance', in *Performativity and Performance*, ed. A. Parker and E. Kosofsky Sedgwick (New York and London: Routledge, 1995), p.154.

60. Enright, *Making Babies*, p.19.

61. Enright, *The Gathering*, p.227.

62. Lacan, *The Ethics of Psychoanalysis*, p.46.

63. Enright, *Making Babies*, p.20.

64. Ibid., p.178.

65. Enright, 'Muscular Metaphors', p.17. For a more technical discussion of this arhetorical aspect as one mode of the 'Real', see Schwall, 'Lacan or an Introduction to the Realms of Unknowing', pp.127–32.

66. Enright, *The Gathering*, p.125.

67. Ibid.

68. The link between Liam and the sea is underscored in the passage when Veronica goes through the books in the parental home, where she finds 'stories by Guy de Maupassant, one called 'La Mer' in which ... a sailor stores his severed arm in a barrel of salt', Enright, *The Gathering*, p.196. This is exactly what Liam will do professionally: deal with severed body parts.

69. Coincidence: in French sea waves are 'vagues'.

70. Lacan, *The Ethics of Psychoanalysis*, p.46.

71. Enright, *The Gathering*, p.1.

72. Ibid., p.246.

73. Quoted in Diamond, 'The Shudder of Catharsis', p.155.

74. This point is somewhat more elaborately argued in my brief analysis of the novel in H. Schwall, 'Anne Enright, *The Gathering*', *Irish University Review*, 37, 2 (2007), pp.594–8.

75. Enright, *The Gathering*, pp.155–6.

76. Slavoj Žižek's *Looking Awry: An Introduction to Jacques Lacan through Popular Culture* (Cambridge, MA and London: MIT Press, 1997) is all about the reading of the 'object o', and is very useful to analyze Enright's work.

77. Braidotti, *Metamorphoses*, p.124.
78. Enright, 'Muscular Metaphors', p.19.
79. Braidotti, *Metamorphoses*, p.124.

Select Bibliography

WORKS BY ANNE ENRIGHT

'Smile', 'Felix', 'Thirst', and 'Seascape', in *First Fictions Introduction 10* (London: Faber and Faber, 1989), pp.121–50.

The Portable Virgin (London: Vintage, 1991).

The Wig My Father Wore (London: Jonathan Cape, 1995).

The Wig My Father Wore (New York: Grove Press, 1995).

The Wig My Father Wore (London: Minerva, 1996).

What Are You Like? (London: Jonathan Cape, 2000).

What Are You Like? (London: Vintage, 2001).

The Pleasure of Eliza Lynch (London: Jonathan Cape, 2002).

The Pleasure of Eliza Lynch (New York: Grove Press, 2002).

The Pleasure of Eliza Lynch (London: Vintage, 2003).

Making Babies: Stumbling into Motherhood (London: Jonathan Cape, 2004).

Making Babies: Stumbling into Motherhood (London: Vintage, 2005).

The Gathering (London: Jonathan Cape, 2007).

Taking Pictures (London: Jonathan Cape, 2008).

Yesterday's Weather (New York: Grove Press, 2008).

Yesterday's Weather (London: Vintage, 2009).

OTHER WORKS BY ANNE ENRIGHT: ARTICLES AND INTERVIEWS

'Bored Out of Our Boxes', *Fortnight*, 323 (1993), p.32.

'Pumping up the Parish', *Fortnight*, 330 (1994), p.41.

'Green Hearts', review of F. O'Toole, *Meanwhile Back at the Ranch: The Politics of Irish Beef*, *London Review of Books*, 17, 15 (1995), pp.26–7.

'Diary', *London Review of Books*, 17, 18 (1995), p.25.

'Gate crasher: Who wants to be a billionaire', *The Irish Times*, 9 September 1995.

'The Body Royal', Irish Times, 18 November 1995.

'Lonely Lament of a Small-screen Orphan', Irish Times, 10 August 1996.

'Colour Codes in Darkest Dakar', Irish Times, 24 August 1996.

'Diary', London Review of Books, 19, 1 (1997), p.33.

'Going, Going, Gonne', Irish Times, 5 April 1997.

'Diary: Bombings in Baghdad', London Review of Books, 21, 12 (1999), p.41.

'What's Left of Henrietta Lacks?', London Review of Books, 22, 8 (2000), pp.8–10.

'My Milk', London Review of Books, 22, 19 (2000), pp.34–5.

'The Last Book I Bought', Daily Telegraph, 9 December 2000.

'Loved and Lost', Daily Telegraph, 26 January 2002.

'Anne Enright Interview by Caitriona Moloney', in Irish Women Speak Out: Voices from the Field, ed. C. Moloney and H. Thompson (Syracuse, NY: Syracuse University Press, 2003), pp.51–64.

'When we were 10', Daily Telegraph, 7 August 2004.

'At the Sharp End', Independent (UK), 24 November 2004.

'The 00s: Anne Enright', in Magnum Ireland, ed. B. Lardinois and V. Williams (London: Thames & Hudson, 2005), pp.226–7.

'Introduction', in K. O'Brien, As Music and Splendour (London: Penguin, 2005), pp.v–xi.

'Here's Looking at You', Guardian, 20 August 2005.

'Written in the Stars', Guardian, 27 August 2005.

'Diary: Listen to Heloïse', London Review of Books, 29, 9 (2007), p.43.

'An Identity Withheld', Irish Times, 2 June 2007.

'Seeing is Believing', Irish Times, 2 June 2007.

'Fallen Nun: Michale Ondaatje's In the Skin of a Lion', Guardian, 15 September 2007.

'Anne Enright Reading from her Novel', Boston College Irish Seminar, Boston College Front Row, Boston College, 27 September 2007, http://frontrow.bc.edu/program/enright/, accessed 1 July 2010.

'Diary: Disliking the McCanns', London Review of Books, 29, 19 (2007), p.39.

'Muscular Metaphors in Anne Enright: An Interview by Hedwig Schwall', The European English Messenger, 17, 1 (2008), pp.16–22.

Interview by Mark Lawson, Front Row, BBC Radio 4, 7 March 2008.

Interview by Matthew Sweet, Night Waves, BBC Radio 3, 11 March 2008.

'Writers' Rooms: Anne Enright', Guardian, 16 May 2008.

'Author, Author: Almost Written', *Guardian*, 31 May 2008.

'Anne Enright in Conversation at the Sydney Writers' Festival', ABC Radio Transcript, 8 June 2008.

'Author, Author: Final Thoughts', *Guardian*, 5 July 2008.

'Author, Author: Name that Plume', *Guardian*, 9 August 2008.

'Author, Author: Answering the Question', *Guardian*, 13 September 2008.

'Author, Author: Combining Creation with Procreation', *The Guardian*, 18 October 2008.

'Author, Author: Life Lessons', *Guardian*, 22 November 2008.

'Christmas Appeal: Giving Birth in Katine', *Guardian*, 20 December 2008.

'Author, Author: Creative Blockage', *Guardian*, 3 January 2009.

'Author, Author: A Writer's Treasure Trove', *Guardian*, 7 February 2009.

'Diary: A Writer's Life', *London Review of Books*, 31, 10 (2009), p.31.

'Sinking by Inches: Anne Enright on Ireland's Recession', *London Review of Books*, 32, 1 (2010), pp.21–2.

'Diary: Mrs Robinson Repents', *London Review of Books*, 32, 2 (2010), pp.34–5.

Rev. of *Hand in the Fire* by Hugo Hamilton, *Guardian*, 17 April 2010.

CRITICAL MATERIAL ON ANNE ENRIGHT AND SELECTED REVIEWS

Annan, G., 'Twin Peaks' (review of *What Are You Like?*), *New York Review of Books*, 47, 14 (2000), p.90.

Battersby, E., Review of *The Portable Virgin*, *Irish Times*, 25 February 1991.

Birne, E., 'What Family Does to You' (review of *The Gathering*), *London Review of Books*, 29, 20 (2007), pp.30–1.

Bracken, C., Review of *Making Babies: Stumbling Into Motherhood*, *Irish Studies Review*, 13, 3 (2005), pp.436–8.

Cahill, S., 'Doubles and Dislocations: The Body and Place in Anne Enright's *What Are You Like?*', in *Global Ireland: Irish Literatures for the New Millennium*, ed. O. Pilný and C. Wallace (Prague: Litteraria Pragrnsia, 2005), pp.133–44.

———— '"A Greedy Girl" and a "National Thing": Gender and History in Anne Enright's *The Pleasure of Eliza Lynch*', in *Irish Literature: Feminist Perspectives*, ed. P. Coughlan and T. O'Toole (Dublin: Carysfort Press, 2008), pp.203–22.

Carroll, E., Review of *The Gathering*, *Estudios Irlandeses – Journal of Irish Studies*, 3

(2008), http://www.estudiosirlandeses.org/indexnavy.htm, accessed 25 June 2010.

Cherry, K., 'The Laying Out of Bones' (review of *The Gathering*), *American Book Review* 30, 1 (2008), pp.24–5.

Coughlan, P., 'Irish Literature and Feminism in Postmodernity', *Hungarian Journal of English and American Studies*, 10, 1–2 (2004), pp.175–202.

———— '"Without a blink of her lovely eye": *The Pleasure of Eliza Lynch* and Visionary Scepticism', *Irish University Review: a Journal of Irish Studies*, 35, 2 (2005), pp.349–73.

Craciun, D., 'The Pleasure Anne Enright Took in *The Pleasure of Eliza Lynch*', *B.A.S.: British and American Studies/Revista de Studii Britanice si Americane*, 11 (2005), pp.211–17.

Craig, P., Review of *The Gathering*, by Anne Enright, *Independent* (UK), 7 June 2007.

Cronin, M. 'Inside Out: Time and Place in Global Ireland', *New Hibernia Review*, 13, 3 (2009), pp.74–88.

Dallas, L., 'A Love Like This' (review of *Making Babies: Stumbling into Motherhood*), *Times Literary Supplement*, 5 November 2004.

Dell'Amico, C., 'Anne Enright's *The Gathering*: Trauma, Testimony, Memory', *New Hibernia Review*, 14, 3 (2010), pp.59–74.

D'hoker, E., 'Reclaiming Feminine Identities: Anne Enright's *The Wig My Father Wore*', in *Irish Literature: Feminist Perspectives*, ed. P. Coughlan and T. O'Toole (Dublin: Carysfort Press, 2008), pp.185–201.

Ebest, S.B., 'These Traits Also Endure: Contemporary Irish and Irish-American Women Writers', *New Hibernia Review*, 7, 2 (2003), pp.55–72.

Ettler, J., 'The Twins of the Father' (review of *What Are You Like?*), *Observer*, 16 April 2000.

Ewins, K., 'Original Sins' (review of *The Gathering*), *Times Literary Supplement*, 11 May 2007.

Felter, M., 'Anne Enright', in *Dictionary of Irish Literature, Revised and Enlarged Edition* Vol. 1, ed. R. Hogan (Westport, CT: Greenwood, 1996.), pp.410–11.

Finucane, K.P., 'Touched by an Angel?' (review of *The Wig My Father Wore*), *American Book Review*, 24, 1 (2002), p.25.

Fitzgerald, P., 'Bringers of Ill Luck and Bad Weather' (review of *What Are You Like?*), *London Review of Books*, 22, 5 (2000), p.8.

Fogarty, A., 'Uncanny Families: Neo-Gothic Motifs and the Theme of

Social Change in Contemporary Irish Women's Fiction', *Irish University Review*, 30, 1 (2000), pp.59–81.

Frye, J., 'Narrating Maternal Subjectivity: Memoirs from Motherhood', in *Textual Mothers/Maternal Texts: Motherhood in Contemporary Women's Literatures*, ed. E. Podnieks and A. O'Reilly (Waterloo, ON: Wilfred Laurier UP, 2010), pp.187–201.

Gardam, S.C., '"Default[ing] to the Oldest Scar": A Psychoanalytical Investigation of Subjectivity in Anne Enright's *The Gathering*', *Études Irlandaises*, 34, 1 (2009), pp.99–112.

Gilling, T., 'Earth Angel' (review of *The Wig My Father Wore*, by Anne Enright), *New York Times*, 18 November 2001.

Gruss, S., 'Sex and the City?: Ecofeminism and the Urban Experience in Angela Carter, Anne Enright and Bernardine Evaristo', in *Local Natures, Global Responsibilities: Ecocritical Perspectives on the New English Literatures*, eds L. Volkman, N. Grimm, I. Detmers and K. Thomson (Amsterdam: Rodopi, 2010), pp.321–36.

Guest, K., 'Review of *Taking Pictures*, by Anne Enright', *Independent* (UK), 28 March 2008.

Hansson, H., 'To Say "I": Female Identity in *The Maid's Tale* and *The Wig My Father Wore*', in *Irish Fiction since the 1960s: A Collection of Critical Essays*, ed. Elmer Kennedy-Andrews (Gerrards Cross: Colin Smythe, 2006), pp.137–49; 314–16.

———— 'Anne Enright and Postnationalism in the Contemporary Irish Novel', in *Irish Literature since 1990: Diverse Voices*, ed. M. Parker and S. Brewster (Manchester: Manchester University Press, 2009), pp.216–31.

Harte, L., 'Mourning Remains Unresolved: Trauma and Survival in Anne Enright's *The Gathering*', *LIT: Literature Interpretation Theory*, 21, 2 (2010), pp.187–204.

Heinegg, P., 'The Past Is Not a Happy Place' (review of *The Gathering*), *America Magazine*, 25 February 2008.

———— 'Desperate Housewives, Irish-Style' (review of *Yesterday's Weather*), *America Magazine*, 8 December 2008.

Imhof, R., Review of *The Wig My Father Wore*, *The Linen Hall Review*, 12, 2 (1995/96), pp.12–14.

Ingman, H., *A History of the Irish Short Story* (Cambridge: Cambridge University Press, 2009).

Jeffries, S., 'I Wanted to Explore Hatred and Desire', *Guardian*, 18 October 2007.

Kennedy, A.L., 'The Din Within' (review of *The Gathering*, by Anne Enright), *The Guardian*, 28 April 2007.

Lee, H., 'All Reputation' (review of *The Pleasure of Eliza Lynch*) *London Review of Books*, 24, 20 (2002), pp.19–20.

———— 'Pawed, Used, Loved and Lonely' (review of *Taking Pictures*, by Anne Enright), *Guardian*, 1 March 2008.

MacFarlane, R., 'Separated at Birth' (review of *What Are You Like?*), *Times Literary Supplement*, 3 March 2000.

McGlynn, M., 'New Irish New York: Contemporary Irish Constructions of New York City', in *Ireland and Transatlantic Poetics: Essays in Honor of Denis Donoghue*, ed. B. Caraher, R. Mahony and D. Donoghue (Newark, NJ: University of Delaware Press, 2007), pp.205–21.

McNeill, J., 'The Shadows of Elisa Lynch' (review of *The Pleasure of Eliza Lynch*), *Independent* (UK), 18 January 2003.

Merritt, S., 'Sex and Death and Caravans' (review of *Taking Pictures*), *The Observer*, 6 April 2008.

Mills Harper, M., 'Flesh and Bones: Anne Enright's *The Gathering*', *The South Carolina Review*, 43, 1 (2010), pp.74–87.

Moloney, C., 'Re-Imagining Women's History in the Fiction of Éilís Ní Dhuibhne, Anne Enright, and Kate O'Riordan', *Postcolonial Text*, 3, 3 (2007), pp.1–15.

———— 'Anne Enright', in *Twenty-first-Century British and Irish Novelists*, ed. Michael R. Molino (Detroit, MI: Gale, 2003), *Dictionary of Literary Biography Vol.* 267, Literature Resource Center, accessed 25 June 2010.

———— and Thompson, H. (eds), *Irish Women Speak Out: Voices from the Field* (Syracuse, NY: Syracuse University Press, 2003).

O'Donoghue, B., 'Anne Enright's Tales of the Ordinary' (review of *Taking Pictures*), *Times Literary Supplement*, 5 March 2008.

———— 'From an Unreliable Place' (review of *Taking Pictures*), *Times Literary Supplement*, 7 March 2008.

Padel, R., 'Twin Tracks and Double Visions' (review of *What Are You Like?*), *The Independent* (UK), 26 February 2000.

Powell, K.T., *Irish Fiction: An Introduction* (New York: Continuum, 2006).

Rustin, S., 'What Women Want', *Guardian*, 15 March 2008.

Saunders, K., Review of *The Gathering*, *The Times*, 16 June 2007.

Schwall, H., 'Anne Enright, *The Gathering*', *Irish University Review*, 37, 2 (2007), pp.594–8.

———— 'The Portable Virgin: Anne Enright's Translations of Philosophy into Literature', in A New Ireland in Brazil: Festschrift in Honour of Munira Hamud Mutran, ed. L.P.Z. Izarra and B. Kopschitz X. Bastos (Sao Paulo: Humanitas, 2008), pp.339–50.

———— 'Distance and Desire: Civilisations and their Discontent', in To Touch or Not to Touch? Interdisciplinary Perspectives on the Noli me tangere, ed. R. Bieringer, B. Baert and K. Demasure (Annua Nuntia Lovaniensia, Leuven: Peeters, 2010).

Scurr, R., 'Novel of the Week: What Are You Like, by Anne Enright', New Statesman, 10 April 2000.

Shriver, L., 'Still Life with Thumb on Lens' (review of Taking Pictures), Telegraph, 15 March 2008.

Shumaker, J., 'Uncanny Doubles: The Fiction of Anne Enright', New Hibernia Review/Iris Éireannach Nua, 9, 3 (2005), pp.107–22.

Smyth, G., The Novel and the Nation: Studies in the New Irish Fiction (London and Chicago, IL: Pluto Press, 1997).

Stenson, S.E., 'Anne Enright', in Irish Women Writers: An A–Z Guide, ed. A.G. Gonzalez (Westport, CT: Greenwood, 2006), pp.120–4.

Tague, J., 'Glowing from the cathode-ray tube' (review of The Wig My Father Wore), Times Literary Supplement, 31 March 1995.

Thompson, S., 'Still Life with Parrot' (review of The Pleasure of Eliza Lynch), Times Literary Supplement, 6 September 2002.

Tóibín, C., 'Introduction', in The Penguin Book of Irish Fiction, ed. C. Tóibín (London: Penguin, 1999), pp.ix–xxxiv.

Weekes, A.O., 'Anne Enright', in Unveiling Treasures: The Attic Guide to the Published Works of Irish Women Literary Writers (Dublin: Attic Press, 1993), pp.120–1.

Wood, J., 'To Thrill – A Mockingbird' (review of What Are You Like?), Guardian, 11 March 2000.

OTHER REFERENCES

Abraham, N., 'Notes on the Phantom: A Complement to Freud's Metapsychology', trans. Nicholas Rand, Critical Inquiry, 13 (1987), pp.287–92.

Agreement Reached in the Multi-Party Negotiations, Belfast, 10 April 1998 otherwise known as the 'Good Friday Agreement' (Dublin: Government Information Services, 1998).

Anderson, B., *Imagined Communities: Reflections on the Origin and Spread of Nationalism* (London: Verso, 1991).

Armand, L., *Technē: James Joyce, Hypertext and Technology* (Prague: Karolinum Press, 2003).

Barker, P., *The Ghost Road* (Harmondsworth: Penguin, 1996).

Berman, M., *All That is Solid Melts into Air: The Experience of Modernity* (London: Verso, 1983).

Box, P.H., *The Origins of the Paraguayan War* (New York: Russell and Russell, 1967).

Braidotti, R., *Nomadic Subjects: Embodiment and Sexual Difference in Contemporary Feminist Theory* (New York: Columbia University Press, 1994).

———— *Metamorphoses: Towards a Materialist Theory of Becoming* (Cambridge: Polity, 2002).

Butler, J., *Precarious Lives: The Power of Mourning and Violence* (London: Verso, 2004).

———— *Antigone's Claim: Kinship Between Life and Death* (New York: Columbia University Press, 2000).

————'Antigone's Claim: A Conversation with Judith Butler', an interview by P. Antonello and R. Farnetti, *Theory & Event* 12, 1 (2009), Project Muse, http://muse.jhu.edu.eproxy.ucd.ie/journals/theory_and_event/v012/12.1.antonello.html, accessed 1 July 2010.

Carter, A., *The Bloody Chamber* (London: Vintage, 1979).

———— *Black Venus* (London: Chatto and Windus, 1985).

Cixous, H., 'The Laugh of the Medusa', trans. K. Cohen and P. Cohen, in *New French Feminisms: An Anthology*, ed. E. Marks and I. de Courtivron (Brighton: Harvester, 1981), pp.245–64.

Cixous, H. and Clément, C., *The Newly Born Woman* (Minneapolis, MN: University of Minnesota Press, 1985).

Cleary, J., 'Introduction: Ireland and Modernity', in *The Cambridge Companion to Modern Irish Culture*, ed. J. Cleary and C. Connolly (Cambridge: Cambridge University Press, 2005), pp.1–21.

———— *Outrageous Fortunes: Capital and Culture in Modern Ireland* (Dublin: Field Day Publications, 2007).

Connolly, C., 'The Turn to the Map: Cartographic Fictions in Irish Culture', in *Éire-Land*, ed. Vera Kreilkamp (Chicago, IL: McMullen Museum of Art and University of Chicago Press, 2003), pp.27–33.

Conrad, J., *Nostromo: A Tale of the Seaboard*, ed. J. Berthoud and M. Kalnins (Oxford: Oxford University Press, 2008).

Cooppan, V., 'World Literature and Global Theory: Comparative Literature for the New Millennium', symploké, 9, 1–2 (2001), pp.15–43.

Damrosch, D., What is World Literature? (Princeton, NJ: Princeton University Press, 2003).

———— How to Read World Literature (Chichester: Wiley-Blackwell, 2009).

Deane, S., Celtic Revivals: Essays in Modern Irish Literature (London and Boston, MA: Faber and Faber, 1985).

———— Strange Country: Modernity and Nationhood in Irish Writing Since 1790 (Oxford: Oxford University Press, 1997).

De Alencar, J., O Guaraní: Romance brasileiro, ed. Darcy Damasceno (Rio de Janeiro: Instituto Nacional do Livro, 1958).

Deleuze, G. and Guattari, F., Anti-Oedipus: Capitalism and Schizophrenia, trans. R. Hurley, M. Seem and H. Lane (London and New York: Continuum, 1984).

De Kesel, M., Eros and Ethics: Reading Jacques Lacan's Seminar VII, trans. Sigi Jottkandt (New York: State University of New York Press, 2009).

De Nooy, J., 'Reconfiguring the Gemini: Surviving Sameness in Twin Stories', AUMLA - Journal of the Australasian Universities Language and Literature Association, 97 (2002), pp.74–95.

Derrida, J., Specters of Marx, trans. P. Kamuf (New York and London: Routledge, 1994).

Diamond, E., 'The Shudder of Catharsis in Twentieth-Century Performance', in Performativity and Performance, ed. A. Parker and E. Kosofsky Sedgwick (New York and London: Routledge, 1995), pp.152–72.

Eagleton, T., Crazy John and the Bishop and Other Essays on Irish Culture (Cork: Cork University Press and Field Day, 1998).

Ellmann, M., 'Skinscapes in "Lotus-Eaters"', in Ulysses: En-Gendered Perspectives – Eighteen New Essays on the Episodes, ed. K.J. Devlin and M. Reisbaum (Columbia, SC: University of South Carolina Press, 1999), pp.51–66.

Ettinger, B., The Matrixial Borderspace (Minneapolis, MN and London: University of Minnesota Press, 2006).

———— 'Neighbourhood and Schechina', in 'Seduction into Life: Co-responding with Bracha L. Ettinger', ed. N. Giffney, A. Mulhall and M. O'Rourke, Studies in the Maternal, 1, 2 (2009), http://www.mamsie.

bbk.ac.uk/back_issues/issue_two/bracha_ettinger.html, accessed 25 January 2010.

Fanon, F., *The Wretched of the Earth*, trans. R. Philcox (New York: Grove Press, 2004).

Felman, S., *Jacques Lacan and the Adventure of Insight* (Cambridge, MA. and London: Harvard University Press, 1987).

Fornos Peñalba, J.A., 'Draft Dodgers, War Resisters and Turbulent Gauchos: The War of the Triple Alliance against Paraguay', *The Americas*, 38, 4 (1982), pp.463–79.

Freud, S., *The Uncanny*, trans. D. McLintock and H. Haughton (London: Penguin, 2003).

Freyne, P., 'We're Back to Normal Service', *Sunday Tribune*, 26 April 2009.

Gibbons, L., 'The Global Cure? History, Therapy and the Celtic Tiger', in *Reinventing Ireland: Culture, Society and the Global Economy*, ed. P. Kirby, L. Gibbons and M. Cronin (London: Pluto, 2002), pp.89–106.

Graham, C., *Deconstructing Ireland: Identity Theory Culture* (Edinburgh: Edinburgh University Press, 2001).

Grigg, R., *Lacan, Language, and Philosophy* (New York: State University of New York Press, 2008).

Grosz, E., *Space, Time, and Perversion: Essays on the Politics of Bodies* (New York: Routledge, 1995).

—————— 'Deleuze's Bergson: Duration, the Virtual and a Politics of the Future', in *Deleuze and Feminist Theory*, ed. I. Buchanan and C. Colebrook (Edinburgh: Edinburgh University Press, 2000), pp.214–34.

Hall, S., 'Introduction', in *Modernity: An Introduction to Modern Societies*, ed. S. Hall, D. Held, D. Hubert and K. Thompson (Malden, MA and Oxford: Open University Press, 1996), pp.3–18.

Hanratty, D.M. and Meditz, S.W. (eds), 'Library of Congress Country Study on Paraguay', *Library of Congress*, http://memory.loc.gov/frd/cs/pytoc.html, accessed 26 September 2005.

Hanson, C., *Short Stories and Short Fictions, 1880–1980* (London: Macmillan, 1985).

Hutcheon, L., *A Poetics of Postmodernism: History, Theory, Fiction* (New York: Routledge, 1992).

'Indian Mutiny', *Encyclopaedia Britannica*, 2000.

Irigaray, L., *Speculum of the Other Woman*, trans. G.C. Gill (Ithaca, NY: Cornell University Press, 1985).

———— This Sex Which Is Not One, trans. C. Porter and C. Burke (Ithaca, NY: Cornell University Press, 1985).

———— Marine Lover of Friedrich Nietzsche, trans. G.C. Gill (New York: Columbia University Press, 1991).

———— 'Volume Without Contours', in The Irigaray Reader, ed. M. Whitford (Oxford: Blackwell, 1991), pp.53–68.

———— 'Women-Mothers, the Silent Substratum of the Social Order', The Irigaray Reader, ed. M. Whitford (Oxford: Blackwell, 1991), pp.47–52.

———— Elemental Passions, trans. J. Collie and J. Still (New York: Routledge, 1992).

———— Sexes and Genealogies, trans G.C. Gill (New York: Columbia University Press, 1993).

———— I Love To You: Sketch of a Possible Felicity in History, trans. A. Martin (New York and London: Routledge, 1996).

———— 'The Wedding Between the Body and Language', in Luce Irigaray: Key Writings, ed. L. Irigaray (London and New York: Continuum, 2004), pp.13–22.

James, P., 'Globalisation and Empires of Mutual Accord', Arena Magazine, 85 (2006), pp.41–5.

Joyce, J., Ulysses, intro. D. Kiberd (Harmondsworth: Penguin, 1992).

———— Dubliners (London: Penguin, 1992 [1914]).

Kearney, R., Postnationalist Ireland: Politics, Culture, Philosophy (London and New York: Routledge, 1997).

Kirkland, R., '"That Car": Modernity, Northern Ireland and the DMC-12', Field Day Review, 3 (2007), pp.94–107.

———— 'Ballygawley, Ballylynn, Belfast: Writing about Modernity and Settlement in Northern Ireland', Irish Review, 40–41 (2009), pp.18–32.

Kristeva, J., 'The True-Real', in The Kristeva Reader, ed. T. Moi (Oxford: Blackwell, 1986), pp.214–37.

———— 'Women's Time', in The Kristeva Reader, ed. T. Moi (Oxford: Blackwell, 1986), pp.187–213.

Lacan, J., Écrits (Paris: Seuil, 1966).

———— The Ethics of Psychoanalysis: The Seminar of Jacques Lacan, Book VII, 1959–1960, ed. J. Miller and trans. D. Porter (London: Routledge, 1999).

——— 'The Mirror Stage as Formative of the Function of the I as Revealed in Psychoanalytic Experience', in Écrits: A Selection, trans. Alan Sheridan (London and New York: Routledge, 2001), pp.1–8.

Lillis, M. and Fanning, R., The Lives of Eliza Lynch: Scandal and Courage (Dublin: Gill and Macmillan, 2009).

Lloyd, D., Irish Times: Temporalities of Modernity (Dublin: Field Day, 2008).

Lyotard, J., The Postmodern Condition: A Report on Knowledge, trans. G. Bennington and B. Massumi (Manchester: Manchester University Press, 1984).

Marx, K., The Communist Manifesto, ed. M. Cowling and trans. T. Carver (Edinburgh: Edinburgh University Press, 1998).

Meaney, G., 'Sex and Nation: Women in Irish Culture and Politics', in The Irish Women's Studies Reader, ed. A. Smyth (Dublin: Attic Press, 1993), pp.230–44.

——— 'Race, Sex and Nation', The Irish Review, 35, 1 (2007), pp.46–63.

McCarthy, C., Modernisation: Crisis and Culture in Ireland 1969–1992 (Dublin: Four Courts Press, 2000).

Nickson, R.A., Historical Dictionary of Paraguay, 2nd edn (Metuchen, NJ and London: Scarecrow Press, 1993).

Ní Dhuibhne, E., Fox, Swallow, Scarecrow (Belfast: Blackstaff Press, 2007).

Norquay, G. and Smyth, G., 'Waking Up in a Different Place: Contemporary Irish and Scottish Fiction', in Across the Margins: Cultural Identity and Change in the Atlantic Archipelago, ed. G. Norquay and G. Smyth (Manchester: Manchester University Press, 2002), pp.154–70.

Onega, S., 'British Historiographic Metafiction in the 1980s', in British Postmodern Fiction, ed. T. D'haen and H. Bertens (Amsterdam: Rodopi, 1993), pp.47–61.

O'Toole, F., Black Hole Green Card: The Disappearance of Ireland (Dublin: New Island Books, 1994).

——— The Lie of the Land: Irish Identities (London and New York: Verso, 1997).

——— After the Ball (Dublin: New Island Books, 2003).

——— Ship of Fools (London: Faber and Faber, 2009).

——— 'Fear of the Future Set Aside as Ireland Embraces its Present', Irish Times, 23 May 1998.

Parker, I., Slavoj Žižek: A Critical Introduction (London: Pluto Press, 2004).

Pettersson, A., 'Transcultural Literary History: Beyond Constricting

Notions of World Literature', *New Literary History*, 39 (2008), pp.463–79.

Plá, J., *The British in Paraguay 1850–1870*, trans. B.C. McDermot (Richmond and Oxford: Richmond Publishing and St Antony's College, 1976).

Pollock, G., 'Art/Trauma/Representation', *Parallax*, 15, 1 (2009), pp.40–54.

Potts, D.L., '"When Ireland was Still Under a Spell":The Poetry of Nuala Ní Dhomhnaill', *New Hibernia Review* 7, 2 (2003), pp.52–70.

Robertson, R., 'Glocalization: Time-Space and Homogeneity-Heterogeneity', in *Global Modernities*, ed. M. Featherstone, R. Robertson and S. Lash (London and Thousand Oaks, CA: Sage Publications, 1995), pp.25–44.

Robinson, M., 'Cherishing the Irish Diaspora', Address to the Houses of Oireachtas on a Matter of Public Importance, 2 February 1995, http://www.oireachtas.ie/viewdoc.asp?fn=/documents/addresses/2Feb1995.htm.

Rohy, V., 'Ahistorical', *GLQ: A Journal of Lesbian and Gay Studies*, 12, 1 (2006), pp.62–83.

Rosendahl Thomsen, M., *Mapping World Literature: International Canonization and Transnational Literature* (London: Continuum, 2008).

Ryan, M., 'Abstract Homes: Deterritorialisation and Reterritorialisation in the Work of Colm Tóibín', *Irish Studies Review*, 16, 1 (2008), pp.19–32.

Schwall, H., 'Lacan or an Introduction to the Realms of Unknowing', *Literature & Theology, An International Journal of Theory, Criticism and Culture*, 11, 2 (1997), pp.125–44.

Sharp, G., 'Intellectuals in Transition', *Arena Journal*, 65 (1983), pp.84–95.

Shaw, V., *The Short Story: A Critical Introduction* (London: Longman, 1983).

Sherry, N., *Conrad's Western World* (Cambridge: Cambridge University Press, 1971).

Sontag, S., *On Photography* (New York: Picador, 1977).

Sophocles, *Antigone*, trans. R.C. Jebb, *MIT Internet Classics Archive*, MIT, http://classics.mit.edu/Sophocles/antigone.html, accessed 1 July 2010.

Spark, M., *The Hothouse by the East River* (London: Macmillan, 1973).

Stavrakakis, Y., 'The Lure of Antigone: Aporias of an Ethics of the Political', *Umbr(a)*, 1 (2003), pp.117–29.

Sullivan, M., 'Feminism, Postmodernism and the Subjects of Irish and

Women's Studies', in *New Voices in Irish Criticism*, ed. P.J. Mathews (Dublin: Four Courts Press, 2000), pp.243–50.

———— 'I am, therefore I'm not (Woman)', *International Journal of English Studies*, 2, 2 (2002), pp.123–34.

———— 'The Treachery of Wetness: Irish Studies, Seamus Heaney and the Politics of Parturition', *Irish Studies Review*, 13, 4 (2005), pp.451–68.

———— 'Boyz to Menz(own): Irish Boy Bands and the Alternative Nation', *Irish Review*, 34 (2006), pp.58–78.

Swift, J., *Gulliver's Travels* (New York: Dell Publishing, 1974).

Tóibín, C., 'Selling Tara, Buying Florida', *Éire-Ireland*, 43, 1 and 2, (2008), pp.11–25.

Tomlinson, J., 'Cultural Globalisation: Placing and Displacing the West', in *Cultural Perspectives on Development*, ed. V. Tucker (London and Portland, OR: Frank Cass, 1997), pp.22–35.

Urry, J., 'Inhabiting the Car', *The Sociological Review*, 54, s1, (2006), pp.17–31.

Waugh, P., *Practising Postmodernism, Reading Modernism* (London: Edward Arnold, 1992).

Whitford, M., *Luce Irigaray: Philosophy in the Feminine* (London: Routledge, 1991).

Žižek, S., *Looking Awry: An Introduction to Jacques Lacan through Popular Culture* (Cambridge, MA: MIT Press, 1992).

Index

S

Schwall, Hedwig, 179
sex, 24–5, 27, 127, 171
  Catholicism and, 207–8
  in *The Gathering*, 15, 132, 140–1
  in *The Pleasure of Eliza Lynch*, 10, 24–5,
    111, 120, 131, 171, 172
  in short fiction, 34–5, 37, 40, 47, 212
  Victorian double standard, 116
  in *The Wig My Father Wore*, 27, 69, 172,
    174, 212
Shakespeare, William, *King Lear*, 132
Shaw, Valerie, 37
Shumaker, Jeannett, 44, 167
Smyth, Gerry, 52
Sontag, Susan, 60
Spark, Muriel, *The Hothouse by the East River*,
  149
St Louis High School, Rathmines, 1
Stalin, Joseph, 29
Steinam, Gloria, 20
subjectivity, 87, 89, 92, 97, 98, 186,
    194–5, 197, 198–9, 209
  femininity, 8, 22, 27, 89, 90, 92, 93,
    94–5, 98, 154, 186, 195, 199
  in psychoanalytic discourse, 26, 70–1,
    74–5, 76, 77–8, 79, 82, 98, 213–14
  repression of mother as subject, 7–8,
    68–9, 70–2, 74–5, 80–3, 89–90, 93,
    98–101, 210
  see also intersubjectivity
Sukenick, Ronald, 53
Sullivan, Moynagh, 69, 197
Swift, Jonathan, 165, 166, 168

T

technology *see* machines and technology

television, 2, 51, 58, 59, 61–2, 172–4,
    185, 187–9
Thomsen, Mads Rosendahl, 52
Tóibín, Colm, 2, 3, 17, 18, 29, 54, 166,
    170
trauma, 3, 7, 8, 79–83, 94–5, 98, 101,
    158–9
Trinity College Dublin, 1–2, 20

U

Urry, John, 190

V

Victoria, Canada, 1
Victorian era, 116, 120
  see also Enright, Anne, WORKS,
    The Pleasure of Eliza Lynch

W

Waugh, Patricia, 114
Whitaker, T.K., 170
Whitford, Margaret, 101
Winterson, Jeanette, 9
women *see* female body; femininity;
  feminism; motherhood; pregnancy;
  repression of femininity
Woolf, Virginia, 37

Y

Yates, Richard, *Revolutionary Road*, 19
Yeats, W.B., 22

Z

Žižek, Slavoj, 74, 80, 82, 154